11-1-73

CAMBRIDGE STUDIES IN
CHINESE HISTORY, LITERATURE AND INSTITUTIONS

General Editors
PATRICK HANAN AND DENIS TWITCHETT

Wage Patterns and Wage Policy
in Modern China 1919-1972

Other books in the series

Wage Patterns and Wage Policy in Modern China
1919-1972

by

CHRISTOPHER HOWE

CAMBRIDGE
AT THE UNIVERSITY PRESS
1973

Published by the Syndics of the Cambridge University Press
Bentley House, 200 Euston Road, London NW1 2DB
American Branch: 32 East 57th Street, New York, N.Y.10022

© Cambridge University Press 1973

Library of Congress Catalogue Card Number: 72-97875

ISBN: 0 521 20199 3

Printed in Great Britain
at the University Printing House, Cambridge
(Brooke Crutchley, University Printer)

*To Patricia, Emma
and Roderick*

'Now, this is what I want to ask you about – to wit, how you get people to work when there is no reward of labour, and especially how you get them to work strenuously?'

'No reward of labour?' said Hammond, gravely. 'The reward of labour is *life*. Is that not enough?'

WILLIAM MORRIS
News from Nowhere

Contents

Diagrams

Tables

Preface

This book is an attempt to provide a statistical analysis of changes in the level and structure of Chinese wages from the 1920s to the early 1970s. It also seeks to elucidate both the mechanisms responsible for these changes and their economic significance.

We begin our enquiry in Chapter 1, by exploring some basic theoretical and empirical aspects of the wage structure with particular reference to the relevance of these in planned economies and low income countries; and in Chapter 2, we examine the history of wage movements in the period before the establishment of the Chinese People's Republic in 1949.

The statistical data on the structure and level of wages in the post-1949 period are relatively plentiful up to 1958. After that year, data on the wage structure consist mainly of reports by visitors and official statements of a fairly general kind. But in 1971 and 1972 important information on the level of wages was released, so that, in this respect, the information in Chapter 3 – which summarises the post-1949 developments – is fairly complete. In total, although the data for the whole period from the 1920s are not as ample as those for the Soviet Union or the mature capitalist economies, by comparison with what is available for many other low income countries, the detail and historical range of the Chinese data are impressive.

The statistical aspects of the wage system are interesting, since they can tell us how the Chinese experience of wage change relates both to the experience of other developing countries in recent years and to the historical experience of economies that have now achieved high levels of per capita income. In making such comparisons, however, we are immediately up against the problem of whether there is a 'normal' pattern of wage change (determined perhaps by changes in per capita income or the degree of industrialisation) against which we can compare the Chinese or other cases. This question is discussed in Chapter 1, and our conclusion is that although individual histories of wage change may have their unique features, some broad patterns are discernible. Thus we are able in Chapters 2 and 3 to consider such questions as whether or not occupational wage structures in China have widened or narrowed in response to industrialisation; whether the inter-industry wage structure resembles that found elsewhere; whether the level of real urban wages has moved inexorably upward; and whether large differentials have emerged between rural and urban areas and between privileged and less privileged groups within the cities.

All these questions – especially those relating to the level of wages and the nature of inter-sectoral differentials – have been of considerable practical consequence in developing countries in the post-war period. Many contemporary developing countries, for example, are experiencing social and political stress that is directly attributable to failures to control the distribution of income. The extent to which such lack of control and income inequalities are inevitable, and the advantages and disadvantages of radical efforts to solve these problems are topics about which the Chinese experience can tell us much. China is the only large, low income country that has experimented with both centralised and partially decentralised systems of socialist planning, and the effectiveness of wage policy within the framework of these systems is the subject matter of Chapters 4 to 7.

In Chapter 4, we describe the evolution of wage policy and use both quantitative and qualitative indicators to appraise the degree to which wage movements have conformed to policy intentions. In Chapters 5 and 6, we describe the two main components of the wage determination mechanism – the normal process of planning and the wage reform movements – and finally in Chapter 7, we analyse the factors that have determined the limits of wage control in the Chinese system.

Up to this point in the book, we are solely concerned with the wage system and its efficiency as an instrument of economic control. To many people, this may seem something of a distortion, since in the popular consciousness it is precisely the Chinese reputation for eschewing reliance on wage systems that is exciting and worthy of investigation. We would argue, however, that the failure of most students of this phenomenon to relate their ideas on incentive policy to any serious examination of the efficiency of the wage system, distorts their analysis of the Chinese experience to a point where it is of slight academic or practical interest. To redress the balance a little we start with wages and then, in Chapter 8, we widen our enquiry to consider first the significance of different forms of wage payments (i.e. piece-work, bonus schemes etc.) and then to discuss other components of the incentive system such as variations in job security and emulation campaigns.

In Chapter 9, we try to draw the threads of the previous chapters together by assembling some analytical concepts that enable us to put the past evolution of the incentive system in perspective, and to make some suggestions about the nature and problems of its future development. In this as in other chapters, we have restricted our attention to the economic implications of the incentive system. This is, of course, artificial, but we think legitimate. It is artificial because economic controls are bound to reflect and should in some sense be congruent with the total system of social control. The relationship between this larger system and its economic component is beyond the scope of this book, but since the problems of the sub-system must be reflected in the broader issues, its study in relative isolation seems justified and should provide materials for those who are trying to draw the complete picture.

The sources for this study are economic and industrial journals, newspapers, legal compilations and other literature published in China. We have also made use of one group of publications that proved particularly difficult to evaluate. These are the newspapers, broadsheets, pamphlets and journals produced during the Cultural Revolution. These publications, with their confessions, accusations and revelations about the past provide insights comparable in a way with those provided in Soviet studies by the Smolensk Archive and the revelations of Milovan Djilas. They are bound, therefore, to make a considerable impact on our understanding of China. Their interpretation, however, involves many problems. The documents are one-sided and contain many factual (especially chronological) errors. Some of these are easily spotted, others can only be appreciated by specialists and there are doubtless others that are at present undetectable. In spite of this, the use of Red Guard and Cultural Revolution materials seemed worthwhile since they are particularly rich in their revelations about the history of the incentive system. At this stage, however, the provisional nature of conclusions based on these sources must be borne in mind.

Although the literary sources for our subject are vast, it remains unhappily true that the nature of incentive systems is such that these sources can never be an adequate basis for analysis. This is a particular problem in the Chinese case, where the possibility of a cultural bias in our methods and assumptions is so great. Unfortunately, little fieldwork was done on relevant topics before 1949 or, to the best of our knowledge, has been since. The reports of visitors to China are, of course, useful as sources of qualitative and quantitative information and we have drawn freely on the experience of others as well as on our own observations in China in 1965 and 1966. It would, however, be idle to pretend that our understanding of the problems discussed in this book would not be much deeper if access to China was less restricted.

Many people have contributed to the preparation of this book and I should like to mention in particular Professor D. C. Twitchett and Professor K. R. Walker, both of whom read the whole manuscript and made valuable comments. I have also had the benefit of expert advice on earlier manuscripts from Professor Janet Chapman.

Professor Ezra Vogel generously gave me access to interview materials on wages and I am indebted to Professor Michel Oksenberg for first pointing out to me the value of the finance and currency law compendiums as sources for the study of the Chinese wage and salary system.

I also wish to thank Professor C. J. Dunn, Professor P. G. O'Neil and the late Mr C. Yanada for the trouble they have been to and the interest they have taken in enabling me to read Japanese materials. Mr J. P. Emerson has kept me supplied with useful references, and together with Mr K. Kobayashi, facilitated my research in the Library of Congress. Finally, my thanks to Mrs P. A. Pettitt and Mrs L. M. A. Wilkinson for the care with which they handled the problems of typing the manuscript.

CHRISTOPHER HOWE

London 1973

Abbreviations

CCCP	*Ching chi chou pao*
CCJP	*Ch'ang ch'un jih pao*
CCYC	*Ching chi yen chiu*
CFJP	*Chieh fang jih pao*
CHCC	*Chi hua ching chi*
CHJP	*Chiang hsi jih pao*
CHKY	*Chi hsieh kung yeh*
CKCN	*Chung Kuo ch'ing nien*
CKCNP	*Chung Kuo ch'ing nien pao*
CKKY	*Chung Kuo kung yeh*
CLJP	*Chi lin jih pao*
CTJP	*Ch'eng tu jih pao*
FCJP	*Fu chien jih pao*
HC	*Hung ch'i*
HEPJP	*Ha erh pin jih pao*
HH	*Hsüeh hsi*
HHPYK	*Hsin Hua pan yüeh k'an*
HHYP	*Hsin Hua yüeh pao*
HLCJP	*Hei lung chiang jih pao*
HNJP	*Ho nan jih pao*
HPJP	*Hu pei jih pao*
HTJP	*Hsi ts'ang jih pao*
HWJP	*Hsin wen jih pao*
JMJP	*Jen min jih pao*
JMTY	*Jen min tien yeh*
KCJP	*Kuang chou jih pao*
KHJP	*Kuang hsi jih pao*
KJJP	*Kung jen jih pao*
KMJP	*Kuang ming jih pao*
KSJP	*Kan su jih pao*
LNJP	*Liao ning jih pao*
LT	*Lao tung*
LTJP	*Lü-Ta jih pao*
NCJP	*Nan ching jih pao*
NCNA	*New China News Agency*
NFJP	*Nan fang jih pao*

NMKJP	*Nei meng ku jih pao*
SCJP	*Szu ch'uan jih pao*
SCMP	*Survey of the China Mainland Press*
SHJP	*Shan hsi jih pao*
TCJP	*T'ien chin jih pao*
TCKT	*T'ung chi kung tso*
TCP	*Ta chung pao*
TKP	*Ta kung pao*
TPKY	*Tung pei kung yeh*
WHP	*Wen hui pao*

1

Wage structure and development

The comparative study of economic systems shows that the mechanisms for allocating economic resources are capable of considerable variation. It is interesting to observe, however, that there are hardly any significant examples of economies which in modern times have allocated labour resources irrespective of the preferences of the individuals who comprise the labour force, or given rewards irrespective of individual performance. The implication of this is that the structure of incentives is an important determinant of the efficiency with which labour resources are allocated, the creativeness and intensity of work effort and the speed with which new skills are acquired.

The main focus of this study is the structure of money wages in urban industry. However, a correct understanding of this will lead us into some consideration of the wages in the modern bureaucratic and services sectors and also the question of the relationship between the wage structure and the wage level and to the analysis of wage forms and non-wage incentives.

The Chinese economy is unique in many ways, and its enormous population alone ensures that the scale of labour market issues makes comparative judgement of any kind difficult. None the less, since both the history of all wage structures and the key issues of wage policy in both low income and socialist economies do seem to exhibit some common characteristics, we begin this chapter by reviewing what these characteristics are, and we then in Chapter 2 relate these to an analysis of wage structure trends in pre-Communist China.

The value of this preliminary exercise is that it gives us an initial, three-dimensional framework within which to consider Chinese wage experience since 1949. Consider for example, the question of skill differentials. Although, as we have said, the Chinese economy has some unique features, it largely shares with other countries the technology, and therefore the occupational structure of modern industry. This means that the labour skills and technical organisation found in Chinese industry should be broadly similar to those found in other countries. If, therefore, the occupational wage structures in Chinese industry were found to be significantly different from those found elsewhere, we should clearly be on to something very interesting, and we should then have to consider whether these deviations had obvious efficiency implications. On the other hand, if Chinese experience corresponded closely to that found elsewhere, then this too would have important theoretical and policy implications.

The relevance of socialist wage experience arises from the fact that Soviet advisers in China encouraged, and in the early stages directed the creation of a Soviet style machinery for wage administration. This was done in spite of the wide economic and cultural differences between China and Russia. Much of this book is concerned with the consequences of this policy and these cannot be properly understood without prior understanding of the working of the Soviet system in its own environment.

The point of the historical materials is that we know from the history of other labour markets that, apart from technology, the boundaries of possible wage reform are strongly affected by the nature of the pre-existing wage pattern. This is because past wage relationships, however themselves determined, become norms by which the workforce judge the equitableness of changes in the wage structure. Reforms that ignore this and do violence to the inherited structure and its logic run grave risks. Thus to form even a *prima facie* judgement of the rationality of the wage reforms in China after 1949, some knowledge of the historic wage structure is indispensable.

THE DEVELOPMENT OF WAGE STRUCTURES

The structure of wages is a totality composed of a series of structures that differentiate wages by skill or occupation, industry, firm, sector and area. Of all these, skill and occupational differentials are probably the most fundamental and the area (or geographical) the most empirically elusive. The fundamental character of skill differentials arises from the fact that while differentials due to imperfect information and barriers to mobility are usually eroded with the passage of time, skill differentials are likely to persist for as long as there is any heterogeneity in labour force quality. This is because market forces and commonly shared concepts of equity will both tend to remove differentials between persons of equivalent skills, irrespective of the industry, sector or firm in which they work. Thus in the long run, the inter-industry, inter-sector and inter-firm wage structures will each be a reflection of their respective variations in skill requirements.[1]

[1] M. W. Reder, 'Wage differentials: theory and measurement', in *Aspects of labor economics* (National Bureau of Economic Research, Princeton: Princeton University Press, 1962), p. 276.

The elusiveness of the area differential arises from the point that, in order to identify a 'pure' area differential, it is necessary to eliminate from the nominal data the effects of inter-area variations in the sector or industry occupational mix, as well as any regional price differences. In practice this is very difficult, and little effective work has been done on this subject in respect of low-income countries.

There are two related and broadly consistent propositions about the development of wage structures that have received a lot of attention. These are (*a*) that in individual economies there is a tendency for inter-industry wage differentiation of all types to reach a maximum in the early stages of industrialisation and then to decline; and (*b*) that cross-country comparison shows that wage differentiation is greater, 'the lesser the degree and the greater the rate of industrialization'.[1]

The explanation of these phenomena is that in the early stages of industrialisation the supply of manpower capable of industrial work is small – with progressive scarcity as one moves up the skill order – and that constraints on labour mobility, such as imperfect knowledge of job opportunities and customary or legal barriers, are at their most effective. As time passes, however, the pool of labour containing various levels of skills may be expected to grow and social modernisation undermines constraints on mobility. Thus, at a certain point, the long phase of declining differentials begins.

The evidence for these hypotheses is fairly impressive, although important exceptions and anomalies can be found. In this chapter we shall consider this evidence with respect to the cases of the skill and inter-industry wage structures, starting with that for skill.

Skill differentials

Skill and occupational differentials in the industrial sector are usually measured in one of two ways. These are: (i) calculation of the ratio between the wage of the average skilled worker and that of the average unskilled worker; (ii) calculation of the size of the overall wage span within enterprises or industries – either inclusive or exclusive of unskilled workers.[2] In this

---

[1] Lloyd G. Reynolds and Cynthia H. Taft, *The evolution of wage structure* (New Haven: Yale University Press, 1956), p. 356. Clark Kerr, in John T. Dunlop (ed.), *The theory of wage determination* (London: Macmillan, 1957), p. 187.

[2] The data rarely allow us to get beyond these commonly used measures for any significant period of history. Unfortunately the simplicity of the measures seems to lead to ambiguous results in some cases. For example, it would appear that fluctuations in Japanese occupational differentials between 1881 and 1919 moved in opposite directions according to which of the two measures is used. Koji Taira, *Economic development and the labor market in Japan* (New York and London: Columbia University Press, 1970), Chart 1, p. 16.

study we shall refer to (i) as the skill differential and (ii) as the occupational differential.

Using the first of these measures (the ratio of average skilled to unskilled wages), an important survey of industrial wages in fifteen relatively in-dustrialised countries, in 1954, found that in the four industries examined, 80% of the skill differentials fell in the range of 1:1.1 to 1:1.3 and that over the period 1936 to 1954, the median ratios for all four industries declined. It was further noted that there was some evidence of a contraction in the size of inter-industry variations in the skill differential.[1]

These data for industrialised countries indicate that the countries con-cerned were all in the phase of declining skill differentials and constitute impressive evidence of the uniformity of size, as well as of direction, of skill differentials in this phase.

Data for low-income countries show greater variation in both the size and trend direction of skill differentials. Table 1 summarises data on the ratios of average skilled to unskilled workers in selected Asian, African and Latin American economies.

It is probable that some of these inter-country variations arise solely from problems of data definition and comparability – but there are probably some real differences as well. The table shows that skill differentials in 1958–62 ranged from 1:1.32 (Argentina) to 1:2.87 (Congo Brazzaville). There is no systematic relationship between the size of differentials and per capita income in the nineteen countries. However, when countries are ranked by size of differential there is a clear tendency for them to fall into geographical groupings, with African countries exhibiting the highest differentials, Asian the lowest and Latin American falling in between. When one considers the magnitude of intra-group differences in resources, real income and economic structure, this point is of considerable interest.

Of the nineteen countries for which there are data for 1958–62, it is possible to compare these with data for 1948–52 in thirteen cases. Of these, eight had declining and five increasing skill differentials.

The overall impression given by these data is that strong inter-country similarities in the size and trend of skill differentials do not assert themselves in industry until the economy is relatively mature. In the early stages of development, skill differentials may be widening or narrowing, but although inter-country variations are marked, differentials are likely to be sub-stantially higher than in more industrialised economies. All of this is

---

[1] 'Changing wage structures: an international review', *International Labour Office Review* (hereafter *I.L.O. Review*), no. 3, March 1956, pp. 275–83.

TABLE I. *Ratio of skilled to unskilled workers' wages, various developing countries, 1948/52 and 1958/62 (unskilled wage = 100)*

	Year	Ratio	Year	Ratio
Asia				
Hong Kong	1952	196	1962	175
India	—	—	1959	168
Pakistan	1952	169	1962	159
Africa				
Algeria	—	—	1960/2	201
Congo (Brazzaville)	—	—	1960/2	287
Congo (Kinshasa)	1954	338	1960/2	268
Ghana	1954	229	1960/2	240
Ivory Coast	1954	190	1960/2	197
Nigeria	—	—	1960/2	157
Senegal	—	—	1960/2	253
Tanzania	1954	218	1960/2	211
Tunisia	1954	195	1960/2	179
Latin America				
Argentina	1948/52	144	1958/62	132
Brazil	1948/52	206	1958/62	184
Chile	1948/52	194	1958/62	209
Colombia	—	—	1958/62	181
Mexico	1948/52	219	1958/62	212
Peru	1948/52	167	1958/62	171
Venezuela	1948/52	154	1958/62	186

SOURCE: Elliot Berg, 'Wage structures in less-developed countries', in Anthony D. Smith (ed.), *Wage policy issues in economic development* (London: Macmillan, 1969), pp. 334–5.

broadly consistent with our two propositions about the natural history of wage structures.

Apart from industry, data for the overall span of occupational differentials, both in the public sector and throughout the economy as a whole, show much greater differentials than those for industrial workers alone, although in recent years there has been a greater tendency to compression, due to the pervasiveness of minimum wage legislation and an increased supply of literates to the labour force. The public sector span is usually in the range of 1:8 to 1:11, and economy-wide spans of 1:30 have been reported.[1]

[1] Elliot Berg, in Anthony D. Smith (ed.) (1969), p. 320. Koji Taira, 'Wage differentials in developing countries', *I.L.O. Review*, no. 3, March 1966, p. 287.

Industry differentials

Our knowledge of the histories of inter-industry wage structures is rather inadequate, but the 1956 International Labour Office survey did produce some interesting material. The survey showed, for example, that in most countries printing, machinery manufacture and transport equipment manufacture were 'high wage' industries, while textiles, tobacco and clothing were 'low wage' industries. The survey then took one representative from each group (the metals and textile industries) and analysed the ratio between average earnings in them in eleven countries in 1938 and 1954. The eleven countries included Argentina, Japan, Mexico and India, which may be considered as representatives of the low-income, industrialising countries.[1]

The results showed that the 1938 ratio invariably favoured the metals industry and that it varied from 1:1.7 (Mexico) to 1:3.73 (Japan). In nine cases the ratio had declined by 1954, in which year the range was from 1:0.99 (Argentina) to 1:2.14 (Japan).

Unlike the skill ratio, the survey showed that the inter-industry ratio did not exhibit any tendency to vary according to the degree of economic development. In 1938, for example, Japan had the largest ratio and Mexico the smallest, with India and the Argentine ranking sixth and tenth, in the middle.

Although these data are limited in terms of country and time coverage, they do at least confirm the very widespread tendency for wages in the heavy industry sector to exceed those in light industry. This can probably be explained in terms of the relative skill requirements of the two types of industries and of the high proportion of female labour in the textile industry whose earnings are adversely affected by a socially determined sex differential.

Apart from this, it should be noted that inter-industry differentials may not only depend on the composition of skill requirements at any one time, but also on inter-industry variations in rates of technical progress. For where rates of technical progress are higher, it will be necessary to pay for adaptive ability as well as for dexterity and experience, and a premium may also be necessary to ensure the stable commitment of workers trained in new skills which are not generally available in the labour market. In Japan, this latter premium is paid in heavy industry in the form of seniority payments which give the lifetime income curve a much more pronounced shape than is usually the case. This type of technical progress effect has

---

[1] 'Changing wage structures', *I.L.O. Review*, no. 3, March 1956.

probably been a factor in variations in the size of the heavy industry wage differential.[1]

The other factor in inter-industry wage variations will be inter-industry variations in rates of growth. In situations where the supply of industrial labour is scarce and the existing industrial labour force to any degree immobile, fast-growing industries may be expected to have above average rates of wage increase.

WAGE POLICY ISSUES IN DEVELOPING COUNTRIES

The policy issues raised by changing wage structures call ultimately for some means of defining the optimal structure in any given case. Given the complexity of the issues involved in each type of structure and their close interdependence, this is obviously impossible. However, where workers have freedom of job choice and are responsive to wage variations, differentials are indispensable, and unless policy makers have faith in totally unregulated markets, some judgements are bound to be made. Clearly a limiting case where decisions are easy is that where changes in the wage structure have no observable effects on decisions relating to mobility or skill acquisition. The real problems arise when the effects are positive but small. The policy makers then have to decide the extent to which it is worth increasing the wage bill in order to improve the quality and utilisation of the labour force, rather than limiting wage increases and intervening directly by some form of employment direction or changes in training and educational programmes.

Most writers agree that complete lack of regulation is unlikely to lead to satisfactory structures. In India, for example, unregulated markets caused wage structure instability that had costs in terms of productivity losses due to excessive mobility.[2] In Japan on the other hand, historical evidence suggests that at one time unregulated markets tolerated sectoral/skill differentials that were *too low* to enable firms to achieve the levels of commitment necessary for skill acquisition in the modern sector.[3]

Since the Second World War the main issues in wage policy in developing economies have arisen from government intervention that was inappropriate rather than absent. The development of minimum wage legislation and

---

[1] Tsuji Hideo, *Chinkin kōzō* (The structure of wages), (Tokyo: Rōmu Gyōsei Kenkyū Sho, 1955), p. 336.

[2] Morris D. Morris, *The emergence of an industrial labor force in India: a study of the Bombay cotton mills, 1854–1947* (Berkeley: University of California Press, 1965).

[3] Koji Taira (1970), Chap. 5. Both Morris and Taira found that from an early stage the industrial workforce was very mobile in response to wage differentials.

public sector wage policies reflecting political rather than economic considerations, have kept pushing up the wages floor. At the same time there
has in some cases been a tendency to keep some parts of the ceiling high by
maintaining substantial differentials for clerical work – differentials that
reflected the social values of late colonial society rather than contemporary
trends in labour supply.[1] The net effect of these policies has been to keep
real wages in the modern urban sector rising steadily, to keep the skill
differential low, and to increase sectoral differentials both between agriculture and industry and between modern public and traditional sectors in
the cities.[2]

The question of distortions in the inter-sectoral wage structure is particularly important. Reynolds has suggested that skill requirements should
make the appropriate urban–rural differential 25% to 30%. Observed
differentials of 100% to 200% are therefore completely inappropriate, even
if per capita incomes are adjusted for the higher dependency denominator
in urban areas.[3] Sectoral differentials in urban areas have been less discussed, but these too are clearly a growing problem. It has been argued that
the modern industrial and bureaucratic sectors do require substantial
differentials, including those that take the form of seniority payments,
security of tenure and fringe benefits. However if these premiums are
excessive and inflexible, their costs in terms of unemployment and social
divisiveness can be too high.[4] Even in Japan, the *nenkō jōritsu* system,
whose contribution to Japanese industrialisation has been so persuasively
argued, was operated as part of a total system in which at least 20% of the
industrial labour force were temporary workers who were excluded from
its privileges and who moved between the modern and domestic sectors in
response to economic fluctuations.[5]

In conclusion, then, it can be seen that the development of wage structures

---

[1] H. A. Turner, *Wage trends, wage policies, and collective bargaining. The problems for
underdeveloped countries* (Cambridge: Cambridge University Press, 1965).
[2] Between 1956 and 1964 the median increase per annum in real wages in manufacturing
industry in developing countries was 2.7%. A. D. Smith (ed.) (1969), Table 1, p. 44.
[3] Lloyd G. Reynolds, 'The general level of wages', in A. D. Smith (ed.) (1969), p. 78.
[4] Typical fringe benefits in the modern sector amount to 25% to 50% of total remunera-
tion, Elliot Berg in A. D. Smith (ed.) (1969), pp. 305–6. The case for fringe benefits and
tenure security is argued in Koji Taira (1966), pp. 292–4. Discussions of the unemployment costs of erroneous wages policy are in Lloyd G. Reynolds, *Wages, productivity and
industrialization in Puerto Rico* (Homewood: Irwin, 1965), and *Towards full employment*
(Geneva: International Labour Office, 1970), esp. Chaps. 13 and 14.
[5] Miyohei Shinohara, *Structural changes in Japan's economic development* (Economic
Research Series no. 11, The Institute of Economic Research, Hitotsubashi University,
Tokyo: Kinokuniya Bookstore, 1970), p. 315. Koji Taira (1970), pp. 161–3. Shinohara
Miyohei, Funahashi Naomichi (eds.), *Nihon gata chinkin kōzō no kenkyū* (Studies in
Japanese wage structure) (Tokyo: Rōdō Hōgaku shuppan, 1963), Chap. 6.

since the Second World War has become a major policy issue in developing countries. But although awareness of the problem has become more acute and better informed, there is no example of the successful implementation of a comprehensive wage structure policy. For although some social and political factors reinforce the economic case for regulation, the vested interests involved and the intrinsic complexity of implementation have so far prevented any significant achievements.[1]

WAGE CONTROL IN THE COMMAND ECONOMY

Up to now our discussion has dealt with the wage problems of economies in which resource allocation as a whole is left to a significant degree to market mechanisms. In the Soviet Union and other societies whose econo-mies are operated on the basis of 'command' rather than 'market' social-ism, the landscape is rather different. In these economies it is basically true to say that outputs and inputs are determined for the enterprise in physical terms as part of the enterprise's *technical–industrial–financial plan*.[2] Inputs here include labour requirements which are structured in the labour plan by skill categories. The enterprise plan, which is negotiated between the enterprise and its ministry, is in turn part of the national economic plan negotiated between the ministries and co-ordinating agencies of a functional or general character (Ministries of Finance, Labour, State Planning Com-mission, etc.). Thus the enterprise labour plan is part of a unified national labour plan which *is* the demand for labour. On the supply side however, unlike capital equipment and materials, labour is not centrally allocated. Wartime apart, the command economies have allowed substantial freedom of job choice. This probably reflects both deeply ingrained social values and the experience of costly and ineffective labour control experiments.[3]

[1] Most of the contributors to the I.L.O. symposium agreed on the need for a positive wages policy. 'The purpose of wage policy in developing countries', A. D. Smith (ed.) (1969), p. 174. An early, persuasive case for a wage structure policy was put in S. A. Palekar, *Problems of wage policy for economic development, with special reference to India* (London: Asia Publishing House, 1962).

[2] The main sources for this account are, Abram Bergson, *The economics of Soviet planning* (New Haven and London: Yale University Press, 1964), Chaps. 5 and 6. W. Galenson, 'Wage structure and administration in Soviet industry', in J. L. Meij (ed.), *Internal wage structure* (Amsterdam: North Holland Publishing House, 1963), Chap. 6. Janet Chapman, *Wage variation in Soviet industry: the impact of the 1956–1960 wage reform* (Memorandum RM–6076–PR, Santa Monica: The Rand Corporation, 1970), pp. 24–33.

[3] Labour control in the 1920s and 1930s is discussed in Isaac Deutscher, *The Soviet trade unions* (London: Royal Institute of International Affairs, 1965); Solomon M. Schwarz, *Labour in the Soviet Union* (London: Praeger, 1953); S. Swaniewicz, *Forced labour and economic development* (London: Royal Institute of International Affairs, 1965); Margaret Dewar, *Labour policy in the USSR 1917–1928* (London: Royal Institute of International Affairs, 1956).

Thus at the heart of the command economy we find one side of a real market. And although the socialist state has exceptional power to influence directly the composition and motivation of the labour force, wage differentiation has been found to be an indispensable instrument for securing the planned distribution of the labour force and stimulating skill acquisition.

The implication of this for the inter-industry structure of wages is that it must be planned to ensure that it reflects inter-industry variations in skill requirements, geographical location and any factors that create variations in work disutility. If this is not done, the inter-industry distribution of labour will be incorrect and particularly serious problems will arise if there is an overall excess demand for labour. The means to achieve the desired structure take the form of ministry and enterprise plans that have the average wage and the wage bill as their main indicators. At the enterprise level, these indicators are subject to inspection and supervision by the State Banks as well as by the enterprise's controlling ministry.

The size of skill differentials is also planned and control over these takes the form of grade systems whose extent and variation are determined according to the importance of the enterprise's industry, its size and geographical location. Individuals are placed within a grade system in accordance with detailed technical criteria provided in handbooks. Most of these handbooks are on an industry basis, but some relate to occupations and may be used in any industry. Changes in the skill wage structure have to be limited to what is possible within the average and wage bill targets.

In view of the basic differences in the mechanics of wage determination in socialist and non-socialist countries, the question as to how far income distribution and the history of socialist wage structures conform to those of non-socialist countries is of the greatest interest. In the Russian case, the data suggest that the similarities are more important than the differences. Bergson, for example, in his classic study of the distribution of earnings among Soviet industrial wage earners, found a striking similarity between the distribution in Russia in 1928 and that in the United States in 1904. And his data suggested that Stalin's attack on trade union egalitarianism in 1931 led to changes that made the Russian wage distribution approximate even more closely to the market-determined American distribution.[1]

The long-run trends in Russian skill differentials also appear to have followed the pattern of increasing during the early plans and then beginning to decline. Thus the latest reform of 1956–60 reduced the differential

---

[1] Abram Bergson, *The structure of Soviet wages* (Cambridge, Mass.: Harvard University Press, 1954).

between top and bottom grade rates for industrial workers to 1:2 in the case of heavy industry and 1:1.8 in the case of light industry.[1] Some data on this are presented in Table 2.

TABLE 2. *The structure of basic wage scales in Soviet industry, 1962 (post reform)*

Branch of industry	Number of grades	Ratio of top to bottom grade (bottom grade = 100)	Ratio of top to bottom basic rate including special allowances for labour hardship conditions, etc.
Coal			575
Underground mining	8	375	
Surface mining	8	320	
Repair shops	8	280	
Iron and Steel			442
Ore mining underground	8	320	
Metal production	10	320	
Auxiliary work	8	280	
Non-ferrous metallurgy			443
Ore mining	7	286	
Metal production	7	260	
Auxiliary	7	244	
Cement	7	240	277
Chemicals	7	230	351
Petroleum and gas			347
Underground	6	242	
Refineries	6	200	
Drilling	6	200	
Most branches of heavy industry, printing, machine building and metal working	6	200	328
Light industry			
Food industry, non-mechanised work in state farms	6	180	
Textiles	6	180	240
Food	6	180	200
Rural grain and milk processing	6	180	180
All industry			575

SOURCE: Janet Chapman (1970), p. 26.

[1] Janet Chapman (1970), pp. 7–14, 29–30.

The data in Table 3 show differentials between workers, office staff and Engineering–Technical personnel. These are seen to have reached a peak in 1933 and to have since steadily declined. Although the latest reform was purportedly a reflection of egalitarian ideals, observers have pointed out that the compression of skill differentials could plausibly be explained by changes in the labour supply that have lessened the comparative scarcity of many skills.

TABLE 3. *The relationship between earnings of wage earners, Engineering–Technical personnel and office workers in Soviet industry, 1932–66 (average earnings of workers = 100)*

	Average earnings of Engineering–Technical personnel	Average earnings of office workers
1932	263	150
1933	271	151
1935	236	126
1940	213	111
1945	230	101
1950	176	93
1955	166	89
1960	148	82
1962	144	84
1965	142	83
1966	144	84

SOURCE: Janet Chapman (1970), p. 99.

The Russian inter-industry structure, after the initial reform of the First Five Year Plan, has also exhibited considerable uniformity with structures in non-socialist economies. In the initial reform there was a radical restructuring of inter-industry rankings that corresponded to the labour allocation priorities of the plan. Since then, in Russia as elsewhere, textiles and clothing have been prominent 'low wage', and heavy industry and printing prominent 'high wage' industries.

The behaviour of the industry structure through time has also shown some tendency to compression, although the exceptional growth of earnings in the coal industry obscures this.

Table 4 shows that if we include all eleven industries for which data are available for the relevant years, both the overall span and the coefficient of variation widened between 1928 and 1966. However, the exclusion of the

TABLE 4. *Inter-industry differentials in the average earnings of Soviet wage earners, 1928, 1935, 1966 (average of all industrial earnings = 100)*

	1928	1935	1966
Coal	90	115	184
Ferrous metallurgy	106	113	121
Electric power	125	117	98
Chemicals	117	104	100
Machinery and metal working	130	116	99
Paper	95	84	100
Woodworking	87	87	90
Light industry including textiles	82	83	81
Shoes	124	88	82
Garments	114	79	73
Food	97	77	84
Overall span	100–158	100–152	100–252
Coefficient of variation	15.2%	16.4%	28.8%
Coefficient of variation excluding coal	—	—	14.0%

SOURCE: Basic data from Janet Chapman (1970), p. 47.
NOTE: The average of 100 includes earnings in industries not shown in this table.

coal industry from the calculation of the coefficient of variation in 1966 reduces the size of this dramatically.

Wage problems in the command economy

Despite the broad similarity of wage structures and their trends in socialist and non-socialist economies, the wage problems of the command economy are in many ways peculiar to it. By comparison with the wage structure in a market economy, socialist wage structures (particularly rate structures) have a tendency to inertia and rigidity. In practice, however, continuous changes in supply are able to exert some influence on the structure of *earnings*, and when the disparity between earnings and rates becomes excessive, or a major new trend in the wage structure is required, an official wage reform takes place. This combination of unplanned movements in relative earnings and periodic reforms of basic rates seems to enable the wage structure to perform its functions without the emergence of grave anomalies.

However, looking at labour utilisation in its widest perspective, it is arguable that the segmentation of labour markets created by ignorance and mobility impediments is so serious that reliance on the wage structure in the Soviet Union has been excessive. Emily Clark Brown suggested in 1966 that the efficiency of labour utilisation would be improved if labour exchanges were revived to provide information on job opportunities, and in 1969 this became official policy.[1]

Apart from this, the fundamental problem of socialist wage systems is the inability of the planners to ensure optimal utilisation of labour at the enterprise level; that is, to ensure that the labour input used to produce a planned level of output is minimal. This partly arises from the long history of pressures on managers to fulfil physical in preference to financial and cost targets and the effects of this have been reinforced by lax financial control, particularly as exercised by the State Bank.[2] A further problem arises from the point that even if managers *were* responsive to incentives to minimise labour costs, the specification of the occupational structure of the employment plan prevents them from doing so in a rational way.

At bottom, of course, the truth is that both in the Soviet Union and Eastern Europe, all this has not mattered too much, because the supply of labour prior to the 1960s has in general not been severely constrained. And even in the 1960s, overmanning has probably had its socially beneficial aspects.[3] It was however no accident that one of the most radical reforms of a command economy in the 1960s took place in Czechoslovakia, where labour supply was for the first time becoming a serious brake on economic growth. And that a basic part of the Czechoslovakian reform was an attempt to increase productivity and squeeze surplus labour from enterprises. This was to be done by making *increments* to individual income directly dependent on cost and wage indicators of enterprise performance. This policy was of course bound to lead to increased income inequality.[4]

---

[1] Emily Clark Brown, *Soviet trade unions and labor relations* (Cambridge, Mass.: Harvard University Press, 1966), p. 45.

[2] In the Soviet system as it operated before the reforms of the 1960s, the enterprise could usually obtain the funds necessary for excess wage expenditures if it had the support of its ministry.

[3] This point emerges clearly from the survey of East European economies contained in P. J. D. Wiles (ed.), *The prediction of Communist economic performance* (Cambridge: Cambridge University Press, 1971).

[4] B. Levcik, 'Wages and employment problems in the new system of planned management in Czechoslovakia', *I.L.O. Review*, 110, no. 65, 1967, pp. 299–314. According to one source, in the unreformed economy, when income distribution was divided into six strata, the incomes at the bottom of the top stratum were only double those at the top of the bottom. See Ernest Gellner's review of Pavel Machonin's *Czechoslovak society: the sociological analysis of social stratification* (Bratislava), in *New Society*, 5 Aug. 1971.

A move in a similar direction is also visible in some of the recent, more conservative reforms in the Soviet Union.[1] And it seems probable that this problem will arise in other East European economies fairly soon unless it is alleviated by relaxation of intra-bloc controls on labour migration.

[1] Galina Danilovna Soboleva, 'The new Soviet incentive system: a study of its operation in Kiev', *I.L.O. Review*, 101, no. 1, 1970, pp. 15–33.

2

The structure of industrial wages
before 1949

In this chapter we begin by making a statistical sketch of the pre-1949 wage structure and we then attempt to explain this structure in economic terms and consider its relevance to wage policy after 1949.

There are no satisfactory national data that can be used to ascertain the structure of industrial wages in the pre-Communist period. There are however important data for Shanghai and Manchuria, and fragmentary but interesting material for the cities of Canton and Kunming. The Shanghai data are the result of a series of surveys carried out between 1928 and 1946. The coverage and definitions used in these pioneering studies are not completely consistent, but we know sufficient about them to enable us to make use of their results. Certainly, this work reflects the efforts of some of the best Chinese social scientists working in the pre-war period.

The Manchurian data are in some respects even more valuable and impressive. Wage surveys of various kinds were carried out by Japanese research organisations from the end of the First World War up to the mid-1940s and some of these materials are as remarkable in quality as in quantity.[1] In contrast to this, with the exception of Shih Kuo-heng's survey in Kunming, other industrial wage data produced in this period are of problematic value.

The relatively small geographical area covered by good data is not important, since we are concerned with the industrial wage structure, and the share of industrial output and employment accounted for by Shanghai and Manchuria was very large. Only crude estimates of this preponderance are possible at present, but in terms of output, one estimate for 1933 puts the shares of Shanghai and Manchuria in total industrial output at 50% and $12\frac{1}{2}$% respectively. Shortly after this, Manchurian growth accelerated very

---

[1] John Young, *The research activities of the South Manchurian Railway Company, 1907–1945 – A history and bibliography* (New York: The East Asian Institute, Columbia University, 1966). This bibliography alone lists 136 items related to wages and labour, many of which run to hundreds of pages.

rapidly, so that by the early 1940s the combined share of these areas was probably 75%–80%.[1]

Despite the availability of data for these areas, their reconciliation for the purposes of making inter-regional and inter-temporal comparisons presents many problems; such comparisons have therefore to be treated with care and only the most striking evidence can be accepted as relevant for analytical purposes.

OCCUPATIONAL AND SKILL DIFFERENTIALS

Shanghai

In Table 5, we summarise the findings of a survey of the factory labour force in Shanghai in 1946. It can be seen from this table that the skill differential was only 1:1.5. This is low, compared for example with the average differential of 1:2.04 for the thirteen African, Asian and Latin American countries for which we have data for the years 1948–52. The average span of 1:2.37 between the highest and lowest paid workers is also lower than the 3 to 4 fold spans reported in many developing countries in the post-war period.

The analysis of inter-industry aspects of occupational differentials reveals two interesting phenomena. The first is that inter-industry variations in the size of differentials was large – ranging from 1:1.1 in the gas industry to 1:5.2 in matchmaking. Further, the data show that differentials tended to be higher in the light than in the heavy industry sector; and this is true even when the differential is restricted to male workers.

More detailed information about inter-industry aspects of the occupational differential is shown in Table 6, and this table also enables us to draw some conclusions about the way these changed between 1930 and 1946. Clearly, the pattern of change was complex. In six industries the occupational differential increased while in six it declined. When the data are weighted, however, the average span shows a significant decline from 1:1.77 to 1:1.49.[2]

---

[1] This is based on material in John K. Chang, *Industrial development in pre-Communist China* (Chicago: Aldine Publishing Co., 1969) and Yuan-li Wu, *An economic survey of Communist China* (New York: Bookman Associates, 1956), Chap. 2.

[2] A curious feature of these data is that inspection of the changing occupational categories in the twelve industries shows that in eight cases a new occupation reflecting increased mechanisation appeared, and in six of these, the new occupation provided a new top rate. However, when industries are ranked by degrees of increased differentiation, these eight industries fill *the bottom* eight places. Thus technical progress appears to be associated with compression of the occupational wage structure.

TABLE 5. *The structure of skill and occupational wage differentials in Shanghai, 1946 (hourly rates)*

Occupational differentials (average ratios of lowest to highest paid occupations in industry with lowest occupation = 100)		The skill differential (ratio of average wages of skilled workers to average wages of unskilled workers, unskilled average = 100)
All workers[a]	237	150[d]
All skilled workers[b]	215	
All male skilled workers	159	
Male skilled workers in heavy industry (weighted)[c]	119	
Male skilled workers in light industry (weighted)[c]	142	

SOURCE: *Shang hai kung ch'ang lao kung t'ung chi* (Statistics of Shanghai's factory labour) (Shanghai: Shanghai Bureau of Social Affairs, 1947), Tables 13–52, pp. 37–65.

NOTES:
(a) This figure is an unweighted average derived from data for 40 industries. It includes wages of male and female, skilled and unskilled workers.
(b) This figure is the same as the above except that data for 'miscellaneous' and 'packaging' occupations have been excluded. Unfortunately some earlier surveys excluded these categories altogether.
(c) Heavy industry comprises electricity generation, electrical machinery manufacture, machinery, shipbuilding, metallurgical trades and gas. Light industry comprises flour, tobacco, cotton spinning, cotton weaving, paper and matches.
(d) Unskilled workers are those described as 'miscellaneous' and 'packaging workers'.

Manchuria

Our starting point for the skill differential in Manchuria is a survey of manual workers' wages in Dairen, Mukden, Antung and Changchun between 1919 and 1927. As with most Manchurian surveys, the wages of Chinese and Japanese (and sometimes Korean) workers are given separately – even though their occupational designations are identical. For our purposes, it seems appropriate to concentrate on the structure of Chinese wages and leave the question of the racial wage structure on one side.[1]

[1] The racial differential was approximately × 3. However, Japanese sources claimed that Japanese workers were more productive than Chinese and that the 'pure' racial differential was actually × 2. This differential was justified in the mid 1930s as being essential to secure sufficient migration from Japan to alleviate Japanese problems and to establish a large Japanese population in Manchuria for political purposes. These problems are discussed with remarkable frankness in *Nichi-Man rōdō mondai zadankai yōroku* (A summary record of a conference on Japanese–Manchurian labour problems held at the

TABLE 6. *The range of skill differentials in twelve industries in Shanghai, 1930 and 1946 (average hourly rates; lowest occupation = 100)*

Industry	1930	1946
Machinery	133	109
Shipbuilding	128	169
Matchmaking	305	262
Enamelling	221	237
Cotton spinning	191	136
Cotton weaving	208	150
Underwear manufacture	200	437
Flour	147	132
Oil pressing	124	148
Tobacco	130	147
Paper manufacture	181	145
Printing	225	314
Average (weighted)	177	149

SOURCE: Data for 1946, as Table 5, 1930 data from *Wage rates in Shanghai* (Shanghai: The Shanghai Bureau of Social Affairs, 1935), Tables I–XVI, pp. 128–72.

NOTE: The data are for skilled, male, time workers in identifiable occupations.

In order to estimate the size of the skill differential in this case, we have compared the average wage of metal workers and carpenters with the wage for miscellaneous labourers. The results are shown in Table 7. This table

TABLE 7. *Skill differentials in Changchun, Dairen and Antung, 1919–27 (average unskilled wage = 100[a])*

Area	1919	1927
Changchun	250	258
Dairen	428	244
Antung	300	350

SOURCE: *Kako jūgonenkan no Manshū ni okeru Nihonjin oyobi Chūgokujin shukōgyō rōdōsha chingin no sūsei* (Wage trends of Chinese and Japanese manual workers in Manchuria during the past fifteen years) (Dairen: Minami Manshū Tetsudō Kabushiki Kaisha (South Manchurian Railroad Company) [hereafter *MMT*] Shachōshitsu Jinjika, 1927), pp. 5–8.

NOTE: (a) The source does not make clear whether these data are rates or earnings.

Yamato Hotel, Hsinking) (Hsinking: Keichō Dai Ichibu, 1934). See also Takei Gōichi, *Manshū no rōdō to rōdō seisaku* (Manchurian labour and labour policy) (Tokyo: Ganshō Shōten, 1941).

TABLE 8. *Skill differentials in the coal, steel and textile industries in Manchuria, 1939 (earnings of Chinese workers) (average unskilled wage = 100^a)*

Industry					
			Textiles		
Coal	Steel	Textiles	(males)	(females)	Average
136	113	111	(101)	(113)	120

SOURCE: *Manshū kōgyō rōdō gaikyō hōkoku* (Report of a survey of industrial labour conditions in Manchuria) (Hsinking [Changchun]: *MMT* Shinkyō Shisha Chōsashitsu, 1944), pp. 43, 83–5, 166–8.

NOTE:
(a) The basic labour force classification used by the Japanese, distinguishes between regular, apprentice and low-level miscellaneous workers (*honkō, hojo* and *zatsueki*). In estimating the skill differential in this table we have used average wage data for *honkō* and *zatsueki* workers.

suggests, that apart from the Dairen figure for 1919, the skill differential exhibited substantial inter-temporal and inter-city stability in the region of 1:2.5 to 1:3.5, with some tendency in Changchun and Antung for the differential to increase.

Data for these areas in 1928 and 1931, suggest that the skill differential was still increasing,[1] but when we turn to the late 1930s and early 1940s, a distinct narrowing is indicated. Material for 1936, for example, suggests a differential of 1:1.33 and figures of this order are found in later materials

TABLE 9. *The skill differential in the construction industry in Peking, Tientsin, Tsingtao and Tsinan, 1939–42 (average unskilled wage = 100)*

Year	Peking	Tientsin	Tsingtao	Tsinan
1939	191	171	141	157
1940	150	145	138	157
1941	141	147	132	157
1942	140	113	134	114

SOURCE: *Man-shi ni okeru rōdōryoku jijō ni kansuru chōsa* [Gokuhi] (A survey of the labour situation in Manchuria and China) [Top secret] (Tokyo: *MMT* Tōa Keizai Chōsakyoku, 1944), p. 71.

[1] *The Manchoukuo yearbook 1934* (Tokyo: East Asian Economic Research Bureau, 1934), pp. 660–1.

summarised in Tables 8 and 9. The data on the skill differential in construction between 1939 and 1942 shown in Table 9 are confirmed by qualitative reports that link the rapid decline of the skill differential in Manchuria with the development of the Sino-Japanese war after 1937.

Other cities

One other interesting source of information on the skill differential is that produced by Shih Kuo-heng in his survey of labour conditions in an electricity generating plant in the city of Kunming. Here the skill differential was reported to have been 1:2.43 in 1939.

TABLE 10. *Skill and occupational differentials in a Kunming factory, 1939 (minimum unskilled wage = 100; hourly rates)*

Skilled workers	
Maximum	323
Average	292
Minimum	200
Unskilled workers	
Maximum	138
Average	120
Minimum	100
The skill differential	243

SOURCE: Shih Kuo-heng, *China enters the machine age* (Cambridge, Mass.: Harvard University Press, 1944), p. 65. These data were collected from a government owned electricity generating establishment.

Judgements based on these materials must be tentative, but the main conclusions seem to be as follows.

(i) In Manchuria, the only area for which we have long-term data, the skill differential at first increased, and then declined, with an acceleration in this decline towards the end of the period.

(ii) By the late 1930s the skill differential in Manchuria had been compressed to a level that was low by comparison with either Shanghai or international standards.

(iii) In the relatively small, newly industrialising city of Kunming, the skill differential was noticeably higher than in either Manchuria or Shanghai. And finally:

(iv) In inter-industry terms, the Shanghai 1946 data show occupational differentials to be greater in light than heavy industry, while in Manchuria, skill differentials appear greater in the heavy sector, and this tendency appears to have become more pronounced after 1937.

THE INTER-INDUSTRY WAGE STRUCTURE

Our knowledge of the pre-1949 inter-industry wages structure is summarised in Tables 11–13. The Shanghai inter-industry wage structures for 1930, 1936 and 1946 are set out in Table 11. In Table 12, we have data on the Manchurian inter-industry structure for 1924 and 1936. And finally, in Table 13 we have inter-industry data for Canton in 1936.

TABLE 11. *The inter-industry structure of wages in Shanghai 1930, 1936, 1946 (highest ranking industry = 100; average monthly earnings)*

Industry	1930	Industry	1936	Industry	1946
Printing	100	Shipbuilding	100	Shipbuilding	100
Shipbuilding	86	Printing	88	Printing	77
Machinery	63	Machinery	64	Flour	74
Silk weaving	56	Underwear manufacture	49	Wool weaving	72
Oil pressing	52	Enamelling	47	Machinery	72
Enamelling	52	Silk weaving	46	Cotton weaving	66
Hosiery knitting	46	Flour	41	Tobacco	65
Flour	45	Paper manufacture	40	Underwear manufacture	60
Underwear manufacture	44	Wool weaving	39	Cotton spinning	58
Paper manufacture	41	Oil pressing	38	Hosiery knitting	57
Cotton weaving	36	Cotton weaving	38	Paper manufacture	56
Tobacco	36	Tobacco	36	Enamelling	53
Wool weaving	32	Hosiery manufacture	33	Silk weaving	51
Cotton spinning	26	Matchmaking	29	Oil pressing	48
Matchmaking	26	Cotton spinning	25	Matchmaking	43
Silk reeling	21	Silk reeling	20	—	
Overall span	1:4.76		1:5		1:2.33
Coefficient of variation	45%		45.3%		21.2%

SOURCE: *Shang hai kung ch'ang lao kung t'ung chi* (1947), Table 10, p. 35.

Three points emerge from these data. The first is that if we take 1936 as the pre-war norm, a substantial similarity in the ranking of industries is apparent. In all these areas, the metal and machinery sector ranks high relative to textiles; and as Table 14 shows, in Manchuria and Shanghai the metals to textile wage ratio moved to a point in 1936 where the ratio was very close to the average ratio reported for the four developing economies surveyed in 1938.

Following from this, the second phenomenon of note is that whereas the Manchurian inter-industry wage structure reportedly remained fairly stable, in Shanghai there was sharp upward movement of all branches of

TABLE 12. *The inter-industry structure of wages in Manchuria, 1924 and 1936 (highest ranking industry = 100)*

Industry	1924[a]	1936[b]		1936[c]	
Machinery and metals	100	Utilities	100	Metals	100
Utilities	61	Machinery	81	Electricity	84
Chemicals	57	Food	68	Oil pressing	80
Food	57	Chemicals	64	Glass	68
Dyeing	41	Textiles	50	Gas	67
				Cement	54
				Cotton spinning	54
				Hemp bag manufacture	52
Overall span	1:2.44	1:2.0		1:1.92	
Coefficient of variation	31.2%	23.15%		22.8%	

SOURCES AND NOTES

(a) Average basic earnings of Chinese workers in Japanese owned factories from *Manshū kōgyō rōdō jijō* (Labour conditions in Manchurian industry) (Dairen: *MMT* Shomubu Chōsaka, 1925), pp. 52–3.
(b) There is no indication as to whether these data are rates or earnings, see Takei Gōichi, *Manshū no rōdō to rōdō seisaku* (1941), pp. 200–1.
(c) Earnings data for Chinese workers from *Manshū keizai tōkei nempō 1936* (The Manchurian yearbook of economic statistics for 1936) (Dairen: Dairen Chamber of Commerce and Industry, 1937), pp. 156–9.

TABLE 13. *The inter-industry structure of wages in Canton, 1936 (highest ranking industry = 100; monthly earnings)*

Industry	Canton	Industry	Canton
Machinery	100	Wire	43
Glass	69	Shoes	39
Tyres	59	Matches	37
Rice milling	59	Textiles	37
Food	54	Overall span	1:2.71
Soap	50	Coefficient of variation	35.4%
Light industry	49		
Tobacco	49		

SOURCE: *Kuang chou jih pao* (Canton daily) (hereafter *KCJP*), 13 Oct. 1957.

TABLE 14. *The average wage ratio between the machinery and textile industries in Manchuria, Shanghai and Canton, 1924/30 and 1936*

Year	Manchuria	Shanghai	Canton
1924/30	1:1.62	1:2.03	—
1936	1:2.44	1:2.00	1:2.7

SOURCES: As Tables 11–13.

the cotton textile industry during the war. And finally, a further point in the inter-regional comparison, is that in 1936 the span and degree of dispersion of the inter-industry wage structure was greater in Shanghai than in Manchuria or Canton. However, as Table 11 shows, the Shanghai span was compressed during the war by almost half.

MOVEMENTS IN REAL WAGES

Our knowledge of real wage movements in China is still very slight. We do, however have one series (Table 15) that shows movements of real wages, by industry, in Shanghai between 1930, 1936 and 1946. These show that real wages were tending to decline during the 1930s, due probably to the impact of the world depression. But during the wartime period, a very rapid growth of real wages is indicated. It is probable that although upward pressure on wages was also strong in Manchuria at this time, the wage controls exercised by the Manchurian Government were more effective than the wartime controls operated in other parts of China.[1]

THE PRE-WAR WAGE STRUCTURE: CONCLUSIONS

The general picture of the wage structure that emerges from this chapter is one of declining differentials, although both the speed and direction of these movements were subject to significant variations according to the period or industry under consideration.

In the case of occupational and skill differentials, the process of compression had by the 1940s reached a point where Chinese differentials seem low by appropriate international comparison. However, it is important to emphasise that this was partly a consequence of wartime conditions, rather

---

[1] Accounts of these controls are in Takei Gōichi, *Manshū no rōdō to rōdō seisaku* and *The Manchoukuo yearbook 1942* (Hsinking: The Manchoukuo Year Book Company, 1942).

TABLE 15. *Index of real earnings in Shanghai industries 1930–46 (1936 = 100)*

Industry	1930	1936	1946
Machinery	93.33	100	199.23
Shipbuilding	81.09	100	175.71
Matches	84.18	100	263.45
Enamelling	105.54	100	199.26
Silk reeling	98.81	100	—
Cotton spinning	99.80	100	412.65
Silk weaving	116.30	100	197.99
Cotton weaving	90.39	100	308.05
Wool weaving	77.10	100	328.61
Underwear manufacture	85.52	100	218.62
Hosiery knitting	130.37	100	298.58
Flour	103.84	100	324.59
Oil pressing	128.04	100	220.39
Tobacco	93.57	100	317.12
Paper manufacture	97.92	100	244.76
Printing	106.49	100	152.25
Average for all industries	98.74	100	315.20

SOURCE: *Shang hai kung ch'ang lao kung t'ung chi* (1947), Table 12, p. 36.

than being solely the outcome of a steady process reflecting supply factors and the elimination of impediments to mobility.

In Manchuria, the outbreak of the Sino-Japanese war in 1937 and the Pacific War in 1941, were associated with an acute labour shortage. This was mainly due to the acceleration of a war-based programme of industrialisation which had no realistic labour plan incorporated in it. It was also related to an important change in the migration patterns of the Chinese workers who formed an overwhelming proportion of the unskilled workforce.[1] This labour shortage and the consequent drive to recruit Chinese workers was in sharp contrast to the situation in the mid-1930s. For, in this earlier period, the Japanese had attempted to limit the inflow of Chinese workers into Manchuria in order to keep employment opportunities

[1] Matsumura Takao, 'The formation and development of labour and immigration policy after the foundation of Manchoukuo', in *Nihon teikoku shūgi ka no Manshū* (Manchuria under Japanese imperialism) (Tokyo: Manshū Shi Kenkyū Kai, 1972). Migration issues are discussed in *Shōwa jūgonendo nyū-Man kuryokusho tōkei* (Statistics on labourers entering Manchuria in 1940) (No place: Tōya Haigun Kabushiki Kaisha, 1941); *Jihen to nyū-Man rōdōsha mondai* (Problems relating to workers entering Manchuria after the 'China Incident') (Harbin: MMT Hokkei Keizai Shiryō, 1938); *Manshū kōgyō rōdō gaikyō hōkoku*, as cited.

open for their own urban unemployed and rural 'surplus labour', whom it was hoped could be encouraged to migrate from Japan.[1]

The marked decline in the skill differential that accompanied this transformation can thus be explained in terms of two mutually reinforcing factors. The first is that migration trends led to a greater relative shortage of unskilled workers. The second is that the wage controls introduced to control the wage–price inflation were probably more effective at the wage ceilings touched by the more skilled workers than at the lower levels. If this was so, then the presence of an institutional rather than psychological or conventional upper wage limit may have given a special twist to the 'Reder effect'. That is, to the tendency in conditions of labour shortage for employers to lower hiring (or promotion) standards for the more skilled jobs, thus ultimately creating an acute shortage of supply at the lower end of the skill range and thereby driving up wage rates for less skilled workers more than proportionately.

The relationship between war and the skill differential in Shanghai differed somewhat from that suggested above, the main distinction being that in Shanghai a dominant factor in the situation was a rapid inflation. In inflationary conditions, one generally finds that the main tactic of organised labour is to push up the average wage as rapidly as possible, and that in the process of doing this, differentials are eroded. However, as in Manchuria, wage control was also probably more effective at the top of the wage–skill range than at the bottom, and this would have reinforced the other factors that were tending to reduce differentials.

The significant exception to these generalities about the small size of the skill differential in the 1940s is the result of Shih Kuo-heng's 1939 Kunming survey shown in Table 10. In this case, the skill differential is close to that found in Manchuria in the early 1920s.

One explanation of this is that whereas by the late 1930s in Shanghai and Manchuria there existed an established market for labour of all skill levels, in Kunming, industry was established as a wartime measure, so that although unskilled labour could be drawn from local urban and rural sources, skilled labour had to be imported from Shanghai at very high wages. A second consideration is that the transfer costs for migrants moving into the unskilled urban labour market may have been higher in the case of a large city such as Shanghai than in the case of a relatively small city such as Kunming. If this was so, it would tend to increase the unskilled wage in large cities such as Shanghai, relative to that in the smaller ones such as Kunming.

[1] A very good account of this is in Ueda Teijirō, *Nihon jinkō seisaku* (Japan's population policy) (Tokyo: Chikura Shobō, 1937).

Our main conclusion about the inter-industry wage structure is that the 1936 structure was similar in all areas and broadly the same as that found in other economies at comparable levels of development. What has to be explained about this structure is why a sharp geographical difference in it developed during the wartime period, so that, while in Manchuria heavy industry remained high in the inter-industry ranking, in Shanghai it fell. A major factor here was that whereas in Manchuria the wartime inter-industry pattern of output growth favoured heavy industry and thus reinforced the fundamental skill factor in keeping heavy industry high in the rankings, in other areas the rise of light industry is explained both by the different inter-industry pattern of growth, and by the fact that wage controls in these areas were more effective in the publicly controlled heavy sector than in the private, light sector.[1]

From the findings of this chapter, it can be argued that the industrial wage structure as it crystallised in the late 1940s was a complex, spatially fragmented phenomenon, that the post-1949 reformers understandably described as chaotic. But it is also clear that this structure can be at least partially explained in economic terms, only some of which pertain to specifically wartime conditions. Thus a rapid imposition of geographically uniform, standardised wage structures that failed to take account of the economic forces at work in the historic wage structure could be expected to encounter difficulties, and also perhaps to create anomalies as peculiar as those that were supposedly being remedied.

[1] The pattern of inter-industry output growth is indicated in 'An estimate of industrial electricity consumption in Shanghai and the rate of industrial output', *Ching chi chou pao* (The economic weekly) (hereafter *CCCP*), ser. 3, no. 5 (1946).

3

The level and structure of wages
since 1949

In this chapter we describe the evolution of the Chinese wage structure since 1949 and indicate how this structure and the level of wages have interacted during the same period. The data we have drawn on are sometimes fragmentary and ambiguous, so that using them seems as difficult as deducing the characteristics of a lost civilisation from a mass of broken pots. However it is probably true that, by comparison with the standards of other low income countries, the range and even the quality of wage statistics relating to the years before 1958 are quite good. There is a certain mystique about the lack and low quality of Chinese economic data. But most scholars who have attempted serious comparative work would agree that this can be exaggerated. The statistical blackout of the 1960s, in contrast, presents real problems since it has only been relieved by a few isolated flashes of information.

One factor that is an aid to the interpretation of wage information is that the rules governing wage calculation and accounting have remained constant over lengthy periods. For example we know that the rules for calculating minimum wages in 1957 were exactly those developed in 1948. Similarly, the accounting rules for defining the components of the enterprise wage bill remained virtually unchanged between 1951 and 1965.[1]

A possible break in accounting continuities is the Cultural Revolution. For this seems to have been accompanied by important changes in incentive organisation and occupational nomenclature. But since the details and permanence of these changes are not clear and may be less than they seemed at the time, it seems appropriate to continue to assume that the fundamentals of the pre-1966 system have remained unaltered up to the present.[2]

---

[1] Liu Yi, 'The system of wage grades for workers', *Lao tung* (Labour) (hereafter *LT*),1957, no. 7, pp. 24–5; The regulations on wage bill accounting are in *LT*, 1951, no. 8, pp. 9–10; *Kung yeh k'uai chi ho suan* (Industrial accountancy calculation) (Peking: Chinese People's University Publishing House, 1965), pp. 121–4. These regulations also applied in the private sector, *Szu ying ch'i yeh k'uai chi chih tu* (The accounting system in private enterprises) (Peking: The China Book Bureau, 1954), Chap. 5.
[2] *1969 Shin Chūgoku nenkan* (The new China yearbook) (Tokyo: Chūgoku Kenkyū Shō, 1969), pp. 89–91.

THE CLASSIFICATION OF THE LABOUR FORCE

Let us now define the main groups of persons whose wages we are interested in. Several classifications are possible and below we list some of the most important ones found in Chinese wage literature. The employed population in urban areas may be divided into four sectors. These are: (I) workers and staff employed in State Administrative Organs, Mass Organisations, Welfare and Educational establishments; (II) workers and staff in economic enterprises in the public sector; (III) persons employed in cooperativised handicraft and trade activities and (IV) persons engaged in private economic activity in either the modern or traditional sector. Since the socialisation of industry and trade in 1956, there has been no modern private sector, but a residual, unorganised private sector has remained in existence.

Workers and staff in (I) are divided into occupational categories which in 1956 spanned thirty wage grades. At the top of the range are senior officials of the State Council, Judiciary, etc., and at the bottom, miscellaneous persons engaged in the lowest levels of office work, i.e. messengers, cleaners, etc.[1]

Within the cooperative sector (III), the most important distinction is that between wage earning staff who administer the cooperatives and the cooperative members themselves, the incomes of the latter being variable – depending on the fluctuating income of the cooperatives and the allocation of income between accumulation, welfare and personal income.

For our purposes the most important group of occupational categories is that comprising workers and staff in industry (sector II). In wage accounting this group is divided into the following categories: (*a*) production workers; (*b*) apprentices; (*c*) skilled and managerial staff; (*d*) ordinary staff; (*e*) miscellaneous personnel (sweepers, etc.), and (*f*) guards.[2] Within the production worker category there is an important distinction between skilled workers on the permanent establishment and unskilled labourers, many of whom would be employed on a temporary basis. Category (*c*) is similar to the Soviet Engineering–Managerial–Technical Personnel class, although the criteria for inclusion in this category are much looser in China than in the Soviet Union.[3]

[1] *1955 Chin jung fa kuei hui pien* (The 1955 compendium of currency laws and regulations) (Peking: Currency Publishing House, 1956), pp. 550–2; *1956 Chung yang ts'ai cheng fa kuei hui pien* (The 1956 compendium of Central Government financial laws and regulations) (Peking: Financial Publishing House, 1957), pp. 228–39.
[2] *Lao tung t'ung chi kung tso shou ts'e* (Handbook of labour statistics) (Peking: Statistical Publishing House, 1958), p. 17.
[3] This will be discussed in John Philip Emerson's forthcoming work on Chinese technical manpower.

In some instances industrial personnel are further classified into: (1) production personnel (including skilled and unskilled workers, ordinary, skilled and managerial staff and apprentices); (2) personnel not connected with production, and (3) personnel not included in the enterprise labour record.[1]

We have referred several times to the category of workers and staff. This is a basic manpower term and it refers to all persons employed in public administration, economic enterprises, education, health and Mass Organisations, in rural and urban areas, who have a regular wage or salary. It therefore *excludes* capitalists, cooperative members and others in occupations where incomes are variable.

TABLE 16. *Workers and staff by branch of the economy 1949, 1952 and 1957 (millions)*

Branch	1949	1952	1957
Material production total	5.203	10.446	17.865
of which:			
1. Industry	3.059	5.263	7.907
2. State farms, etc.	0.088	0.282	0.925
3. Construction	0.200	1.048	1.910
4. Transport and communication	0.634	1.129	1.878
5. Trade, food and drinks	1.222	2.724	5.245
Non-productive branches total	2.801	5.358	6.641
Total productive and non-productive	8.004	15.804	24.506
Workers and staff as a percentage of all non-agricultural employment	30.5%	43.0%	61.8%
Industrial employment as a percentage of total urban employment	12.9%	20.2%	24.4%

SOURCES: John Philip Emerson, *Nonagricultural employment in mainland China 1949–1958* (Washington: U.S. Department of Commerce, 1965), Tables 1 and 2, pp. 128–9. 'Statistical materials on our country's population', *TCKT*, 1957, no. 11, pp. 24–5; 'A tentative discussion of the relationship between socialist urban population increase and the development of agricultural and industrial production', *Kuang ming jih pao* (The enlightenment daily) (hereafter *KMJP*), 7 Oct. 1963; 'The gap between the rise in the living standards of workers and peasants is not excessive', *Ho nan jih pao* (Honan daily) (hereafter *HNJP*), 27 Sept. 1957; 'A preliminary research survey into the difference in living standards of peasants and workers in Kiangsu province', *LT*, 1957, no. 21, pp. 18–21; 'The standard of living of the city's workers and peasants is gradually rising', *Lü-Ta jih pao* (Lushun-Dairen daily) (hereafter *LTJP*), 15 July 1957.

[1] Chou Feng-ching and Wang Hung-ting, 'The compilation of enterprise wage and labour plans', *Chung Kuo kung yeh* (Chinese industry) (hereafter *CKKY*), 1957, no. 2, p. 61; 'We do research into the problem of calculating the number of temporaries to be included in the enterprise labour record', *T'ung chi kung tso* (Statistical research) (hereafter *TCKT*), 1957, no. 4, p. 19.

To give some idea of the magnitudes involved we show in Table 16 data on the growth of employment of workers and staff by branch of the economy for the years 1949 to 1957.

From this table one can see that persons classified as workers and staff were not a majority, even of non-agricultural employment, before the mid 1950s, and that industrial employment was still less than a quarter of total urban employment in 1957 – the last year of the First Five Year Plan. None the less, workers and staff, particularly industrial workers and staff, were obviously the dynamic sector in terms of employment growth in these years. But perspective plans made in the 1950s and the *hsia fang* (sending down) campaigns of the 1960s, both suggest that the rate of growth of these sectors has declined in the past twelve years.[1]

TABLE 17. *Money wages of workers and staff, 1949–72 (annual average wage, yuan)*

	1949	1950	1951	1952	1953	1954	1955	1956	1957	1958	1959	1963	1971	1972
Wage	262	322	379	446	496	519	534	610	637	(657)	(690)	607	650	715
Index	100	123	145	170	189	198	204	233	243	(251)	(263)	232	248	273
% change on previous quoted year		23	18	18	11	5	3	14	4	n.a.	n.a.	−5	7	10

SOURCES

1949–59. *Ten great years* (Peking: Foreign Languages Press, 1960), p. 216; *New China News Agency* (hereafter *NCNA*), 26 Jan. 1960; *Average annual money earnings of workers and staff in Communist China* (Washington: Central Intelligence Agency, 1960). The figure for 1958 is not comparable with earlier figures because it excludes new entrants to the labour force. The same is probably true of 1959.

1963. This is an estimate based on data for the wages growth of workers and staff in Peking. Since Peking was a 'key point' city, wages growth there would tend to be a little above average, but we have made no allowance for this. *NCNA*, 27 July 1964, translated in *Survey of the China Mainland Press* (hereafter *SCMP*), 1964, no. 3269.

1971. 'Living standards in China improve', *Peking Review*, 30 Sept. 1971. This figure is a maximum in the sense that it probably excludes recent entrants to the labour force and temporary workers.

1972. The figure of a 10 % rise in 1972 is based on: (a) an estimate of the effect on the average wage of the reform discussed in Chapter 6 (assuming wages scales published in the 1960s were typical and worker distribution between grades approximately as revealed in the only survey of this, that of 1955), and (b) visitors' reports, for example, 'China: a new tranquillity', *Newsweek*, 19 June 1972. Unfortunately, the data on output and the economy published by the Chinese in May 1972 contained no information on changes in wages.

[1] Christopher Howe, *Employment and economic growth in urban China 1949–1957* (Cambridge: Cambridge University Press, 1971), Chaps. 7–8.

THE LEVEL OF WAGES

Most available data on changes in average wages relate to the average money earnings of all workers and staff. In Table 17 we show these for the period 1949 to 1972.

In addition to this basic series we have data for industrial workers and staff only.

TABLE 18. *Money wages of workers and staff in industry, 1949/50–1957 (annual average wage, yuan)*

	1949/50	1952	1957
	350	525	694
Index	100	150	198

SOURCES: Chao Yi-wen, *Hsin Chung Kuo ti kung yeh* (New China's industry) (Peking: Statistical Publishing House, 1957), pp. 32–3. The 1957 figure is estimated on the assumption that workers and staff in industry had the same percentage rise as *all* workers and staff.

The changes in real average wages represented by these figures can be calculated from retail price and cost of living indexes shown in Table 19. In this table we show the official retail price index and another index compiled on the basis of data from eight major cities. We also show price data from five provinces and three cities.

Finally in Table 20 we summarise official data on money and real wages in terms of growth rates.

These tables indicate how the pace of real and money wages growth has varied between 1949 and the early 1970s. The earliest period (1949–52) is difficult to interpret because the wage data are of low quality and the coverage of the price index unclear. But the First Five Year Plan emerges as a period of rapid real wage growth; the rate of 7.4% per annum achieved by all workers and staff and 5.7% per annum by industrial workers and staff being significantly higher than the median 2.7% real wage growth reported by manufacturing industry in developing countries in a similar period. The fall in real wages between 1957 and 1963 reflects both price rises and a fall in money wages. The cause of the latter is unclear, but it seems unlikely that it was due to a fall in basic rates. The most probable explanation is that it reflects very tight control of promotion. For if, as older, highly paid, workers retired, they were replaced by new entrants

TABLE 19. *National and local indexes of retail prices and the cost of living, 1952–63*

	1952	1956	1957	1963
Retail prices in eight cities	100	107.8	109	118.2 ⎱ ᵃ
National retail price index	99.9	106.3	108.6	⎰
Shanghai cost of living index	100	108.2	109	— ᵇ
Shanghai retail prices	100	109.1	110.5	— ᶜ
Changchun retail prices	100	106.4	110.5	— ᵈ
Hupei price index (unspec.)	100	105.1	—	— ᵉ
Kansu wholesale price index	100	98.6	—	— ᶠ
Kwangsi price index (unspec.)	100	112.1	—	— ᵍ
Liaoning price index (unspec.)	100	—	107.5	— ʰ
Nanking cost of living index	100	112.0	—	— ⁱ
Shantung retail price index	100	110.1	—	— ʲ

SOURCES
(a) *Ten great years* (1960), pp. 171 and 174; 'In the fifteen years since liberation commodity prices have remained stable', NCNA (Peking), 3 Dec. 1964, *Ta kung pao* (hereafter *TKP*) (Hong Kong), 4 Dec. 1964.
(b) *Shang hai chieh fang ch'ien hou wu chia tzu liao hui pien* (A compendium of Shanghai commodity prices before and after liberation) (Shanghai: Shanghai People's Publishing House, 1958), p. 463.
(c) Ibid. p. 460.
(d) *Ch'ang ch'un jih pao* (Changchun daily) (hereafter *CCJP*), 17 Nov. 1957.
(e) *Hu pei jih pao* (Hupei daily) (hereafter *HPJP*), 11 Aug. 1957.
(f) *Kan su jih pao* (Kansu daily) (hereafter *KSJP*), 10 July 1957.
(g) *Kuang hsi jih pao* (Kwangsi daily) (hereafter *KHJP*), 10 Nov. 1957.
(h) *Liao ning jih pao* (Liaoning daily) (hereafter *LNJP*), 1 Oct. 1957.
(i) *Nan ching jih pao* (Nanking daily) (hereafter *NCJP*), 1 July 1957.
(j) *Ta chung pao* (Masses daily) (hereafter *TCP*), 16 Aug. 1957.

without replacement promotions, the effect would be to lower the average money wage.

The official figures for 1971 and 1972 suggest that real wages began to grow again in 1972, although this is subject to the assumption that the price level has been stabilised in recent years.

Over the period 1952–72, the wages of workers and staff are estimated to have grown at 1.9% per annum in real terms. This is lower than the 2.7% mentioned above. However it would be wrong to jump to any hasty conclusions about the implications of these data for the welfare of the labour force. The absolute level of consumption of workers and staff reached by the late 1950s was fairly high, and the total welfare implications of wage levels and changes thereof cannot be evaluated without analysis of supple-

HWP

TABLE 20. *Growth rates of real and money wages of all workers and staff and industrial workers and staff, 1949/50 – 1972 (per cent per annum)*

	Money wages		Real wages	
	All workers and staff	Industrial workers and staff	All workers and staff	Industrial workers and staff
1949/50 – 1952[a]	17.5	14.5	21.2	17.0
1952 –1957	7.4	5.7	6.0	4.0
1957 – 1963	− 0.8	n.a.	− 2.1	n.a.
1963 – 1972[a]	1.9	n.a.	1.9	n.a.
1952 – 1972[a]	2.4	n.a.	1.9	n.a.

SOURCES: As for Tables 17, 18, 19.
NOTE: (a) real wage data after 1963 assume no net rise in retail prices. The price data for 1949/50 – 1952 are based on 1950 (March) = 100, wage data start in 1949.

mentary benefits, income security and other factors outside the scope of this analysis.

An important qualification to these tables is that it is likely that official, national data do not tell the whole story. It will be observed, for example, that in 1956, five out of the six local price indexes stood above the official retail price index. These discrepancies suggest that the official index understates the price movements relevant to real wage estimates and this may be due to different handling of the commodity composition and price choices involved in index composition. There is evidence, for example, that in the crucial case of food, national indexes gave excessive weight to primary foodstuffs and official prices.

Local indexes on the other hand gave more realistic treatment to secondary foodstuffs although they probably did not include the prices of illicit transactions. One index of secondary foodstuffs prices reportedly rose 13.48% between 1952 and 1956 and probably nearly half as much again in 1957,[1] and the importance of this can be judged from the fact that according to consumption surveys, these foodstuffs accounted for 41% of all food and 24% of all consumption expenditure.[2] In other cases too – for

[1] Chiang Chen-wu, 'Some views on the wage reform', *Jen min tien yeh* (People's electricity) (hereafter *JMTY*), 1956, no. 21, pp. 5–9. The impact of secondary foodstuffs on retail prices is illustrated by the fact that while the eight-city retail price index stood at 101.1 in 1956 (1950 = 100), the Taiyuan retail price index (which included secondary foodstuffs) stood at 129.53 in 1956 (1950 = 100), *Shan hsi jih pao* (Shansi daily) (hereafter *SHJP*), 18 Aug. 1957.
[2] Hsieh Chien-yün, 'The change of livelihood in a worker's household', *Hsin Hua pan yüeh k'an* (The new China semi-monthly) (hereafter *HHPYK*), 1957, no. 10, p. 87.

example rent expenditure – official real income calculations used controlled prices in public accommodation where a more realistic approach would have to take account of higher prices actually being paid in licit and illicit transactions.[1]

Apart from the problems raised by price indexes, official real wage information does not take account of the effect on real incomes of changes in subsidies, utility prices and certain types of bonus payments. The importance of these factors was widely discussed in 1956 and these discussions throw some further doubt on the meaning of real wage changes calculated from official data. For example in 1954, it was reported that workers and staff in public sector economic departments had average money wage increases of 5.2% and the official data for workers and staff money wages in 1955 show a small but positive movement.[2] Yet evidence from as far apart as Changchun city and Kwangtung province later reported substantial wage declines in these years due to changes in bonus procedures, etc.[3] Conversely, in 1956 the real effect of the national wage reform was greater than official data show, due to changes in public sector pricing and subsidy payments not reflected in these series.[4]

The above remarks justify qualification – rather than rejection – of official estimates of changes in the wage level and there does not seem adequate reason to doubt that the changing pace of wage trends for workers and staff was broadly as shown in Table 20.

1777685

THE STRUCTURE OF WAGES

Occupational and skill differentials in industry after 1949

In this section we are mainly concerned with changes in the occupational wage structure in industry, and there are three aspects of this of interest to us: the overall span of incomes within enterprises; the relationship *between* the average incomes of the main occupational groupings within enterprises; and the degree of differentiation *within* the main occupational groups.

The span of incomes within enterprises before 1949 was very large, and

[1] For example, 'The change in the standard of living of Shanghai workers in the past 27 years', *TCKT*, 1957, no. 13, pp. 6–7. Official rents were used in this survey although many Shanghai workers were actually paying above these, see Christopher Howe, 'The supply and administration of urban housing in mainland China: the case of Shanghai', *The China Quarterly*, Jan.–Mar. 1968, pp. 73–97.
[2] 'The rate of increase of wages should be lower than that of productivity', *TKP*, 3 Feb. 1955 and Table 17.
[3] Shen Ya-kang, 'The wage reform must be put into an important place', *LT*, 1956, no. 7, pp. 31–2; *Nan fang jih pao* (Southern daily) (hereafter *NFJP*), 4 Aug. 1956.
[4] *Hsin wen jih pao* (Daily news) (hereafter *HWJP*), 2 Sept. 1957.

TABLE 21. *Intra-enterprise wage differentials 1948, 1956, 1957 and 1972* (*top rate/earnings* = *100*)

Occupation	Manchuria 1948[a]	Szechuan 1956[b]	Liaoning 1957[c]	Shenyang 1972[d]
Managerial staff	33–100	67–100	59–100	n.a.–78
Skilled technical staff	25–100	42–66	51–85	15–100
Ordinary staff	n.a.–60	25–40	37–56	
Skilled production workers }				
Unskilled production workers }	20–60	20–65	14–47	14–45
Miscellaneous personnel	n.a.	19–33	n.a.	n.a.
Overall span	× 5.00	× 5.26	× 7.15	× 6.98

SOURCES
(a) *Chung yang ts'ai ching cheng ts'e fa ling hui pien*, First Collection, vol. 2 (1952), p. 710.
(b) 'Struggle to eliminate the phenomenon of egalitarianism in the wage system', *LT*, 1956, no. 3, pp. 16–17.
(c) Ishikawa Shigeru, 'Changes in the structure of employment and wages in the Second Five Year Plan', in *Chūgoku keizai hatten no tōkei kenkyū II* (Studies in the statistics of China's economic development) (Tokyo: Ajia Keizai Kenkyū Sho, 1962), pp. 52–3.
(d) Mitch Meisner, 'The Shenyang transformer factory – a profile', *The China Quarterly*, no. 52, Oct.–Dec. 1972, p. 731.

40 to 50 fold spans between top and bottom incomes were reported as common. Differentials of this order were popularly regarded as unacceptable and after Liberation, local, spontaneous reforms led to their being reduced to spans of 2 to 3.5 fold. These in turn were considered by the planners as too narrow and the official guideline was that spans should normally be 6 to 7 fold, while in Manchuria they could be up to 10 fold.[1] The latter figure involved a substantial increase in differentiation, because the official rates for Manchurian industry in 1948 stipulated that top rates for managers and technicians should only be five times the rate for unskilled workers[2] (see Table 21).

In Table 21 we have data on actual enterprise wage structures in the 1950s and in 1972, together with an example of the official planned rate structure for public sector enterprises in Manchuria in 1948.

[1] Wang Ya-ch'iang, *Kung yeh ch'i yeh kung tzu ti li lun yü shih chien* (The theory and practice of wages in industrial enterprises) (Peking: Machinery Publishing House, 1955), Chaps. 7 and 12.
[2] *Chung yang ts'ai ching cheng ts'e fa ling hui pien* (Compendium of Central Government financial laws), First Collection, vol. 2 (Peking: New China Bookstore, 1950), pp. 710–13.

TABLE 22. *Salary coefficients for selected occupations in iron and steel enterprises, 1956*

Occupation	Number of salary rates	Salary coefficient Class I enterprises
Factory level leadership personnel		
Factory director, chief engineer	1	3.00–2.55
Assistant directors, assistants to the director, assistant chief engineer, chief smelting engineer, chief rolling engineer, chief power equipment engineer	2	2.55–2.10
Department level leadership personnel		
Production, technical, technical control department chiefs	1	2.52–2.10
Senior dispatcher, and planning, design, labour organisation, supply accounting and safety department chiefs	2	2.10–1.74
Industrial education, personnel, welfare and secretariat chiefs	3	1.78–1.48
Engineering and technical personnel		
Shift dispatcher	1	1.78–1.48
Senior engineers, senior designers (smelting, rolling, machinery, electricity, planning technical norms, safety, technical control, technical education, supply)	2	1.74–1.45
Engineers	3	1.45–1.20
Higher grade technicians (norm calibrating, labour organisation, technical control, equipment control, product control, designing, safety)	4	1.10–0.86
Technicians (technical personnel of other departments)	5	0.86–0.66
Administrative personnel		
Warehouse chief, cost accountants, summary statisticians, economists	1	1.10–0.86
Warehouse section chief, records chief, warehouse administrator, statisticians, draftsmen	2	0.86–0.66
Bookkeepers, cashiers, sales personnel, timekeepers	3	0.72–0.62
Bill collectors, copiers, examiners, transport personnel, freight inspectors, packaging controllers, general affairs and welfare personnel, clerks	4	0.66–0.55
Telephone operators, typists, mail clerks, stencillers, copyists, labellers and markers	5	0.60–0.50

SOURCE: K'o Pe, 'A tentative discussion of the professional duties salary system for senior administrators, engineers, and technicians, and staff personnel', *CKKY*, 1956, no. 2, p. 3.

TABLE 23. *Wage differentials between selected occupations in heavy industry,*
1948 and 1956 (top rate = 100)

Occupation	1948	1956
Factory manager and chief engineers	76–100	85–100
Department chiefs	81–100	50–84
Skilled technical staff	63–81	22–59
Accountants	40–76	29–37
Typists	40–56	17–22
Miscellaneous personnel	22–40	18–22
Skilled production workers	14–45	n.a.

SOURCES: Data for 1948 from 'The wage system in Lushun-Dairen', *CKKY*,
1950, vol. 2, no. 2, pp. 11–19.
Data for 1956 as Table 22.

A more detailed account of the structure of industrial staff salary rates is
given in Table 22. This shows official rates for persons in different occupations in enterprises of the largest and most modern character. In the
following table we compare the salary standards of selected occupations in
heavy industry in Lushun-Dairen in 1948 with rates proposed for the iron
and steel industry in 1956. Table 22 illustrates the specialisation and detail of
official salary structures and Table 23 indicates how inter-occupational
salary differentials moved in the 1950s and gives us a more controlled
measure of wage spans within industrial enterprises.

These tables show that in the 1950s, intra-enterprise wage spans were
reduced to the range of 4 to 7 fold – approximately in line with early plans,
except that the planned 10 fold spans in Manchuria do not seem to have
been achieved.

In the 1960s, scattered data indicate that there was some further contraction of the overall span. For example, in 1963 a Wusih tyre factory was
reported as having the occupational wage structure summarised in Table 24.

The overall span here is only 3.7 and another article, published in 1965,
confirmed that a 4 fold span was normal in heavy industry. However,
our data for 1971/2 suggest that the acceleration of industrial growth
after the Cultural Revolution was accompanied by a widening of the span
back to the 5 to 7 fold level.[1]

---

[1] 'A Peking shopper's guide', *The Sunday Times*, 9 May 1971; *Peking Review*, 30 Sept.
1971. Another interesting income span is that found within Communes. It was reported
that in Tibetan Communes the span between the Commune head and the average
Tibetan labourer was ninefold, *The Times*, 23 Dec. 1970.

TABLE 24. *The occupational wage structure in a Wusih tyre factory, 1963 (top rate = 100)*

Occupation	Monthly wage (yuan)	Rate
Party secretary	110	100
Factory manager	95	86
Department chief	60–65	55–59
Department staff	40–50	36–45
Workers	30–68	27–62
Overall span	—	×3.7

SOURCE: 'The treatment of workers and staff in a Wusih tyre factory', *Yüan tung kuan ch'a* (Far east perspective) (Hong Kong), 16 June 1963.

We turn now to the relationships between the main occupational groupings and trends in these. A feature of the situation in the early 1950s was that top rates for managerial and technical staff were the same, and technical staff *earnings* may well have been higher. At the time, this was seen to be a concession to the acute shortage of technical staff. By 1955 however, the relative shortages had changed and there were complaints of various compressions and confusions in the enterprise wage structure. Senior managerial staff felt they had lost ground to all other groups, and at a lower level, foremen (*ch'e chien chu jen*) were falling behind skilled workers. One survey of 244 enterprises, for example, found that 77 % of foremen were on rates below top skilled workers.[1] As a result, the 1956 reform gave preferential rises to managerial staff at all levels. Thus by 1958, the data shown in Table 25

TABLE 25. *The growth of incomes of persons in the major occupational categories in industrial enterprises, 1952–7*

Occupation	Increase (%)
Managerial staff	86.89
Ordinary staff	76.11
Skilled technical staff	70.50
Workers	52.67

SOURCE: Shu Jui-ho and Chou Fei-kuang, 'The wage problem adjustment programme of some factories', *LT*, 1958, no. 2, p. 22.

[1] Sung P'ing, 'Why is it necessary to introduce wage reform?' *HHPYK*, 1956, no. 10, p. 75.

on the relative growth of incomes of persons in different occupational categories were being given.

This table reflects the increased inter-group differentiation achieved in the 1956 wage reform. In the 1970s, however, there seems to have been a renewal of the tendency to lessen differentials between managerial staff and others (Table 24). Even more remarkable, is that our 1972 data (Table 21) indicate that at the top levels, skilled technical staff have again overtaken the managers. This may reflect demand, as well as skill scarcity due to disruption of training in the Cultural Revolution.

Let us now turn to the question of intra-group wage differentiation. In the case of staff, Table 22 gives us a view of the situation in 1956. But unfortunately trends in this type of differentiation are difficult to discern due to definitional problems. From Table 21, however, it would appear that there has been some compression of differentials within the managerial and technical staff groups. This compression is probably due to a growing standardisation of the qualifications for membership. Table 23 indicates that the range of payments possible for each *occupation* also narrowed during the 1950s, presumably for the same reason.

In the case of differentials among skilled workers we are on firmer ground. This is because official data showing the range of rates for skilled workers are more readily available. In column one of Table 26, we show the official, recommended rate spans for skilled workers by industry. And in subsequent columns, we show actual rate spans in 1950 and 1956. These show that rate spans increased during the 1950s, again largely due to the 1956 reform.

There is some evidence that in the mid-1960s differentials between skilled workers were compressed.[1] But the Shenyang data for 1972 (Table 21) suggest that the widening of differentials in enterprises has resulted in the restoration of the 1956 rate spans for the skilled worker class.

The bureaucratic wage and salary structure. Wages and salaries in the bureaucracy are known mainly from tables published in 1955 and 1956. In 1955, there were thirty main wage and salary grades and the overall span was 31.1 fold. For workers employed at the Provincial and Municipal levels of Government, the span was 18.9 fold. In 1956, a reform of this system made the grading process more flexible in the sense that persons with specific occupations could be placed within a wider band of rates,[2] but the

[1] 'The wage income of the Chinese workers increases endlessly', *NCNA*, 3 May 1965.
[2] See above, p. 29, n. 1.

TABLE 26. *Rate spans for skilled workers, 1950 and 1956*

Industry	Recom- mended 1950	South Central 1950	North East 1950	Liaoning post-1956 reform	
Non-ferrous metals	1:3.0	1:2.82	1:2.93	Iron and steel	1:3.2
Heavy chemicals, electricity	1:2.9	1:2.75	1:2.9	Mining	1:3.2
Machinery repair	1:2.85	1:2.7	1:2.87	Glass, cement	1:3.0
Textiles, shoes	1:2.7	1:2.65	1:2.66	Machine tools	1:3.15
Flour, clothes, watches and	1:2.5	1:2.53,	1:2.58	Textiles	1:2.7
cigarettes		1:2.4		Tobacco, sugar, wine	1:2.5

SOURCES: Wang Ya-ch'iang (1955), p. 44; *LT*, 1957, no. 8, p. 26.

reform kept the same income spans. In 1958, however, a further reform reduced the span to 20 fold, and there are references in Red Guard literature to further compressions of the bureaucratic income structure in 1959, 1960 and 1963.[1]

In the Cultural Revolution, the whole structure of governmental and staff occupations seems to have been under pressure and at least partially abolished. But the latest reports suggest that, by autumn 1972, the old system had been revived in modified form.

The occupational wage structure: conclusions. The total impression given by data on the structure of occupational differentials is that these increased between 1950 and 1956, declined in the 1960s, but were restored by 1972. It seems also to be the case that successful changes in intergroup differentials have been made. It must however be remembered that most of our data are official rates rather than earnings and that most of them also refer only to the public sector. The situation in the private sector (which after 1956 became the 'public–private' sector) was far more disorderly – at least in terms of official wage objectives. As late as 1956, interenterprise spans of up to 65 fold and other distortions were being reported[2] and although the most glaring anomalies were corrected in the special wage reform of autumn 1956, immediate conformity to public sector standards

[1] *1966 Shin Chūgoku nenkan* (*benran*) (The 1966 New China yearbook, Compendium), p. 284; 'Why were high wages not reduced?', *Shuang ch'en yüeh* (Frosty morning moon), 1968, no. 1 (10 Jan.).
[2] 'The wage situation in new public–private enterprises', *LT*, 1956, no. 11, pp. 16–18.

TABLE 27. *The skill differential in industry, 1951, 1956 and the early 1960s* (*average unskilled wage = 100*)

	Skill ratio
The chemical sector in Manchuria, 1951	128[a]
The textile industry in Kiangsu, 1956	150–160[b]
The industrial sector in Canton, early 1960s	160–165[c]

SOURCES

(a) 'The path to a rational wage system', *Tung pei kung yeh* (North Eastern industry) (hereafter *TPKY*), 1951, no. 47, pp. 25–9.

(b) 'Some views on the fixing of ordinary workers' wages', *LT*, 1958, no. 6, p. 11; 'Questions and answers on wage reform', *HWJP*, 14 Aug. 1956.

(c) Estimated from ordinary worker rates reported by refugees and data on Canton in *Wen hui pao* (Cultural contact daily) (hereafter *WHP*) (Hong Kong) 8 Dec. 1957.

was unattainable, and Red Guard sources reported that in 1965 the private sector wage structure was still chaotic.[1]

It is difficult to put the post 1949 Chinese occupational wage experience into comparative and historical perspective because although the Chinese data are relatively good on differentials between groups and occupations, international data are mainly in terms of the crude skilled/unskilled differential. It will be recalled that this varied between 1:1.32 and 1:2.87 for a sample of low-income countries and that the typical pattern was for differentials to increase in the early stages of industrialisation and then to decline.

For China, three post-1949 pieces of evidence on the subject are shown in Table 27. This table shows that in every case the differential was below the median differential of 1:1.86 reported for nineteen low-income countries in the survey referred to in Chapter 1.

If we now relate these data to the pre-war Chinese data we see that the differentials reported for Kiangsu and Canton are very close to our estimate of 1:1.50 for Shanghai in 1946, while the Manchurian differential of 1:1.28 is also quite close to the 1936 differential of 1:1.33. Allowing for this regional variation, the table suggests that the skill differential has continued the long run downward trend suggested by pre-1949 data.

It will be recalled that our pre-war data on wage differentials *within* the skilled worker class were fairly comprehensive and some interesting points of comparison with the later structure stand out. The first is that the spans

[1] *Down with Tu Chen-hsiang the chief follower of the capitalist road within the Party in the Canton Finance and Trade system*, pamphlet dated 15 May 1967.

TABLE 28. *The inter-industry structure of wages, 1950–8 (annual average wages, yuan)*

Industry	Sector	Occupation	1950	1951	1952	1953	1954	1955	1956	1957	1958
Electricity	Enterprises controlled by Ministry	Workers and staff	455	551	800	—	—	775[a]	868[b]		
		Production workers	468	572	810						
Coal	Enterprises controlled by Ministry	Workers and staff	—	—	604.8[c]	—	—	—	865[d]	—	932.2[e]
Textiles	Public and public–private enterprises	Workers and staff	455	—	560	595	640	649	654		
		Production workers	422	—	553	591	626	599	627		
Machinery (metal processing)	Public and public–private enterprises	Workers and staff	477	—	586	—	—	665	751		
Iron and Steel	Public and public–private enterprises	Workers and staff	—	—	587.4	679.2	686.2	691.3	797.8		
Paper	All enterprises	Production workers	—	—	597.7	685.5	691.5	674.5	797.1		
		Workers and staff	—	—	496.9	590.2	609.2	624.3	638.4		
Forestry	All enterprises	Production workers	—	—	503.3	573.9	582.7	588.5	596.1		
		Workers and staff	—	—	525[f]	—	—	—	810	—	887[g]

SOURCES

(a) and (b) *JMTY*, 1956, no. 24, p. 8.

(c), (d), (e) Data for 1952 and 1958 from *Hsüeh hsi* (Study) (hereafter *HH*), 1958, no. 7, pp. 25–6. Data for 1956 estimated from official figure for 1958.

(f), (g) From article cited above and *TCKT*, 1957, no. 14, pp. 29–30.

All other data are from *Wo kuo kang t'ieh, tien li, mei t'an, chi hsieh, fang chih, tsao chih kung yeh ti chin hsi* (Our country's iron and steel, electricity, coal, machinery, textiles and paper industries – past and present) (Peking: Statistical Publishing House, 1958) pp. 32, 52, 129, 156, 175, 212.

NOTE: In the cases of Textiles, Machinery and Iron and Steel, the data for 1956 are not strictly comparable with the earlier years because in that year, the private sector was absorbed into the public sector.

of 2.5 to 3.2 fold in the 1950s rate structure involved a considerable increase on the 1946 Shanghai spans which averaged 2.2 fold (or 1.6 fold for male workers only). On the other hand in Manchuria, the new spans involved a *reduction* by comparison with the average 1936 span.

In inter-industry terms, the new skill range involved, in Shanghai at least, a reduction in the size of inter-industry variations in rate spans – since in the pre-1949 period these had ranged from 1:1.1 to 1:5.2 fold. And further, whereas the 1946 spans were greatest in light industry (1:2.3 against 1:1.3 for heavy industry) the new structures required that spans be greatest in the heavy sector. Again however, we find that in Manchuria the inter-industry pattern of occupational wage spans in the pre-war period was more or less in line with the new structures planned for the 1950s. Thus our conclusion is that the reform of the occupational wage structure that took place in the 1950s required in Shanghai (and any similar cities) some substantial modifications of pre-1949 structures, but in Manchuria, the new structure was broadly similar to that already established in the 1930s.

The inter-industry structure of wages

In Table 28 we present data on the inter-industry structure of wages between 1950 and 1958.

In Table 29, we rank industries by average wage and show how this ranking compares with the desired ranking. The desired structure is indicated by an official ranking for production workers published in 1950, and another for staff published in 1955. The 1950 ranking divided industry into five groups, while the 1955 list had seven. Inconsistencies between the groups are negligible. We have used the 1950 desired ranking to evaluate the actual ranking in that year, and the 1955 one to evaluate 1952 and 1956.

The table shows that the desired inter-industry ranking was achieved fairly quickly. In 1950, the main problem was the high position of textiles and the low positions of coal and iron and steel. By 1952, only electricity deviates from the desired ranking. We estimate that this was still so in 1956 and less important, forestry also appears out of place. The persistence of electricity at the top reflects the very rapid rate of wage increase in this industry between 1950 and 1952. Thereafter the growth rate slowed dramatically. This is indicated in Table 30, in which we show indexes of wage growth in seven industries between 1952 and 1956.

There are three qualifications to these tables. The first is that up to 1956 the data refer only to the public sector, and it is possible that in the mid 1950s the wage structure of all enterprises was less satisfactory than that of the public sector taken by itself. Second, the use of metal processing as

TABLE 29. *The actual and desired inter-industry wage structure, 1950, 1952 and 1956 (public sector) (highest wage = 100)*

1950			1952			1956		
Industry	Actual	Desired (1–7)	Industry	Actual	Desired (1–5)	Industry	Actual	Desired (1–5)
Electricity	100	2	Electricity	100	2	Electricity	100	2
Textiles	97	5	Coal	75	1	Coal	100	1
Heavy chemicals	96	3	Iron and steel	73	1	Forestry	94	4
Machinery	89	3–4	Machinery (metal processing)	72	2	Iron and Steel	92	1
Iron and Steel	72	1	Textiles	69	4	Machinery (metal processing)	87	2
Coal	71	1	Forestry	65	4	Textiles	75	4
Flour	70	7	Paper	61	4	Paper	74	4
Clothing	68	6						
Matches	59	7						
Overall span	1:1.7			1:1.64			1:1.35	
Coefficient of variation	19%			17.3%			10%	

SOURCE: Data for 1950 and desired ranking from Wang Ya-ch'iang (1955), pp. 49, 218–19. Data for 1952 and 1956 as Table 28; desired 1955 ranking from *1955 Chin jung fa kuei hui pien* (1956), p. 551.

TABLE 30. *Wage growth in seven industries, 1952–6 (average earnings; 1952 = 100)*

Industry	Wage index in 1956
Forestry	154
Coal	143
Iron and Steel	133
Machinery	128
Paper	128
Textiles	117
Electricity	107
All industry	126

SOURCE: As for Tables 28 and 29.

TABLE 31. *The actual and desired inter-industry wage structure in public enterprises in the South Central Military Region, 1950 (highest average wage = 100)*

Industry	Actual	Desired
Textiles	100	5
Tobacco	98	7
Electricity	86	2
Coal	82	1
Flour	76	7
Machinery making	74	3
Cement	74	1–2
Iron and Steel	70	1
Non-ferrous metals	69	1

SOURCES: 'Report on commodity circulation and wage reform', *Ch'ang chiang jih pao* (The Yangtze river daily), 29 Sept. 1952; desired ranking (1–7) from Wang Ya-ch'iang (1955), p. 49.

a proxy for the whole machinery industry may conceal the slowness of reform in this sector. For it was reported that even in late 1953, average wages in the machinery industry were still lower than those in textiles.[1]

Finally, the national data used in these tables were undoubtedly heavily influenced by enterprises in Manchuria where departures from the desired inter-industry ranking were reported as being rare. As a result they conceal the more serious problems that existed elsewhere. In the South Central Region for example (which included Canton and Wuhan) the situation was particularly unsatisfactory. And in Table 31, we show actual and desired rankings in that region in 1950.

The table indicates that the degree of divergence from the desired structure in this area was far greater than elsewhere. None the less, data for Canton in 1956 suggest that the desired structure had been more or less achieved.[2]

The inter-industry wage structure: conclusions. The development of the inter-industry structure described above fits well into the comparative and historical perspectives developed earlier. The rise of heavy industry, for example, brings China back into line with international experience, and both the rapid transformation of the wage structure and the particularly

[1] Wu Tai, 'Wage problems in our country's machine building industry', *CKKY*, 1954, no. 3, pp. 1–4.   [2] *KCJP*, 13 Oct. 1957.

sharp rise of the coal industry recall the reform of the Russian wage structure during the Russian First Five Year Plan.

In relation to the history of the Chinese wage structure before 1949, we may note first that the narrowing of inter-industry differentials is a continuation of pre-1949 trends – and by 1956, the degree of compression attained was in fact very high by international standards. Second, and a point of great relevance to post-1949 policy, is that the confirmation of heavy industry at the top of the ranking can be seen as a *reversion* to the structure of the 1930s. Evidence from Shanghai, Canton and Chungking all shows that the rise of textiles was a wartime phenomenon.[1] Thus when the Chinese spoke in the 1950s of the necessity of dealing with 'reversals' in the rankings (i.e. higher average wages in light than heavy industry) they were not calling for the inversion of long standing inter-industry wage relationships – only for the correction in certain areas of a situation that had arisen under wartime conditions.

The inter-sectoral wage structure

We have information on inter-sectoral wage structures of three kinds: (1) the inter-sectoral structure for workers and staff; (2) the urban inter-sectoral structure for all employed persons and (3) the rural–urban differential.

The inter-sectoral structure for workers and staff. Table 32 shows the inter-sectoral structure for workers and staff in 1956 and the planned percentage increases for these groups during the First Five Year Plan.

This table is not very informative. Clearly the income of workers and staff in Agriculture and Forestry reflects the policy of not taking urban salary levels to the countryside; and a similar consideration is probably involved in the level of Commerce wages. The important missing figure is the average salary of workers and staff in State Organs. Without this we cannot judge whether the high planned rate of increase for this group was to enable it to catch up, or to get ahead of other workers and staff. Data from Chungking on this topic suggest that it was both. For in Chungking, while the average wage for industrial workers and staff increased from 355 yuan in 1950 to 602 yuan in 1956, that of workers and staff in State Organs increased from 208 yuan to 656 yuan.[2]

---

[1] Shanghai data from Chap. 2; Canton data from *KCJP*, 13 Oct. 1957; Chungking data from *Ch'üan kuo ke chung yao shih hsien kung tzu chih shu* (Index numbers of wages in important cities) (Chungking: Statistical Office of the Ministry of Social Affairs of the National Government, 1945–6).

[2] *Chung ch'ing jih pao* (Chungking daily), 12 Aug. 1957.

TABLE 32. *The inter-sectoral wage structure for all workers and staff, 1956 (average wages or salaries, yuan per annum)*

Sector	Average wage/ salary	Planned increase 1952–7 (%)
All workers and staff	610.5	33.0
Industry	664.9	27.1
Construction	700.9	19.0
Transport and communication	745.8	20.4
Agriculture and forestry	497.8	33.5
Commerce	489.7	28.0
Banking and insurance	586.1	38.2
Health, culture and education	548.1	38.2
State organs	—	65.7

SOURCES: See Nai Ruenn Chen, *Chinese economic statistics* (Edinburgh: Edinburgh University Press, 1966), p. 493; *Chung Hua jen min kung ho kuo fa chan kuo min ching chi ti yi ke wu nien chi hua* (The First Five Year Plan for the development of the economy of the Chinese People's Republic) (Peking: People's Publishing House, 1955), pp. 131–2.

Once again, however, we should bear in mind that local variations in this pattern may have been important. For example we know from the experience of Inner Mongolia that, in key point areas, construction wages grew more rapidly than is indicated by the table. For in this area, construction wages increased by 76.49% between 1952 and 1955, whereas the figure for industry was 29.52%.[1]

Urban inter-sectoral income differentials. Our information on income differentials within cities is restricted to data on Shanghai and the 1956 structure for that city is shown in Table 33.

This table illustrates that the range of incomes in the cities was far greater than is suggested by data for wages in the public sector and for workers and staff quoted in official sources. It is true that in Shanghai, workers and staff were a majority of all employed persons, but in Canton for example, they accounted for only half the labour force.[2] Thus in labour market terms, the wages of persons outside the ranks of workers and staff were very important.

Another interesting point in the table is that the average wages in locally

[1] 'Conscientiously implement wage reform', *Nei meng ku jih pao* (Inner Mongolia daily) (hereafter *NMKJP*), 24 July 1956.
[2] *KCJP*, 29 Sept. 1957; *KCJP*, 13 Oct. 1957.

TABLE 33. *The urban wage structure in Shanghai, 1956 (average annual wages or income, yuan per annum)*

Sector	Wage or income
All workers and staff	852[a]
All employed persons	656[b]
Workers and staff in industry	896[c]
Workers and staff in centrally controlled industrial enterprises (planned)	924[d]
Workers and staff in locally controlled industrial enterprises	1032[e]
Handicrafts	655[f]
Services	636[g]
Transport (traditional)	1320 (maximum)[h]
Secondary and relief work	384–540[i]

SOURCES

(a) *HWJP*, 2 Sept. 1957.
(b) *Chieh fang jih pao* (Liberation daily) (hereafter *CFJP*), 11 Aug. 1956.
(c) *HWJP*, 2 Sept. 1957.
(d) *CFJP*, 18 Aug. 1957.
(e) *CFJP*, 18 Aug. 1957.
(f) *HWJP*, 19 Jan. 1957.
(g) Estimated from *Szu ying shang yeh ti she hui chu yi kai tsao (tzu liao)* (The socialist reform of private commerce: materials) (Peking: San Lien Bookstore, 1963).
(h) Estimated from *WHP* (Hong Kong), 12 Aug. 1955.
(i) *Jen min jih pao* (The people's daily) (hereafter *JMJP*), 19 Aug. 1957.

managed industrial enterprises were higher than those in centrally controlled enterprises. This probably reflects the absorption of the private sector in 1956 and indicates the high level of wages that must have existed in the private sector before socialisation. Finally, the very high potential earnings in the traditional transport sector are important, for although this is not an average figure, the possibility of earnings of this level in a sector where entry was comparatively easy, had far reaching implications for wage management that we shall discuss later.

The rural–urban inter-sectoral differential. We know of only one systematic effort to look at the real income differentials between rural and urban areas. This research utilised data on workers and staff in 1955 together with rural survey data and took two approaches to the differential. In one, the income needed for urban 'non-market expenditures' (defined as rent, internal

TABLE 34. *The ratio of rural to urban per capita income, 1955*

Province	Rural:urban ratio[a]	Rural:urban ratio[b]
Liaoning	1:1.3	1:1.6
Hopei		
excluding Tientsin	1:1.3	1:1.5
including Tientsin	1:1.4	1:1.54
Kiangsu		
excluding Shanghai	1:1.1	1:1.4
including Shanghai	1:1.5	1:1.8
Hupei	1:1.5	1:1.7
Szechuan	1:1.7	1:2.1
Shensi	1:1.7	1:2
National	1:1.5	1:1.8

SOURCE: 'How can it be said that the peasants' standard of living has declined?', *TCKT*, 1957, no. 13, pp. 4–5.

NOTES

(a) urban income adjusted by deducting value of 'non-market expenditure'.
(b) urban income not adjusted for 'non-market expenditure'.

transportation, electricity and water charges etc.) were deducted from incomes, the idea being that expenditure on these goods and services was unnecessary in the rural areas and yielded no utility to urban residents. In the other approach, the income needed for these expenditures was left in the gross wage. The survey used dependency denominators to produce per capita figures, i.e. the income of wage earners was divided by the average number of dependants attached to each worker. In calculating the dependency ratio however, the survey excluded the rural dependants of urban residents. In calculating rural incomes, account was taken of cash incomes and the value of goods produced and consumed within the household, valuing these goods at market prices. The results of this survey are summarised in Table 34.

In evaluating this table one must remember that, although its purpose was to demonstrate that differentials were not as large as commonly supposed, the exclusion of rural dependants from the dependency denominator for urban residents makes the comparison unrealistically favourable to the urban sector. Thus the survey does not tell us what we really need to know, i.e. the size of differentials without any denominator. For this we have to fall back on individual surveys. One of the most persuasive of these was a survey of differentials in Kiangsu, which reported that the wage rate for the *lowest grade* of construction worker was 46% higher than the average income of males in the richest cooperatives in the area of Lake Taihoo.[1] This implies a 1957 differential of 2:1 – which is bigger than the differential of 1955 in Table 34. In relation to Reynolds's figure of 25% to 30% as an appropriate differential, the Chinese differential was high and growing.

We have little information on the way in which the rural–urban differential has changed. Some local attempts were made to measure this, and although the results are not very convincing, the fragments of evidence we have confirm one's impression that for workers and staff at least, the urban–rural differential moved in favour of the cities during the 1950s.[2]

In the 1960s, however, the situation may have changed. Certainly the growth of urban incomes was slowed or halted, and there is some evidence that in the 1960s and 1970s, real rural–urban income differences were narrowed as a result of a differential *price* policy affecting both outputs and inputs.[3]

The regional structure of wages

In Table 35 we illustrate the structure of wages for workers and staff with data for ten provinces and eight cities. Although the period 1952 to 1956 is a very short one, it does include most of the wage change that took place during the First Five Year Plan. The average annual wage is adjusted for each area with the aid of the weightings used to calculate cost of living supplements for workers and staff in 1956. We have had to assume that regional variations in the rate of change of prices did not disturb the structure too much.

In Table 36, we rank ten cities and twelve provinces by order of their growth of workers and staff wages. Data in brackets show real rates – calculated using local price data from the same source as the wage data. It will be seen that the real and money rankings are the same. In both this and Table 35 we have asterisked cities and provinces in which it was reported that there were key point projects during the First Five Year Plan.

The dominant impression given by these tables is that Manchuria was

[1] Wu Pieh-chung, 'Views on the actual fixing of ordinary workers' wages', *LT*, 1958, no. 6, p. 11.
[2] *SHJP*, 23 April 1957.
[3] This is suggested, for example, by the observations in China of Okita Saburo (Director of the Japan Economic Research Centre), reported in *Nihon keizai shinbum* (The Japan economic daily), 25 April 1972, and confirmed by a detailed discussion in 'Market flourishing and prices stable', *Jinmin Chūgoku* (People's China) May 1972, pp. 76–7.

TABLE 35. *The inter-regional structure of real wages of workers and staff, 1952–6 (annual average wage)*

City or Province	Wage		Rank		Rank change
	1952	1956	1952	1956	
Shanghai	612	704	1	3	−2
*Penki	584	876	2	1	+1
*Lushun-Dairen	529	695	3	5	−2
*Liaoning	499	676	4	6	−2
*Harbin	495	700	5	4	+1
Hangchow	470	585	6	9	−3
*Heilungkiang	466	724	7	2	+5
*Kirin	444	632	8	7	+1
Shantung	428	538	9	11	−2
Kaifeng	413	549	10	10	no change
Canton	398	523	11	13	−2
Anhwei	396	590	12	8	+4
Hupei	392	526	13	12	+1
*Chengtu	366	487	14	15	−1
Kwangtung	338	443	15	17	−2
*Kansu	335	503	16	14	+2
Fukien	309	450	17	16	+1
Kwangsi	298	435	18	18	no change
Overall span (excl. Penki)	1:2.05	1:1.66			
Coefficient of variation (excl. Penki)	19.3%	16.64%			

* Key point areas.

The basic data for this table are reported money wages for 1952 and 1956, or, data for 1956 together with information on the change since 1952. In a few cases where data were not available for the required year, we have used national data to adjust what was available. In order to get the structure of real wages, 1956 data were adjusted with the cost of living coefficients used to calculate wages and salaries in the State Bureaucracy.

Data on prices, *1955 Chin jung fa kuei hui pien* (1956), pp. 553–61. An incomplete list of key point areas is Chang Yen-hsing, 'The work of urban construction must be arranged in conformity with the policy of building up the nation economically', *Chi hua ching chi* (Planned economy) (hereafter *CHCC*), 1957, no. 12, p. 4.

SOURCES

Shanghai HWJP, 2 Sept. 1957; HWJP, 28 Aug. 1957; CFJP, 11 Jul. 1957; HWJP, 30 Sept. 1953.

Penki Hei lung chiang jih pao (Heilungkiang daily) (hereafter HLCJP), 29 Aug. 1957.

Lushun-Dairen LTJP, 15 July 1957.

Liaoning Pr. LNJP, 1 Oct. 1957.

TABLE 35 (*cont.*)

Harbin   Ha erh pin jih pao (Harbin daily) (hereafter *HEPJP*), 19 Dec. 1956.
Hangchow   Hang chou jih pao (Hangchow daily), 27 Sept. 1957.
Heilungkiang Pr.   HLCJP 14 Aug. 1957.
Kirin Pr.   Chi lin jih pao (Kirin daily) (hereafter *CLJP*), 14 Aug. 1957; *CLJP*, 8 Dec. 1956.
Shantung Pr.   TCP, 8, 9, 16 Aug. 1957.
Kaifeng   HNJP, 29 May 1957.
Canton   KCJP, 29 Sept. 1957; WHP (Hong Kong), 8 Dec. 1957.
Anhwei Pr.   An hui jih pao (Anhwei daily), 29 Sept. 1957.
Hupei Pr.   HPJP, 11 Aug. 1957.
Chengtu   Ch'eng tu jih pao (Chengtu daily) (hereafter *CTJP*), 11 Sept. 1957.
Kwangtung Pr.   NFJP, 10 Aug. 1957.
Kansu Pr.   KSJP, 5 July 1957; KSJP, 26 Sept. 1957; *KSJP*, 10 Jul. 1957.
Fukien Pr.   Fu chien jih pao (Fukien daily) (hereafter *FCJP*), 5 Aug. 1957.
Kwangsi Pr.   KHJP, 10 Nov. 1957.

initially, and remained, a high wage area. The most striking advance in the rankings is the province of Heilungkiang, but the key point provinces of Kirin and Kansu and the towns Penki and Harbin all made progress. It is true that Lushun-Dairen, Liaoning and Chengtu had below average rises and declined somewhat, but the former two still remain relatively high in the ranking.

The other feature of Table 35 is that in terms of both our indicators, inter-regional income inequalities declined during these years. In view of the short period covered by the data, the decline is substantial.

The difficulty in interpreting these changes in the regional structure of average wages is that such changes may reflect changes in the regional concentration of high and low wage industries, or in the skill composition of the workforce in different enterprises in the same industry, rather than changes in the regional income structure that are independent of such effects. Only the latter type of changes may be considered 'pure' regional wage variations, and only the latter are relevant to the migration decisions of individuals (in so far as these are based on income factors), and therefore to the policy decisions of the planners. The reason for this is that a loom operator in a Canton textile factory is not going to move to the North West simply because that region has an industry mix that yields a higher average wage than Canton. What will count will be the average wages of loom operators in the North West.

In practice, our data must contain both industry, skill and 'pure' differential effects; but unfortunately, it is impossible to separate them out systematically. However, apart from the data in the tables, we do know that some pure differentials were created by regional supplements applicable to

TABLE 36. *The growth of money and real wages of workers and staff by areas, 1952–6 (1952 = 100)*

City or province	Index	
	Money	Real
*Heilungkiang	155	—
*Penki	150	—
*Kansu	150	152
Anhwei	149	—
Fukien	146	—
Kwangsi	146	130
Nanking	145	129
*Inner Mongolia	144	—
*Kirin	143	—
*Harbin	141	—
National average	137	—
*Liaoning	135	126
Hupei	134	—
Kaifeng	133	—
*Chengtu	133	118
Shansi	132	—
Canton	131	—
Kwangtung	131	—
Changchun	131	—
*Lushun-Dairen	131	—
Shantung	126	—
Hangchow	124	—
Shanghai	115	106

SOURCES: As Table 35 and:
Nanking   NCJP, 1 July 1957.
Autonomous Region of Inner Mongolia   NMKJP, 10 Apr. 1957.
Changchun   LT, 1956, no. 7.
Shansi Pr.   SHJP, 23 Apr. 1957.

specific areas and industries;[1] but that in the important case of Shanghai, although average wages grew relatively slowly in the 1950s, the city still maintained 'pure' differentials by comparison with Manchuria. The size of these varied according to industry and occupation, but in 1956 the range was 10%–20%.[2]

[1] According to Wang Ya-ch'iang (1955), pp. 159–62, Manchuria offered area differentials up to 30% from 1952, and the oil and railway systems also had special area supplements. This system of supplements differed from contemporary Soviet practice, according to which special areas had higher basic wage rates.

[2] Data on regional rate variation are in: 'Implement the wage reform on the basis of a small rise', CFJP, 2 Aug. 1956; 'Why the wage increase in Shanghai is smaller than other areas', CFJP, 4 Sept. 1956; Liu Yi, 'The system of wage grades', LT, 1957, no. 10, p. 24.

4

The effectiveness of wage policy

The question we are concerned with in this chapter is, to what extent did the changes in the structure and level of wages described in the last chapter conform to the requirements of official wage policy? In order to answer this, we must first outline the evolution of wage policy and then seek indicators that relate this to the wage changes that actually took place.

In our diagram, we attempt to summarise trends in the main aspects of wage policy. In the case of policy towards the wage level, 'positive' policies refer to policies favourable to raising the average wage, and in the case of the wage structure, they refer to periods when the general attitude appears to have been favourable to the use of the wage structure as an instrument to secure the desired pattern of labour utilisation and to encourage skill acquisition. At some points this diagram necessarily oversimplifies, but in the main, wage policy trends are sufficiently identifiable to make the diagram meaningful.

POLICY TOWARDS THE AVERAGE LEVEL OF WAGES

It can be seen that between 1949 and 1953, policy towards the average level of wages was positive. In this, the period of takeover, rising wages mainly reflected the drive to consolidate political control and recognition of the incentive value of wage rises to stimulate productivity.[1] In the early years of 1949 and 1950, rising wages also reflected the effect on money wages of arrangements to stabilise the real wage during a period of rising prices.

These factors remained operative up to Autumn 1953, subject to some restraint associated with anti-inflationary policy.

By the end of 1953, the emergence of the rural–urban income gap and the problems of financing the First Five Year Plan required that the rapid rise in wages be halted, and the period of strict control initiated at this time lasted until the early summer of 1956.[2] The thaw of reform was how-

[1] 'The rate of wage growth should be lower than the rate of productivity growth', *TKP* (Tientsin), 3 Feb. 1955.
[2] See above and 'We advocate a spirit of bitter struggle and submission to the Plan in order to build the fatherland' (*People's Daily* editorial), *WHP*, 1 Nov. 1953; 'Improve-

[55]

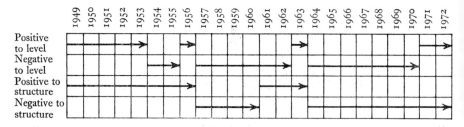

Fig. 1. Trends in policy towards the wage level and wage structure, 1949–72.
SOURCES:
As text of chapter.

ever short-lived, for in November 1956 a *People's Daily* editorial signalled
a cautious return towards stricter controls over wage rises.[1] Seen in perspective, this shift of policy marked the main turning point in policy towards
the average level of wages between 1949 and the present, in that although
there may have been some rises since that year, the dominant thrust of
policy has been to keep average wage rises as low as possible in order to
control the size of the rural–urban differential.

This policy shift initially took the form of a one-year freeze on rises of
wage standards in 1957. This meant that there were to be no across-the-
board increases, but that rises through regrading were theoretically possible.
In the same year, the principles of a new 'rational low-wage policy' were
announced.[2] This policy emphasized the importance of minimising differentiation in general and of controlling the urban average wage level in order
to control both the demand for wage goods, and the size of the urban–rural
inter-sectoral differential.[3]

Important as these developments were, the fundamental nature of the
switch in policy in 1957 and the tensions and controversies that were
stimulated by it are revealed most starkly in the evolution of the Second
Five Year Plan. As originally envisaged, this plan was to be a continuation
of the First Five Year Plan, modified in the light of the institutional framework provided by the socialisation of 1956 and of the growing momentum

---

ments in the standard of living must be subordinate to the advance of production',
WHP, 17 Dec. 1953.

[1] 'The people's livelihood can only be raised gradually', *JMJP*, 28 Nov. 1956.

[2] *1957 Chin jung fa kuei hui pien* (1957 compendium of currency regulations) (Peking:
Currency Publishing House, 1958), p. 94; Sung P'ing, 'Why we must implement the
rational low wage system', *HH*, 1957, no. 23, pp. 14–17.

[3] These points are discussed by Ma Wen-jui (Minister of Labour) in 'An explanation of
the draft temporary regulations on the wages and treatment of miscellaneous and
service personnel and ordinary workers in enterprises, units and State Administration',
HHPYK, 1957, no. 24, pp. 92–3.

of decentralisation in economic administration. In the event, the plan disappeared in the Great Leap Forward and thereafter had no operational function.

According to the original draft of the Plan, published in September 1956, planned wage rises for workers and staff were to be 25%–30%.[1] These figures reflect that the plan was drafted during a period when policy towards the average wage level was positive, although the fact that the planned rises were below the 33% rise planned for the First Five Year Plan shows that the problems of the inter-sectoral wage structure, and of providing the wage-good counterpart of money wages, were already recognised.

During 1957, there was growing controversy over the realism and rationality of the first draft of the Plan, and in the case of wages, the incongruity of the planned rises with the 1957 freeze and with the 'rational low-wage policy' became increasingly embarrassing. This is no conjecture, for the issue was openly and heatedly debated in the journal of the Ministry of Labour.[2] And when, in December 1957, the chairman of the State Planning Commission, Li Fu-ch'un, announced the revised Second Five Year Plan targets, there was no reference at all to the possibility of wage rises during the Plan period.[3] After this, there appears to have been no sustained period when there was a positive policy of increasing the average wage level.

In 1958, there was a planned rise in the average wage of workers and staff of 1.6%, but the Plan out-turn for that year contained no data that suggest that this had been fulfilled.[4] The 1959 Plan suggests that no rises were planned, although a 5% rise was subsequently reported for that year.[5]

[1] Chou En-lai, 'Report on the resolution on the Second Five Year Plan for the development of the national economy', *HHPYK*, 1956, no. 20, pp. 35–49.
[2] Liu Man-shih, 'My views on the rate of increase of wages during the Second Five Year Plan', *LT*, 1957, no. 14, pp. 10–11; Hu Fan-hsüeh, 'I also discuss the problem of the rate of growth of wages in the Second Five Year Plan', *LT*, 1957, no. 18, p. 9; Niu Chung-huang, 'Problems in productivity estimation and wage determination', *HH*, 1957, no. 9, p. 5. This latter article contains an interesting discussion of the point that the rate of growth of the wages of workers and staff should be lower than the rate of growth of per capita *net* output, pointing out that the earlier practice of thinking in terms of gross output productivity indicators had overstated productivity growth, and permitted productivity-based wage plans to be too high.
[3] Li Fu-ch'un, 'Report on the policies and tasks of socialist construction after the fulfilment of the First Five Year Plan in our country', *HHPYK*, 1958, no. 1, pp. 13–18.
[4] Plans and results for 1958 are in: Po Yi-po, 'Report on the National Economic Plan for 1958', *HHPYK*, 1958, no. 5, pp. 12–23; 'State Statistical Bureau report on the outcome of the National Economic Plan for 1958', *HHPYK*, 1959, no. 8, pp. 51–4. *Ten Great Years* recorded an increase of 3% in 1958, but since this figure referred only to those already in employment in 1957, the actual total figure (which would include the low wages of those who joined the workforce in 1958) may have been negative.
[5] The meaning of the 5% rise is ambiguous in this case, 'Workers' standards in China', *NCNA*, 26 Jan. 1960 (*SCMP*, 1960, no. 2188); Li Fu-ch'un 'Report on the National

In 1960, a 6% rise was announced in the National Plan and Provincial targets are also known to have been published, but we have no reports that confirm that these Plans were ever implemented – and if they were, the price data quoted earlier suggest that they must have been more than offset by price increases.[1] The only other years in which there have been rises in the average money wage of workers and staff are 1963 and 1972.

POLICY TOWARDS THE WAGE STRUCTURE

Fig. 1 indicates that policy toward the wage structure remained positive from 1949 to 1956 – a period that includes the policy switch towards the average level of wages that took place in 1954–5. The persistence of this positive policy (that included use of occupational, inter-industry, inter-enterprise and inter-regional wage structures) reflects the continued efforts to implement a Soviet planning system and its corollary, the adoption of an approach to wage work that favoured sharp wage differentiation.

The year 1957 again marked a major turning point. The steam had run out of the reform movement of 1956 and by 1958, the systematic relation of income to skill, work performance or other objective factors, was condemned as capitalist.[2]

According to material produced during the Cultural Revolution, the 1960s were the culmination of a long period of struggle between Maoist and Liuist views on the use of wage systems. Although the Cultural Revolution polarised and personalised the issues, it is probable that the opposing views quoted in these materials represent genuinely contradictory strands in the wage policy thinking of the 1950s and 1960s. The 'Liuist' view (as reported by its opponents) was a social philosophy with implications for industrial organisation; according to Liuists, contradictions concerning 'houses, food, cars and wages' were nothing to do with class struggle, but were 'a question of distribution'; so that, 'if things are distributed more equitably and

Economic Plan for 1959', *HHPYK*, 1959, no. 9, pp. 15–20. Local reports have nothing to say on the subject of wage rises in 1959 so that there is some doubt about the claim at the national level, see 'Hopei) Government work report', *Ho pei jih pao* (Hopei daily), 21 Feb. 1960 (*SCMP*, 1960, no. 17); 'Report of the draft National Economic Plan for Szechuan Province in 1960', *Szu ch'uan jih pao* (Szechuan daily) (hereafter *SCJP*), 27 May 1960 (*SCMP*, 1960, no. 22).

[1] Li Fu-ch'un, 'Report on the Draft Economic Plan for 1960', *JMJP*, 31 Mar. 1960; *SCJP*, 27 May 1960; 'Report on the 1960 Draft National Economic Plan for Kiangsi province', *Chiang hsi jih pao* (Kiangsi daily) (hereafter *CHJP*), 29 June 1960 (*SCMP*, 1960, no. 27).

[2] Particularly revealing articles are: 'A discussion of the way to solve our country's population problem', *JMJP*, 1 Feb. 1958; Liu Shu, 'Sweep away the remnants of the capitalist system of wage grades', *JMJP*, 3 Nov. 1958.

rationally all will be satisfied and this will foster the expansion of productivity'. Equitable and rational distribution here clearly mean distribution that is determined by scarcity and performance factors. The organisational implications of 'equitable' distribution in this sense were reported to be a form of market socialism, in which enterprises would seek profitability and compete in product and labour markets. The 'Liuist' view therefore, is one that took a very positive approach to the use of wage systems.[1]

The 'Maoist' view can be reduced to two propositions. These are (a) that properly stimulated, proletarian enthusiasm does not require the support of material incentives and (b) that the organisational implications of a full 'Liuist' incentive system make it incompatible with state ownership of the means of production, and therefore incompatible with socialism as understood by the Chinese Communist Party. It was claimed that this thinking was a continuation of the policies of the Party before 1949; at which time the Party had been 'basically egalitarian...work being done by effort and courage with absolutely no reliance on material incentives'.[2]

As matters of historical fact, we shall probably never know the detailed inner history of wage policy controversies in the 1950s and 1960s. But it is worth noting that if the 'Maoist' view was authentic, then contrary to the official view, Mao had travelled a long way from his earliest written opinions on the subject, as expressed in his 1942 book on *Economic and financial problems*. Such a change of view is quite possible, but the extent of the reversal is indicated by the following statement taken from the earlier book: 'Next there is the implementation of a ten-hour day and progressive piece-rate wage systems – using wages to increase production and raise labour enthusiasm...the egalitarian, supply wage system obliterates the distinctions between skilled and unskilled labour and between industriousness and indolence – thereby lowering work activism; we must replace the supply system with a progressive piece-rate system to stimulate work activism and increase the quantity and quality of output.'[3]

In this passage, Mao is not only supporting the general proposition that a differentiated wage system was economically efficient, but he is actually advocating the adoption of *progressive* piece-rate systems – systems which

---

[1] The literature on this is extensive and good representative discussions are: 'The fallacy advocated by the top ambitionist in economic work refuted', *KMJP*, 22 April 1967 (*SCMP*, 1967, no. 3928); 'Material incentive is the reaction to bringing proletarian politics to the fore', *KMJP*, 10 Mar. 1970 (*SCMP*, 1970, no. 70–11); *Ch'en shuang yüeh*, no. 1, 10 Jan. 1968.

[2] 'Material incentive is a reaction against proletarian dictatorship', *KMJP*, 25 Nov. 1969 (*SCMP*, 1969, no. 4554).

[3] Mao Tse-tung, *Ching chi wen t'i yü ts'ai cheng wen t'i* (*Economic and financial problems*) (Hong Kong: New Democracy Publishing House, 1949), p. 115.

were bound to lead to extreme income differentiation within enterprises, since progressive piece-rate systems involve the payment of progressively higher unit rewards as more is produced. In the 1950s, even at the height of reforms, progressive systems were considered too inegalitarian and were consistently ignored in favour of constant and diminishing rate systems. In view of this, the Maoist call in the late 1950s and 1960s to revert to Yenan work methods and non-monetary incentives, in opposition to 'Liuist economism', seems very odd.[1]

In the light of these materials it is difficult to define what official policy towards wage structure was in the 1960s. From the evidence of industrial and labour journals, however, it would appear that there was a period between 1961 and 1963 when occupational structures within industries were rationalised, but after this arguments and action in favour of wage structures largely disappear.

THE EFFECTIVENESS OF POLICY

From this account of the fluctuations of wage policy it is apparent that there are no stable criteria that can be applied to measure the effectiveness of wage policy over the whole period. It seems logical therefore to concentrate our initial attention on the effectiveness of wage policy during the years up to 1957, since this was the period during which interest in wage structure and wage forms were high. We shall find that the wage experience of these years is not only interesting in itself, but that the contradictions and problems that emerge throw powerful light on the wage issues of the 1960s and the reasons for the basic switch of wages policy in 1957.

Looking over the whole period between 1949 and 1972, policy towards the average level of wages has been implemented fairly successfully. It is true that at certain times there was some loss of control (especially 1951, 1953 and 1956), but in terms of the policy objectives of control of inflation, the maintenance of high rates of domestic savings, and the fulfilment of the wages targets of the First Five Year Plan, the performance was fairly good. The official data in Chapter 3 show that the average annual price increase in urban areas between 1952 and 1963 was approximately 1.7%. Even allowing for the favourable effects of the choice of base year, and for the exclusion of secondary commodities and unofficial prices, by international standards this performance was still good. Similarly, estimates indicate

---

[1] In the 1970s the pendulum has swung back towards a positive approach to wages and enterprise financial work, see 'Repudiate "Profit in command"; step up socialist accounting', *JMJP*, 14 April 1970 (*SCMP*, 1970, no. 70-17); *JMJP*, 23 Feb. 1970.

that during the First Five Year Plan the proportion of the national income devoted to gross investment was good both by historical standards and by comparison with contemporary developing economies.[1]

Finally, if we measure the results of wage control in terms of the desired outcomes formulated in the First Five Year Plan document, the performance is less striking but still reasonable. The planned increase of money wages for all workers and staff for 1953 to 1957 was 33%; the out-turn was 42.8%.[2] This over-fulfilment was a result of loss of control during the 1956 reform, which in turn was related to the uneven distribution of wage increases within the plan period – a phenomenon that the Chinese themselves criticised. Hard data are rare after 1957, but the estimates in Chapter 3 and other qualitative data appear to confirm that up to 1971, the desired standstill in wage growth – at least in real terms – was basically achieved. During the Cultural Revolution there were reports of illicit wage expenditures by enterprise leaders seeking to retain their power within enterprises. But we have no way of quantifying the effects of this on the average wage level and they were probably only temporary.[3]

We come now to our central interest, the wage structure. Our knowledge of the relationship between actual and desired structure can in some cases be quantified fairly easily. This is especially so in the case of the inter-industry structure, for in this case the desired ranking of industries by average wage was published and remained constant throughout the 1950s. Even in the cases of the inter-sectoral and inter-area structure, we can resort to fairly objective success criteria. In contrast, evaluation of the occupational wage structure presents some difficulties.

It will be recalled, from Table 29 in Chapter 3, that the desired inter-industry ranking appears to have been more or less achieved by 1956 – although this has to be qualified by the point that the official data do not reflect the unfavourable effects on the wage structure that absorption of private industry in 1956 must have had. The desired ranking was rational in the sense that the high-wage industries were relatively skill-intensive and

---

[1] Inflation data are discussed in Anthony D. Smith (ed.), *The labour market and inflation* (London: Macmillan, 1968). Comparative and historical savings data are discussed in Simon Kuznets, 'International differences in capital formation and financing', in *Capital formation and economic growth* (Princeton: Princeton University Press, 1955), and Simon Kuznets, *Modern economic growth* (New Haven: Yale University Press, 1966). Chinese data for the 1950s are estimated in Choh-ming Li, *Economic development of Communist China* (Berkeley and Los Angeles: University of California Press, 1959), pp. 138–40.
[2] 'State Statistical Bureau communique on the results of the First Five Year Plan', *HHPYK*, 1959, no. 8, pp. 48–51.
[3] 'Oppose economism and smash the latest counter attack of the bourgeois reactionary line', *JMJP*, 12 Jan. 1967.

TABLE 37. *The ranking of industries by wages and employment change, 1952–6*

Rank by 1956 average wage	Rank by % employment growth 1952–6
Electricity	Electricity
Coal	Machinery
Iron and Steel	Iron and Steel
Machinery	Coal
Textiles	Textiles
Paper	Paper

SOURCES: As Table 28.

NOTE: Pearson rank correlation coefficient 0.772.

TABLE 38. *Average annual money earnings of workers and staff in the public and private sectors, 1952–6 (yuan per annum)*

	1952	1953	1954	1955	1956
Public sector	439	484	505	525	610
% change on previous year		10	4	4	16
Private sector	453	528	571	585	610
% change on previous year		17	8	2	4

SOURCE: These estimates are based on Chinese and Russian sources. For details see U.S. Central Intelligence Agency, *Average annual money earnings of workers and staff in Communist China* (1960).

relatively fast-growing. The latter point is illustrated by the fact that between 1952 and 1956 there was a relationship between the wage structure and inter-industry variations in employment growth. Thus although labour allocation in these years was partly done by use of direct controls, wages must have performed at least a supportive role in the achievement of the desired inter-industry pattern of employment change. This point is illustrated by Table 37 in which we rank data on inter-industry changes in employment and wages between 1952 and 1956.

In contrast to this relatively satisfactory state of affairs, the behaviour of inter-sectoral differentials was not good. Within the urban sector, for example, the evidence strongly supports the view that the behaviour of the public–private wage differential prior to 1956 was unsatisfactory. In Table 38 we have data that show an inter-sectoral differential in favour of private industry.

During the plan period policy towards the private sector was to combine control with gradual socialisation so that the expanding public sector could achieve rapid dominance in the economy. Given the initial 3% differential in favour of the private sector, this must have implied a policy of reducing the inter-sectoral wage differential to facilitate the expansion of the public sector. In reality by 1955 the differential in favour of the private sector *had increased* to 11%, and there is a mass of partial evidence discussed in Chapter 7 which shows how unplanned private sector wage movements frustrated the achievement of the desired inter-sectoral distribution of employment.

The other urban inter-sectoral differential is that between the modern and traditional sectors (i.e. handicraft, petty commerce and services). Numerically the traditional sector was large, and the evidence again shows that particularly during the periods of rapid expansion, unplanned income movements in the traditional sector took place. And, even after the socialisation in 1956, it was still possible to earn excessive incomes by participating in illicit economic activities.

The rural–urban sectoral differential is very elusive empirically, but we argued in Chapter 3 that the evidence supports the view that during the First Five Year Plan the differential widened in favour of urban areas generally, and certainly in favour of urban workers and staff. It is true that our understanding of rural–urban migration is not sufficient to enable us to say how far this differential explains such migrations, but the Chinese view was that it was very important.[1]

The degree to which the inter-regional wage structure was effective would seem to lie somewhere between that of the industry and sectoral structures. In terms of inter-regional wage rankings, we argued in Chapter 3 that wage movements in the key point areas were generally in the right direction – despite the fact that Manchurian positions in the rankings were already very high. In functional terms we are unable to make any decisive generalisations about the efficacy of this particular wage structure, but it

---

[1] It should be noted that although migration flows were associated with variations in the inter-sectoral income differential, it is also statistically plausible that migration was mainly determined by variations in urban job opportunities. There is certainly qualitative evidence that at times peasants were 'prepared to take jobs at any wage', see 'Fukien province calls on the peasants not to infiltrate into cities', *FCJP*, 10 Mar. 1957 (*SCMP*, 1957, no. 1513). A discussion of migration and the inter-sectoral wage differential that emphasises the wage factor is Ishikawa Shigeru, *Chūgoku keizai hatten no tōkei kenkyū II*, pp. 48–50.

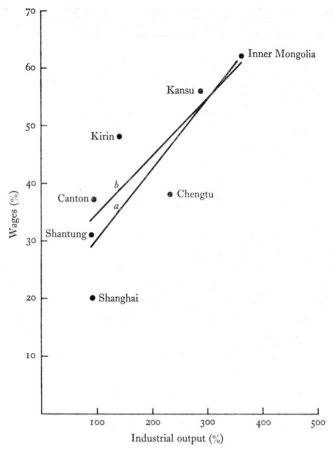

Fig. 2. Inter-regional variations in the relationship between changes in output and wages during the First Five Year Plan.

SOURCES:
Wage data as Table 30 and *NMKJP*, 13 April 1957.
Industrial production data:
   Shanghai various sources quoted in Howe (1971), Table 2, p. 12.
   Kansu KSJP, 12 June 1958.
   Kirin CLJP, 29 June 1957.
   Chengtu CTJP, 11 Sept. 1957.
   Shantung TCP, 3 Aug. 1957.
   Canton KCJP, 22 Nov. 1956.
   Inner Mongolia NMKJP, 10 April 1957.

NOTES:
The correlation coefficient r using all the data = 0.85. If the Shanghai data are excluded, r = 0.886. The Regression line *a* includes all the data. Regression line *b* excludes Shanghai.

   The reason for considering the exclusion of Shanghai is that this is the only area for which we have no firm 1952 data. On the assumption that this conceals a low rate of wages growth, our estimate for 1952 is a conservative one based on reported rises in 1953, 1956 and 1957.

can be seen from the data displayed in Fig. 2 that inter-regional variations in wage growth were significantly related to variations in the growth of industrial output. Thus as a minimum proposition, it is again safe to say that wage changes were working in the right direction. We cannot, however, go beyond this. For although our information about inter-city labour movements is not detailed, we do know that the majority of transfers involved persons of rather atypical character. On the one hand there were skilled migrants subject to direct allocation; and on the other, there were unemployed persons (mainly from the handicraft, commerce, services and transport sectors), who were also moved in a fairly organised way. Thus since a high proportion of migration was of an involuntary nature, only qualitative evidence can definitely tell us whether the manipulation of the inter-regional income structure was an important factor in facilitating these labour transfers. During the First Five Year Plan period, we would suggest that it was not, and this opinion is supported not only by qualitative evidence, but also by the evolution of wage and labour control policy as it affected inter-regional labour movements.[1]

The effectiveness of the occupational wage structure is, as we have already said, particularly hard to measure. In a socialist system the functions of this structure are twofold: its main purpose is to provide incentives for workers to acquire skills, to increase their work intensity and to accept transfers and responsibility; it is also possible that if enterprises are subject to pressures to minimise labour costs and if they have some degree of freedom in hiring, then an appropriate occupational wage structure will ensure that the utilisation of the labour force will be rational. For under such conditions enterprises will not use more skilled labour than they require to fulfil their physical output targets.

The second of these functions is dealt with most easily. The evidence for the First Five Year Plan period overwhelmingly shows that because financial discipline in enterprises was in general loose, the occupational wage structure could not help planners ensure that managers economised in the use of skilled labour. This appears to have been true even in 1954–5, when financial control was particularly tight, and when the authorities had considerable success in controlling the rate of growth of the average wage.[2] It is also true that although managers had some *de facto* freedom in hiring,

---

[1] A representative discussion of workers' resistance to planned migration based on wage factors is 'Lanchow welcomes and thanks Shanghai commercial personnel for their assistance', *HWJP*, 29 May 1956 (*Union Research Institute Research Service*, vol. 4, no. 19).

[2] The best analysis of laxity of financial control and its causes is Dwight H. Perkins, *Market control and planning in Communist China* (Cambridge, Mass.: Harvard University Press, 1966), Chap. 5.

TABLE 39. *The distribution of workers between wage grades by industrial sectors (public), 1955 (% distribution)*

Industry	1	2	3	4	5	6	7	8	Average
				Grade					
Electrical power	6.7	14.7	24.5	21.3	15.2	11.2	5.2	1.2	3.8
Coal	1.1	4.4	13.1	28.3	29.6	18.7	4.5	0.3	4.6
Oil	3.4	10.9	31.2	30.8	14.2	6.2	2.5	0.8	3.7
Iron and Steel	2.9	12.1	27.6	26.9	18.4	8.0	3.2	0.9	3.9
Non-ferrous metallurgy	2.2	12.1	31.7	32.3	14.8	5.3	1.4	0.2	3.7
Metal processing	5.0	19.0	26.7	20.9	14.5	8.9	4.0	1.0	3.7
Chemicals	6.8	20.2	31.2	23.7	10.8	5.0	1.9	0.4	3.4
Construction materials	4.3	15.8	30.6	25.8	14.2	6.7	2.0	0.6	3.6
Textiles	2.1	10.5	21.7	29.0	19.5	12.0	4.4	0.8	4.1
Food and other light industries	6.3	12.5	21.9	24.3	18.0	10.8	4.9	1.3	3.9

SOURCE: 'The numbers, structure and distribution of workers and staff in 1955', *HHPYK*, 1957, No. 2, p.88.

in public sector enterprises the nature of the labour plan must have compromised efforts to make the wage system efficient in this respect.[1]

In order for the occupational wage structure to fulfil its other functions, two conditions are essential: these are (a) that the basic rate schemes reflect the existing structure of skill scarcity and the personal cost of acquiring different skills, and (b) that the machinery of wage administration is efficient. It must be efficient in the sense that it places individuals in their correct occupational categories and that it accurately evaluates personal qualities in determining the precise placing of individuals within the band of rates permitted for each occupation.

Unfortunately there are no obvious quantitative criteria that can tell us how far these conditions hold. It is true that we have some measures of the changing skill level of the labour force, but there is no way of allocating the credit for these changes between the wage system and the other factors which could explain them.

The only interesting quantitative material that we have on this topic are data on the distribution of workers in the public sector in 1955 between different wage grades. These are shown in Table 39. It is apparent from this table that there is a heavy concentration in the middle ranges of the grade structure, but although comparative data suggest

[1] The changing nature of employment control is the main theme of Howe (1971), Part Two.

that the skill distribution shown in the table is about what might be expected, even this cannot be taken as conclusive evidence in favour of the system, since the data themselves do not prove that the positions of individuals within the grade structure were actually related to skills. There is also the problem that the data are restricted to the public sector of industry, where at the time of the survey wage administration could be expected to be most effective.

We turn finally to qualitative evidence on the efficacy of the occupational wage structure, and this mostly suggests that it was not very satisfactory. The evidence reported at the time of the 1956 wage reform pointed to the ineffectiveness and irrationality of wage administration in relation to the occupational wage structure, and the final reports of the reform itself emphasised that in the event, the pressure to increase wages had resulted in the neglect of the original purpose of the reform.[1] It is fair to say that by 1957, these retrospective reports were already reflecting the new line that de-emphasised the wage system in general, and that they must therefore not be taken at face value; but there is no really satisfactory evidence that indicates that the reports were wholly wrong. The one important qualification to these generalisations is that although differentials *within* the main groupings do not appear to have been very effective, differentials *between* groupings did have some effect. This emerges from articles about the results of the 1956 reform and from Cultural Revolution material. These indicate that the differentials achieved by certain technically qualified personnel had a sharp impact on career aspirations and demand for high level education and training.[2]

---

[1] Liu Tzu-chiu, 'The present situation and problems with regard to wage reform', *HHPYK*, 1956, no. 21, pp. 208–10; Lu Ch'an, 'An evaluation of the occupational wage system', *LT*, 1956, no. 10, pp. 36–8.

[2] 'Why were high wages not reduced?', *Shuang ch'en yüeh*, 10 Jan. 1968. In this article it was reported that Liu Shao-ch'i was 'trying to make skilled staff into a special class' and that as a result of the 1956 reform people said, 'future sons will study engineering and daughters will study medicine'.

5

The process of wage determination: plans and evaluation

In this and the following chapters we shall analyse the main components of the official process of wage determination. By official, we mean here that we are concerned with activities conducted within the framework of economic plans, regulations and laws, or specifically organised by Party or governmental authority. The first of these components is the annual wage plan. This is formulated at the national, enterprise and various intermediary levels, and is part of the overall economic plan. The second component is the continuous process of classification and evaluation. This is undertaken to ensure that enterprise job structures conform to those officially recommended, and that the wage standards of individuals have been fixed in accordance with currently prescribed criteria. Finally, in the next chapter, we shall enquire into the various wage reform movements which have taken place between the late 1940s and 1972. In these movements either the direction of official wage policy has been changed, or alleged deficiencies in the regular process of wage determination have been remedied.

For each of these aspects of wage determination we shall try to analyse: (a) the procedures followed; (b) the power relations of the groups involved; and (c) the criteria used to make decisions.[1]

THE WAGE PLAN: SCOPE AND CONTENTS

An article published in 1957 stated that in principle all wage and salary paying units should have annual wage plans, and that these should be capable of aggregation into Ministerial, Industry, Regional and National plans.[2] None the less in practice, it seems that at all times there have been enterprises and units incapable of formulating such plans, and others whose plans were not capable of verification or of aggregation into Regional or National plans.

---

[1] The main general sources for this chapter are Wang Ya-ch'iang, 'The labour and wages plan order', *CHCC*, 1957, no. 10, pp. 29–33; numerous articles in *Chung kuo kung yeh*, esp. 1955–7; *Chung yang ts'ai ching cheng ts'e fa ling hui pien*, Ser. 1, final vol. and Ser. 2, vol. 4.   [2] *CHCC*, 1957, no. 10, pp. 29–33.

The development of wage planning has been a gradual process. In the early 1950s, even in Manchuria, where economic planning was relatively advanced, the first regional labour plans did not include an aggregate wage plan.[1] During the First Five Year Plan, the scope of co-ordinated wage planning gradually broadened. Thus whereas in the State Statistical Bureau Report for 1953, the only wage data referred to were some figures on real wages of workers in state sector industry, by 1957, the Plan was reported as including the wage plans of all industrial and commercial enterprises; state-managed forestry, meteorology and agricultural enterprises; transportation and construction enterprises; urban utilities, Mass Organisations, Banking and State Administration Organs. This plan represented a considerable advance on 1953, but even so, it still completely excluded parts of the traditional sector such as handicrafts and petty commerce. It is clear moreover that this account of the scope of the plan represented an ideal towards which the Ministry of Labour was working, rather than reality.

The heart of the national wage plans in the First Five Year Plan period were the control figures for the total wage bill and the average wage, with the latter broken down by industries and possibly in other ways as well. After 1957, there began a trend towards decentralisation in economic administration, and although this trend has fluctuated in intensity, it has not been reversed. The effect of this on the nature of national wage planning is not really known. Red Guard materials do show that at least rudimentary national labour plans were in existence in the early 1960s and that the Third Five Year Plan for the whole economy (1966–1971) had a labour component. None the less, in wages work it is probable that national plans have not been constructed in the same detail that was attempted in 1957 and that local plans have become much more important; and even in 1972, a time of relative normality, the fate of the Ministry of Labour (the author of earlier wage plans) remains unclear.

At the enterprise level, the wage plan is part of the labour plan, which includes employment and labour productivity targets. The principal wage targets insisted upon are the average wage and the total wage bill. The latter is particularly important because in aggregate, control of enterprise wage bills is fundamental to control of the demand for wage goods. Rules governing the calculation of the wage bill were published in 1951 and 1952, and the 1955 version seems to have remained definitive at least until 1965.[2]

[1] The plan is in *LT*, 1951, vol. 1, no. 6, pp. 35–6.
[2] *Regulations concerning the composition of the total wages bill* in *LT*, 1951, Ser. 1, no. 8, pp. 9–10; *Chung yang ts'ai ching cheng ts'e fa ling hui pien*, Ser. 3, pp. 1060–2; *Kung yeh k'uai chi ho suan*, p. 121.

Basically the wage bill is defined as including all payments to workers except certain categories of prizes and premiums (given in reward for technical innovation or good work performance) and certain kinds of welfare wage supplements.

Although these two targets were the main ones, and in 1958 were retained in the newly simplified industrial planning system, the literature on wage accounting also contains descriptions of various supplementary approaches to the wage plan, which provide techniques for evaluating enterprise wage performance. For example, average wage plans for each category of personnel were required during the 1950s, and a sophisticated wage plan for production workers can be differentiated into time-work, piece-work and premium plans. The value of these latter plans is that they enable an enterprise to ascertain whether movements in the major wage indicators are caused by changes in grading and basic rates, the level of output or the level of premium payments.[1]

Enterprise wage plans are aggregated at various levels, and in total, constitute the national wage plan. The key points of aggregation vary according to the type of control exercised over the enterprise. In the case of industrial enterprises under direct ministry control, the ministry wage plan is the most important, but enterprise plans are also aggregated into Provincial and Municipal plans as well. In the case of locally controlled enterprises, the local level of aggregation becomes the main one, but there must be some aggregation on an industry basis as well, otherwise the Ministry of Labour could not operate on the inter-industry wage structure in a meaningful way.

Outside the industrial sector, the wage plans for other economic enterprises, public utilities, financial, educational, health units etc. are also part of local and national wage plans. However, in the case of personnel in State Administration and Mass Organisations, wage planning has been primarily a matter for the National level.

Wage determination as a continuous process

So far, we have been concerned with those aspects of wage determination that enter into the annual economic plan. Between 1953 and 1957 of course, these plans were constructed within the framework of the First Five Year Plan, and in industrial enterprises, annual plans were often further subdivided into quarterly and even monthly periods. But apart from such plans, there are processes of wage determination that are not supposed to

[1] Wang Ya-ch'iang (1955), p. 206; Yao Ba, 'Talks on enterprise wage work', *CKKY*, 1957, no. 2, pp. 61–4.

Grade	1	2	3	4	5	6	7	8
Occupation/Wage coefficient	1.00	1.16	1.35	1.57	1.82	2.12	2.48	2.90
Moulders			■	■	■	■	■	
Copper smelters			■	■	■	■		
Crane drivers	■	■	■					
Drivers			■	■	■			
Machine tool operators			■	■	■	■	■	■
Metal drilling workers		■	■	■	■			
Fitters		■	■	■	■	■	■	■
Riveters		■	■	■	■	■	■	
Smiths					■	■	■	■
Beaters			■	■	■	■		
Cleaners			■	■	■			
Carpenters			■	■	■	■	■	■

Fig. 3. Occupational wage differentiation in the machine-making industry, skilled workers, China, mid-1950s.

be bound by plan discontinuities at all. These are mainly at the enterprise level, and are the work of classifying jobs and evaluating individuals.

In the case of industrial enterprises, each industry has standardised occupational structures, which together with appropriate definitions and norms can be translated into a structure appropriate to any individual enterprise. In addition to the occupational structure, coefficients are given that determine wage relationships between occupations. Thus in the case of skilled workers, most industries have had eight-grade systems and specific occupations are defined and placed within the grade system. To illustrate this, in Fig. 3 we show the grade structure for the machine-making industry. From this figure it will be seen that individual occupations usually span several grades. Similar grading systems were developed in the 1950s to cover technical and administrative personnel.

Under these systems, once a person's industry and occupation are defined, his basic real wage or salary depends on: (a) his placing within the permitted band of grades; (b) regional cost of living adjustments; (c) the definition of the minimum wage, and (d) in the case of staff, the size and modernity of his enterprise.

We shall see shortly that the criteria for placing individuals within the possible grade band varied, but for most of the First Five Year Plan it depended on technical qualifications. Cost of living adjustments (*b*) were defined in considerable detail in 1955 and 1956 at the levels of the district (*Ch'ü*), municipality (*Shih*) and county (*Hsien*). As finalised in 1956, the system required that each area be placed on a basic scale of eleven possible cost of living adjustments, and some areas were given special supplementary allowances. The basic scale varied from o to 30% and the highest special supplement was 97% – applied in parts of the province of Tsinghai.[1]

With regard to (*c*), the determination of a minimum wage, the principle was that the minimum wage should be adequate to support two adults in an urban area. In monetary terms the minimum wage naturally varied from region to region, and rules were constructed to ensure that in real terms the minimum wage was fairly uniform throughout China.

Finally, in the case of factor (*d*), enterprises were usually grouped into three or five classes and those in the highest class for size and modernity had the highest wage and salary standards. Thus in the case of the proposed grade system for staff in the iron and steel industry in 1956, salary coefficients for factory directors in class 1 enterprises were 2.55 to 3.00, in class 2, they were 1.82 to 2.15 and in class 3, they were 1.52 to 1.80.[2]

To sum up, the process of continuous wage determination consisted of the definition of jobs and the evaluation of individuals. The process was continuous because up to 1957, the implementation of the system was incomplete, and also because even where the system had been established, technical change in production processes and skill acquisition by individuals made existing wage-structures obsolete.

Although this system of wage administration was applied first to industrial enterprises in the public sector, it was intended that similar procedures be followed in the locally controlled public sector and also in private enterprises. In such enterprises, the same system of grades, coefficients and technical standards were valid.[3]

This continuous process of wage determination was subject to two sets of constraints. The first was the annual wage plan, which limited average wages and the wage bill. Any change in wage structure had to be kept within limits imposed by these targets. The second constraint was the existence of Collective Contracts. These contracts were negotiated by representatives of workers, union and management and were initially developed as an instrument for controlling wages, working conditions and managerial practices in the private sector. However, in periods of enterprise

[1] *1956 Chung yang ts'ai cheng fa kuei hui pien*, pp. 239–46.
[2] *CKKY*, 1956, no. 2, p. 3.
[3] At least this was so in the South Central Region, *Temporary regulations on points of principle concerning private industrial enterprise wage adjustment*, *KCJP*, 1 Nov. 1954.

democratisation, Collective Contracts were also introduced into the public sector.[1] In the 1950s, the effectiveness of Collective Contracts was not reported as being very great, the usual criticism being that they were formalities with no real bearing on enterprise organisation and incentive systems. It is none the less interesting that the existence of such contracts was still being reported to visitors as late as the mid-1960s.

The processes described above imply a very technical approach to wage administration. Indeed the whole system as we have described it was essentially the Russian system of wage administration, and it was first implemented on the advice of Russian specialists in Manchuria in the early 1950s. The specialists were reported as quoting Stalin's dictum 'no technical standards, no planned economy'.[2] This technical approach to wage administration has not, however, been consistently followed since 1949. It is probably true to say that up to the end of 1957 this was the *dominant* approach, but between 1958 and 1961 the pressure of the economic crisis and the influences of the prevailing political atmosphere allowed activities such as norm revision, worker evaluation and indeed even basic enterprise economic accounting, to largely disappear. Between 1961 and 1965, this trend was reversed, and both wage and accounting work began to revert to the pre-1958 practices.[3] What has happened during and since the Cultural Revolution is not altogether clear. For on the one hand, regulations defining occupational structures were reported as abolished and were, indeed, obviously contrary to the structural reforms in enterprise management reported during that time and to the traditions of the Paris Commune which was used by the Cultural Revolutionaries as a model organisation. On the other hand, we do also have an important directive, published in 1967, which insisted that reform of the wage system be kept under central control and that changes in nomenclature, grading or rates would be invalid unless undertaken with the authority of the Central

---

[1] *Lao tzu kuan hsi yü chi t'i ho t'ung* (Labour–Capital relations and Collective Contracts) (Shanghai: New China Bookshop, 1950); *Decisions of principle concerning private enterprise wage adjustment*, *T'ien chin jih pao* (Tientsin daily) (hereafter *TCJP*), 19 Dec. 1952; Chang Chih-ang, 'Establish Labour Capital Consultative Committees; do the work of labour–capital relations well', *CCCP*, 1950, Ser. 10, no. 16, pp. 8–9; *Directive on the establishment of Labour–Capital Consultative Committees in private enterprises*, *Hsin Hua yüeh pao* (New China monthly) (hereafter *HHYP*), 1950, no. 6.

[2] 'Research into the compilation of labour plans in mining and industrial enterprises', *TPKY*, 1951, no. 61, pp. 49–53.

[3] 'Work in strict accordance with established systems', *JMJP*, 22 May 1962 (*SCMP*, 1962, no. 2755); 'Fix personnel and labour norms in industrial enterprises', *JMJP*, 18 Nov. 1961 (*SCMP*, 1962, no. 2634). In 1962, a highly significant book on the wage system appeared, in which a case was made for a modest use of the wage structure *subject to the requirements of the urban–rural differential*: Chiang Hsüeh-mo, *She hui chu yi ti fen p'ei* (Socialist distribution) (Shanghai: Shanghai People's Publishing House, 1962), espec. p. 72.

Committee of the Communist Party and the State Council.[1] This suggests that although enterprise level management must have been in disarray and although the Ministry of Labour seems to have virtually disappeared, there was no collapse of wage administration of the kind that had taken place between 1958 and late 1961. We think that this was due, strangely enough, to the desire on the one hand to stop rightist enterprise authorities from abusing the system to preserve their positions by giving extra wages in the form of bonuses, re-evaluation etc. and on the other hand, a determination not to allow leftist attacks to lead to a collapse of wage administration from which it would take years to recover.

The reports of visitors to China in 1971 and 1972 confirm the impression given by documentary evidence. Certainly occupational and grading structures for workers seem to have been retained (or where tampered with, restored). In the case of staff and managerial personnel, it seems that although the old systems of grading were suspended during the Cultural Revolution, visitors to China during 1971 and 1972 were told that the future of these systems was an 'unresolved question' to be settled in the 'final stage' of the Cultural Revolution. This stage appears to have been reached in autumn 1972, when it was reported that a new twenty-four grade system covering the State Bureaucracy and leadership personnel in economic organisations had come into operation. Details of this system are not known but it may well be that apart from some changes in terminology (for example, 'leadership personnel' changed to 'responsible comrades') this system broadly coincides with the old pattern of occupational differentiation.

POWERS AND PROCEDURES

We have tried now to describe the functions of both annual wage plans and the process of continuous wage evaluations. In this section we discuss these procedures with a view to identifying the main groups concerned with wage work and the changing roles they played in it.

---

[1] *Notice from the Central Committee of the Chinese Communist Party, State Council, Central Military Commission and the Central Cultural Revolutionary Group, on dealing further blows to counter-revolutionary economism and speculative, profiteering activities, Kuang t'ieh tsung szu* (Canton Railways General Headquarters), no. 28, Feb. 1968 (*SCMP*, 1968, no. 4129); see also *Notice of the Central Committee of the Chinese Communist Party*, 17 Feb. 1967 (*SCMP*, 1969, no. 4554). This conservatism in relation to the fundamentals of the wage system as they affected workers (as distinct from staff) is also suggested by the best Japanese sources, for example, *Chūgoku sōkan 1971* (The 1971 China compendium) (Tokyo: Ajia Chōsa Kai, 1971), pp. 437–8. It is also supported by an important local directive that stated that wage anomalies 'would be studied and corrected by the Communist Party Central Committee in the last stage of the Cultural Revolution', quoted in *China News Analysis*, no. 695, 1968, from Anhwei Public Broadcasting System, 16 Jan. 1968.

The relationships between enterprises and other planning bodies concerned with their wage work were complex – as indeed were relationships between groups involved within the enterprises themselves. In the case of centrally controlled industrial enterprises, during the First Five Year Plan external control over the formulation of the annual plan was exercised by the enterprise's ministry, and in many cases, by the ministry's local managing bureau as well. In principle, annual wage plans were also subject to local Labour Bureau co-ordination but from discussions on this subject in 1957, it is apparent that up to that time Bureau influence on ministry wage plans was negligible.[1] In the case of locally controlled enterprises, however, the Labour Bureaux were probably more active and capable of meaningful intervention. In the case of State Administration and Mass Organisations it is clear that prior to 1957, the wage plans of these units were a matter for the units themselves under the supervision of the State Council and the State Planning Commission.[2]

External control was also exercised over the process of evaluation described earlier. According to one early source, in the case of industry the rule was that final decisions concerning high level technical and administrative personnel were decided at ministry level, decisions concerning skilled workers and ordinary staff wages were taken by local managing bureaux, while the wages of unskilled workers, temporaries and apprentices were determined within the enterprise itself.[3] Control over wage evaluation in State Administration and Mass Organisations is vested ultimately in the State Council which up to 1959, had subordinate to it a State Personnel Commission which presumably was active in overseeing this work. After 1959, personnel work was taken over by the Ministry of Internal Affairs and it is thought that in 1963 they were handed on to the new State Personnel Organisation Commission.[4]

It can be seen from this discussion that the role of the Labour Bureaux in wage planning has been less than might have been expected from the 1950 directives that established these Bureaux. According to the directives, the Bureaux were to have the research and supervisory functions necessary to facilitate the nationwide unification of wage standards, and they were to work closely with enterprise labour and wage departments.[5] In 1954 and

---

[1] 'The Labour Office chiefs discuss the problem of organisation', *LT*, 1957, no. 12, pp. 2–3 and 13.   [2] *CHCC*, 1957, no. 10, pp. 29–33.
[3] *Chung yang ts'ai ching cheng ts'e fa ling hui pien*, Ser. 2, vol. 4, pp. 1130–2.
[4] Audrey Donnithorne, *China's economic system* (London: George Allen and Unwin, 1967), Chap. 7.
[5] *Hua Tung ch'ü ts'ai cheng ching chi fa ling hui pien* (Compendium of finance and economic regulations for the East China Region) (Shanghai: East China People's Publishing House, 1951), pp. 1678–89.

1955 wage work headed the list of Bureaux tasks and the Bureaux were also closely involved in the 1956 reforms. But it is clear from discussions among Labour Bureau chiefs in 1957 that they had never been able to integrate the different types of enterprise and unit wage plans into consistent, local plans.[1]

Since 1957 the Bureaux have probably played a more important role. For after 1957, the decentralisation of enterprises to local control must have meant that the locally controlled labour force had a predominant position in local labour markets. And we know, further, that at about this time local planning authorities extended their powers over centrally controlled enterprises in various ways.[2]

Apart from plans, the role of the Labour Bureaux in relation to continuous wage determination work in the early 1960s appears to have been of a consultant nature. Since 1965, however, no issue of the Ministry's journal, *Lao Tung* (Labour), is known to have been published, and during the Cultural Revolution the Ministry of Labour came under severe attack, from which its Minister, Ma Wen-jui, seems never to have recovered. What the fate of the Ministry has been during the dissolution of central bureaucracy in recent years is not clear, but it seems unlikely that the store of wage administration skills acquired before 1956 has not found some employment at local levels, even if the old Labour Bureaux have not retained their original title and functions.

The other organisation of considerable importance in wage work is the People's Bank. In Chapter 1 we pointed out that laxness of financial control appears to have been a persistent problem of Soviet wage planning. This laxness was related to the weakness of the banking supervision for the banks appear to have an auditing role, without having the power to insist that infractions of the wage plan be rectified. In the 1950s China seems to have had a similar problem and indeed in some respects it appears to have been even worse. Wage expenditures were described as 'lawless and reckless' and the regulations actually allowed enterprises to overspend their monthly wage plan by up to 10 %. Unlike the Soviet system, this was possible even if they were not fulfilling monthly production targets. In the event of over expenditures continuing for a second month, the People's Bank could call in the enterprise's managing bureau to see what could be done. But even in these cases, it is not clear that if the bureau was satisfied, the bank could do

[1] See the leading article in *LT*, 1955, no. 1.
[2] The growing power of local authorities in wage and welfare work is indicated in *State Council Communication concerning welfare expenditure standards for personnel in State Organs, 1957 Chin Jung fa kuei hui pien*, p. 92; also Christopher Howe (1971), Chaps. 7–8.

anything very effective.[1] Thus, in the 1950s the banks were not effective external controls on the wage plan and this came to a head in 1956, when the unplanned excesses of the 1956 wage reform were attributed in part to the collapse of even vestigial bank supervision.[2]

In the 1960s the situation seems to have been improved, for at the same time as control of the wage bill became the major wage target, the Government made serious efforts to strengthen and multiply external controls over enterprise wage fund management. In 1960, much stricter methods of bank supervision were introduced on a trial basis. These methods were indeed so strict that the banks appeared reluctant to introduce them on the grounds that they would damage their working relationship with enterprises. The system, however, seems to have been consolidated and the banks now have substantial authority to stop excessive wage payments and to enquire closely into reasons for an enterprise's inability to fulfil plans in the required manner.[3]

From our earlier descriptions of the nature of continuous evaluation it can be seen that while external control over the primary wage targets is feasible, the intrinsic character of the work of job description and individual evaluation inevitably leaves discretionary authority at the enterprise level. Since the efficiency of the wage system depends in considerable part on how this work is done, the question of enterprise level authority has always been important.

In the first instance, Manchurian practice was to encourage the establishment of Wage Evaluation Committees at enterprise, municipal and provincial levels. These committees were to include representatives of workers, unions and management and were to draw up draft internal wage structures and negotiate on the basis of these with higher authorities. These committees do not seem to have established much authority and it is clear that the control of evaluation work was quickly taken over by enterprise personnel and wage and labour departments, under the leadership of senior management cadres. Similarly, in the bureaucracy and Mass Organisations, it is reported that effective control over internal wage work was vested in unit leaders. In banking, for example, the official procedure in 1950 was that section chiefs drew up an initial wage scheme which was then democratically

---

[1] Wang Ya-ch'iang (1955), p. 207; 'How we implemented wage fund control', *LT*, 1955, no. 5, pp. 16–17; Li Yo, 'Improve wage fund planning management work', *CHCC*, 1956, no. 5, pp. 7–10.

[2] Cheng K'ang-t'ing, 'A summary of 1956 experience in reforming wages and labour planning', *CHCC*, 1957, no. 8, pp. 9–13.

[3] Hsieh Chi-ch'un, 'Some problems for the People's Bank to concentrate on in the trial implementation method for wage fund control', *LT*, 1960, no. 3, pp. 5–6; Fu Te-huang, 'Do the work of managing the enterprise wage fund well', *LT*, 1962, no. 17, pp. 5–6.

discussed by the method of 'self reporting and public evaluation'. The democratically determined evaluation was then sent to higher levels for ratification. Evidence from the late 1950s however suggests that the democratic aspects of the evaluation system did not in practice count for very much.[1]

In late 1954, the political leadership decided that other influences (apart from managers) should be brought to bear on wage work, and following the first Trade Union Wage Conference in December of that year, there was a drive to set up Union Wage Committees in all industrial enterprises. The attempt to give the unions an active role in wage work reached a peak in 1956. In this year the unions claimed that their role was 'to correct the mistaken activities of management' and instances of union challenges to managerial authority in wage administration were widely reported in the press.[2] However, even in 1956, the unions never achieved any real power and their members were reported as explaining this by the fact that the unions had 'no men, no power and no money'.[3] The rectification of the trade unions in 1957 undoubtedly led to their complete and final exclusion from wage administration and although in the early 1960s, the unions were again reported as being very active in welfare administration, there are few suggestions of any serious wage activity. In 1967 the All China Federation of Trade Unions was abolished and although its reappearance at national level was hinted at in 1971, it seems probable that no union activity of any sort persists at the enterprise level.[4]

From 1956 to the mid 1960s the ultimate authority in wage work has been the Communist Party, and this authority is a natural concomitant of the growing Party role in enterprise management. Before 1956, it was reported that there were serious disputes between managers and Party activists in relation to management matters but from that year on the Party's role became predominant and it acquired new authority in wage matters by promoting wage reform. As we have noted, 1958 to 1961 were

[1] *Chin jung fa kuei hui pien 1949–1952* (Compendium of currency laws and regulations 1949–1952) (Peking: Finance and Economic Publishing House, 1956), pp. 370–2.
[2] 'The All China Federation of Trade Unions calls its first national wage work conference', *LT*, 1955, no. 2, p. 27; 'Firmly implement the system of wage grade supervision', *Kung jen jih pao* (Worker's daily) (hereafter *KJJP*), 26 Aug. 1955. 'Everyone comes and keenly participates in wage reform work', *Chung Kuo hai yuan* (Chinese sailors), 13 June 1956; 'A letter from a Union Wage Committee member', *KJJP*, 17 July 1956.
[3] *LT*, 1955, no. 2, p. 26.
[4] 'Political work in unions', *KJJP*, 7 April 1965 (*SCMP*, 1965, no. 3454). According to Russian sources quoted in a Hong Kong newspaper the dissolution of the *ACFTU* took place on 27 Dec. 1966: 'The Chinese Communists disband the All China Federation of Trade Unions' *Hsing tao wan pao* (The star island evening news), Hong Kong, 3 Jan. 1967.

lean years for wage administration and this can be explained not only by the excessive decentralisation within enterprises of the evaluation processes, but also by the inexperience of Party cadres in handling the practical mechanisms of wage administration. The subsequent revival and centralisation within the enterprise of accounting and technical wage work seems to have led to some revival of managerial powers in the wage field, but it was reported in 1964 that Party Labour and Wage Committees at the enterprise level retained the power to summon senior factory administrators and presumably had the final say in wage decisions.[1]

From 1964–5, the role of the People's Liberation Army in industrial and bureaucratic organisations began to increase in importance, although the significance of this was quickly overshadowed by the whole episode of the Cultural Revolution and the establishment in industrial enterprises of Revolutionary Committees. These committees were composed of Maoist supporters from the ranks of the old managerial cadres together with Army and worker representatives. They had supreme authority within enterprises and it was reported that they were capable of exercising this effectively without recreating the extensive and rule-ridden bureaucracy they had replaced. However, since the disappearance of Lin Piao in 1971, it has become clear that the Party has resumed its key role in enterprise management, although the framework of Revolutionary Committees has been retained.[2]

THE PRIVATE SECTOR

This account of wage determination has been in terms of the public sector. In the private sector as it existed before 1956, the principle was that as far as possible wage work should be modelled on that in the public sector – using the same norms, technical standards etc. The private sector was not however incorporated into local wage plans, so that control of private sector wage work was very important. We have already mentioned one instrument for the exercise of control – the Collective Contracts. These contracts, which governed matters relating to working conditions, wages, discipline, etc. were initially drawn up at the industry or trade level. After they had been approved by the Municipal Government and the local Labour Bureau, they were used as a basis for negotiating contracts in individual enterprises. Enterprise negotiations took place between management and unions in the Labour–Capital Consultative Committee. The

---

[1] 'A record of experience from Shanghai', *LT*, 1964, no. 2, pp. 8–10.
[2] This revival seems to have been initiated from Party Committees at the municipal level, *JMJP*, 4, 6 Feb. 1972 and *JMJP*, 16 June 1972.

secondary contracts resulting from these negotiations had then to be ratified by government and labour authorities at the district (*Ch'ü*) level. Responsibility for registering Collective Contracts and arbitrating disputes arising out of them belonged to the Labour Bureaux and it is reported that a high proportion of these disputes were in fact concerned with wage matters.[1]

In addition to Collective Contracts, another form of external control over private sector enterprises were the district level Private Enterprise Wage Adjustment Committees. Little is known about the activities of these committees, but their main functions would seem to have been to conduct periodic reviews of private sector wages to ensure that these were not distorting local wage structures, and to ensure that private enterprises were conforming to the standards laid down for minimum wages in the public sector.[2]

THE CRITERIA FOR WAGE EVALUATION

There has never been agreement in theory or conformity in practice to a set of stable criteria for determining wages. On the contrary, the issues have been continuously disputed. One conflict has concerned the relative importance of technical and non-technical criteria. By technical criteria, we mean here any criteria that relate a person's income to the specific qualities of his job, or to personal characteristics relevant to his work performance, or to the actual work performance itself. By non-technical criteria, we mean such factors as length of Party service, general work attitude, and degree of current political activism. The other, and related disagreement, has been that between those who would place the main emphasis in wage determination on the *personal* qualities of workers or staff (i.e. length of work experience, formal qualifications, theoretical knowledge etc.) and those who would put the main emphasis on the objective importance and skill requirements of *the job itself*.

The history of the former conflict is in part the history of changing power relations within enterprises, and with qualifications it could be said that when managerial personnel are in charge, technical criteria are preferred, and when the Party has control, political attitudes become important. At times when there is real mass participation in evaluation, differentiation of all varieties tends to be opposed. The use of political criteria is of course completely contrary to the spirit and practice of Soviet wage administration, but none the less it appears to have persisted in various forms and to various degrees for most of the past twenty years.

The history of the other conflict – that between emphasis on the person

---

[1] See above, p. 73, n.1.   [2] *TCJP*, 11 Dec. 1952; *TCJP*, 19 Dec. 1952.

or the job – has, by contrast, been mainly determined by the discovery of objective economic and technological factors relevant to the choice of emphasis.

In the years up to 1955, the main emphasis was on the man not the job, and the criteria used to evaluate the man were mixed, with regular injections of support for technical criteria accompanying the various wage reforms. A good example of the rules for regular evaluation in the early 1950s are those applied in the banking system. In this system (as in industry) the three criteria most often discussed were 'ability', 'character', and 'reputation' (*ts'ai, te, tzu*). In this context ability was defined as technical competence, character as work attitude and prestige among other workers, and under the heading of reputation the main considerations were personal political history and years of Party membership. The banking rules also stated that ability should account for 70% of the total evaluation, character 20% and reputation 10%.[1] Although this could only be a rough guide, it is interesting that where evaluation was subject to formal rules, even at this time, technical considerations were theoretically given the greatest weight. But although this was so, there is also evidence that the technical approach to wages was undermined by emphasising the individual rather than the job. This was particularly the case in the South Central reform of 1952.[2]

The reform of the salary system in State Administration in 1955 and the early stages of the general reform of 1956, marked the high point of the effort to establish complete dominance of a Soviet type system using exclusively technical criteria. And in the case of both workers and staff, the emphasis was also on the establishment of a system in which income was related primarily to the job done and secondarily to personal qualities.[3]

Under this system, accountants, typists, lathe operators, etc. were identified and placed within a band of permissible rates, with only the precise point within the band depending on other criteria. In the case of workers this system is called the job wage system (*kang wei kung tzu chih*) and in the case of staff it is called the responsibility wage system (*chih wu kung tzu chih*).

Within a year, however, both technical criteria and job factors were again demoted and personal qualities – especially 'character' – were restored.

[1] *Chin jung fa kuei hui pien 1949–1952* (1956), pp. 370–2.
[2] *Ch'ang chiang jih pao*, 6 Sept. 1952.
[3] The staff system is described in K'o Pai, 'A discussion of the responsibility wage system for managerial and technical staff in industrial enterprises', *CKKY*, 1956, no. 2, pp. 1–4; the application of the system to workers is discussed in Li Ch'i, 'The Tientsin People's Paper factory implements the job wage system', *LT*, 1956, no. 10, pp. 8–9.

There is no evidence that the use of non-technical criteria has ever been abandoned again. Since 1957, all that has happened has been that its weight in total assessment has fluctuated.[1] Between 1957 and 1960 its weight was considerable, but between 1961 and 1964 it seems to have declined. For students of China's wage criteria this latter period is perhaps the most interesting of all. In the 1950s, wage administration was primarily a question of the struggle between those who wanted to implement a Soviet system and those who wanted to use the wage system as a political and social instrument. But by the 1960s, as a result of reflection on experience, the wage technocrats were beginning to appreciate the shortcomings of the Soviet system and were discussing the principles on which an optimum wage structure should be constructed in the Chinese environment. The main discovery made at this time was that technological variations within and between industries meant that the job-responsibility wage system, in which the job was the main determinant of income, was often unsatisfactory. As a result of these discussions and discoveries, we find in the 1960s a switch back to the use of technical criteria *without* the attempt to fully implement the job-responsibility system. The job-responsibility system was not abandoned, for in some industries it seemed appropriate. In industries where it was not appropriate, however, individuals were classified into broad job-responsibility groups with their personal wage determined by the criteria of practical ability, theoretical ability, work experience, and to some extent, political history.[2]

There is no doubt that as the political temperature rose in the mid-1960s, political criteria revived in importance. As early as 1964, reports claimed that 'thought circumstances' ranked higher than technical considerations in evaluation work, and visitors to China during and after the Cultural Revolution confirm the importance of this.[3] However, we think that it would probably be quite wrong to believe that technical factors ever receded to the extent that some published and reported statements suggest, particularly in the light of the 1967 directive that insisted on keeping central control of the wage system. Some of the most recent information from China reveals that pure skill factors remain very important determinants of income, and we have a report of a *People's Daily* editorial published in

[1] 'Some opinions and views on wage problems', *LT*, 1957, no. 14, pp. 11–13; 'A discussion of the problem of raising the grades of workers and staff', *LT*, 1959, no. 15, pp. 24–6.
[2] The best collection of these discussions is *Kung yeh ch'i yeh kuan li wen hsüan*, vol. 4 (Select documents on management in industrial enterprises) (Peking: Chinese Industry Publishing House, 1964).
[3] 'Mainland workers divided into eight grades', *Hsing tao jih pao* (Star island daily), Hong Kong, 4 Sept. 1964. This article claimed that the three current criteria were (1) 'Thought circumstances', (2) 'Work years' and (3) 'skill'.

November 1972, that states categorically that in rural income evaluation, political factors are in future to be given no weight. If this principle is adopted in industry and other sectors of the economy, the criteria cycle will have moved right back to the position taken in the 1956 wage reform.[1]

---

[1] One article, for example, pointed out that although managerial differentials have declined, the wage range for the occupations in civil aircraft is still sixfold – reflecting the high valuation of the skills of pilots, 'Salary differences, Chinese style', *Mainichi Daily News*, 13 June 1972. 'China drops its political bonus scheme', *The Sunday Times*, 12 Nov. 1972.

6

The process of wage determination: the wage reforms

To complete our picture of the official wage determination process, we turn now to the history of the major wage reform movements. These movements had two main functions. In the first place they were necessary to establish the new structure of wage administration. This was not possible without major, discrete drives that involved the mobilisation of the Party and the Mass Organisations, as well as those parts of the economic bureaucracy directly concerned with wage work. In addition, the wage reforms were a necessary supplement to the regular processes of wage work. Administrative rigidities and the lack of expert, full-time wage personnel meant that under normal conditions these processes could not preserve the combination of flexibility and discipline that rapid, non-inflationary industrialisation required. Thus whenever anomalies in the wage structure became excessive, or whenever circumstances demanded a shift in wage policy, a reform was mounted.

Prior to 1955 there were no reforms that could be described as national. Reforms in this period were either regional or sectoral. In contrast, the reforms of 1956, 1963 and probably 1972, were implemented on a national basis.[1] The main reforms that we shall discuss here are the 1948–51 reforms in Manchuria, the 1952–3 reforms in the South Central Military Region and the national reforms of 1956 and 1963. This list is not exhaustive, but it is sufficient to enable us to analyse the nature of wage reform movements and their significance for the total process of wage determination.

REFORMS IN THE NORTH EAST AND SOUTH CENTRAL REGIONS 1948–53

During the anti-Japanese war, the earliest wage reforms undertaken by the Communist leadership took place in the Shensi–Kansu–Ningsia Border Regions. It was reported that in these reforms, uniform wage standards

---

[1] Shun Szu, 'A discussion of unified central management of wages and labour', *LT*, 1962, no. 13, p. 1.

were imposed in public sector enterprises, and that a simple inter-industry wage structure was created by making average heavy industry wages exceed those in light industry by 10 %.[1] These reforms probably encountered few difficulties. Industry was new to the area so that the problem was the establishment of a new system rather than a reform of a pre-existing one. In addition, only a mild degree of differentiation was imposed, reflecting the fact that wartime conditions made sharp differentiation unacceptably expensive, and reflecting also the fact that high quality work performance could be achieved by the stimulation of patriotic emotion.

The extension of Communist rule into Manchuria in 1948 presented completely new problems. Manchuria was the most industrialised region of China and had long-established wage and industrial relations systems. The earliest efforts to reform Manchurian wages were quite modest. No excessive differentiation was permitted and the reform concentrated on raising real wages to consolidate the Party's political power, and on the removal of the most obvious inequities in inter-enterprise wage relationships.[2]

Once political power was established, the North East Government set about the construction of economic planning and wage systems based on Soviet models; and by 1950, the need for further reform of the existing wage structure and the apparatus of wage administration was pressing, particularly as the wage structure had been adversely affected by the conservative decisions of the Sixth National Labour Congress in Shenyang in 1948. The decisions of this Congress provided that enterprises in areas that came under Communist Government should, pending reform, allow workers and staff to retain their previous wage and salary levels. This decision may have been politically necessary, but its effect was to freeze enterprise wage structures with all their anomalies intact.[3]

The objectives of the reforms that took place in Manchuria between 1950 and 1952 fall into three groups. These were: (*a*) rationalisation of the occupational, inter-industry and inter-enterprise wage structures; (*b*) the introduction of technical rather than political criteria for wage evaluation, and (*c*) the unification of regional wage standards in real terms.[4] The

---

[1] Su Ch'ün, *Kuo chia ch'i yeh kung tzu chih tu ti chi ke wen t'i* (Some problems in the wage system in state enterprises) (place and publisher unknown, 1952).

[2] *Chung yang ts'ai ching cheng ts'e fa ling hui pien*, Ser. 1, final vol., pp. 710–13.

[3] *Chung Kuo chih kung yün tung ti tang ch'ien jen wu* (Present tasks of the Chinese workers and staff movement) (Hong Kong: New China Bookshop, 1949): see also a revealing question-and-answer sequence in *Kung jen yün tung wen t'i* (Problems in the workers movement), vol. 4 (Peking: Worker's Publishing House, 1951), Chap. 6.

[4] Wang Ya-ch'iang (1955), Chaps. 5 and 12; 'The present situation with regard to area wage adjustment and other important experience', *LT*, 1951, vol. 1, no. 10, pp. 21–3; 'The People's Government Ministry of Labour work report for 1950', *LT*, 1951, vol. 2, no. 1, p. 1.

technical standards, norms, etc., necessary for these reforms were worked out at the regional and industry levels first and were finally resolved into a national set of standards at the National Wage Preparatory Conference in September 1950.[1]

The organisational techniques and power relationships involved in the Manchurian reforms have already been alluded to in our earlier section, i.e. the development of Enterprise Wage Committees to work out the framework of reform at the enterprise level, combined with a system of 'guided democratic evaluation' to fix individual wage standards at the shop and small group levels. The problems created by disagreements over criteria and by intra-enterprise power struggles were substantial. But of particular interest was the question of how the reform should affect the average wage. By the time the reform got under way the general level of wages had already been raised once, and through the wage point system money wages were already tied to prices. Thus in the context of an economic situation in which anti-inflationary policy took primacy over all other policies, any manipulation of the wage structure that involved a further rise in the average wage was most unwelcome.[2] But since a major object of the reform was to increase differentiation – particularly in the occupational and industry wage structures – reform could only be compatible with stability of the average wage if the average wage in some sectors and occupational groups actually *fell*. Study of specific sub-regional reforms shows that a policy of selective wage decline was considered.[3] But such opposition developed to this that in November 1951, an all round rise of 15% for public sector workers and staff was announced.[4]

The South Central Military Region was specifically excluded from the recommendations of the 1950 National Wage Preparatory Conference. This decision reflected the late arrival of the Communist armies in the south, and also, the exceptionally unsatisfactory wage structure found in the Region. It will be recalled from Table 31 above, that in the South Central Region the inter-industry structure was particularly troublesome owing to

---

[1] Wang Ya-ch'iang (1955), p. 36; *NCNA* report in *Hsing tao jih pao*, 20 June 1951.
[2] Wang Ya-ch'iang (1955), Chap. 12; *Chung yang jen min cheng fu fa ling hui pien 1949– 1952* (Central People's Government compendium of laws and regulations 1949–1952), vol. II (Peking: People's Publishing House, 1952), p. 666.
[3] In Tsingtao, the increase in differentiation was to take place with a fixed wage bill, and was therefore expected generally to 'lower wages', *Ch'ing tao jih pao* (Tsingtao daily), 28 Nov. 1951. In Lushun-Dairen, there was a similar pattern, with reform involving reduction of wages for middle and lower paid workers. As a result of the reform the average wage was to be reduced by 20%. Wu P'in-chia, 'The wage system in the Lushun-Dairen area', *CKKY*, 1950, vol. 2, no. 2, pp. 11–19.
[4] *The North East People's Government Economic Planning Committee, methods for implementing wage adjustment for workers and staff, LT,* 1951, vol. 2, no. 2, p. 30.

the presence of numerous 'reversals' – that is, instances of light industries with higher average wages than heavy industries. It was also reported that in the occupational wage structure, wages appeared to be completely unrelated to possession of skills.[1] This partly reflected the use of political and seniority criteria in wage determination, and partly the persistence of traditional wage determination practices in which small, natural work groups bargained a fixed sum for a job, and divided this equally upon completion.[2] In addition to correcting the wage structure, the other object of the reform in this region was the unification of the wage point system to ensure that the real wage structure reflected the planners' intentions.[3]

The methods by which the South Central reform were implemented are known in some detail. The technical standards, grade systems, etc. all originated from the Finance and Economic Committee of the Regional Government. At the enterprise level, wage reform was guided by Wage Reform Research Committees and Workers and Staff Representative Committees. The Research Committees were to include representatives of the Party and Mass Organisations as well as managerial and technical staff, and their first job was to draw up a reform proposal by interpreting official wage standards in the light of the specific technical conditions of their own enterprise. The trial reform plan was then to be discussed by the Workers and Staff Representative Committee and when agreed by them, the plan was handed down for evaluation work at the lowest level of formal enterprise organisation, that of the 'small group'. Popular evaluation at this level was subject to guidance from a Wage Reform Evaluation Committee, whose function was to adjudicate disputes arising out of the evaluation of individuals.[4]

In addition to the operation of this formal framework, wage reform at the

---

[1] 'Why implement wage reform? How implement wage reform?' *NFJP*, 14 July 1952; 'Report on wage reform and commodity circulation', *Ch'ang chiang jih pao*, 29 Sept. 1952; 'An initial summary of wage reform in locally managed state industrial enterprises in Canton', *NFJP*, 13 Oct. 1952.

[2] 'Implement wage reform in State sector enterprises; welcome the high tide of economic construction', *NFJP*, 27 Oct. 1952; Four types of traditional group payments systems with egalitarian implications are described in 'Progress in changing to individual piecework systems among the enterprises subordinate to the Hua Hsiang Mining Bureau', *Ch'ang chiang jih pao*, 12 Oct. 1952.

[3] The minimum wage was expressed in terms of 'wage points', and represented the bundle of commodities necessary to support two adults in an urban area. The bundle consisted of quantities of 26 goods and services, divided into 5 main groups. The commodities and quantities could vary by region (on the basis of local commodity availability and expenditure surveys), although the 26 categories were common to the whole country. The cash value of the minimum wage in any area was determined by reference to local price indexes. Wage and salary payments were in cash, kind, or usually, a mixture of the two. Without careful control this system could easily produce unplanned regional wage differentials. A good example of local regulations are those for East China, 'The method for calculating wage points in the East China Region', *FCJP*, 30 April 1952.

[4] 'Methods and policy in the wage reform', *NFJP*, 8 Aug. 1952.

enterprise level was a highly politicised activity. For example the composition of the committees (especially the Evaluation Committee) was carefully controlled, and at the small group level, intensive efforts were made to establish groups of workers committed to taking informal leadership roles at the evaluation stage.[1] The role of the Party in this was strongly emphasised and a typical report stated that the strengthening of Party leadership was the 'chief method of eliminating egalitarian thought'.[2]

In regional reforms such as this, the key link between the regional level of government and the enterprise, was a conference held to initiate the reform and attended by Government, Labour Bureaux, and enterprise staff and others involved in the reform work. At this conference, the aims and methods of the reform were explained and the regional leadership had the opportunity to evaluate the situation at the local and enterprise levels. In the case of the South Central reform this conference was a lively and significant affair, because the report of it reveals again just how powerful was cadre opposition to any lowering of wages.[3] Recalling the substantial divergence of the actual from the desired inter-industry wage structure in the South Central Region, and noting the exceptional egalitarianism reported in the occupational wage structure, it can readily be seen that the prospects for implementing reform without a wage rise were dim. It is true that by comparison with Shanghai and Manchuria, the South Central Region was reportedly a low-wage area, so that in terms of inter-regional equity there seemed to be a case for a rise. But since Shanghai was regarded as an anomaly, and since Manchuria had a concentration of high wage industries, the authorities wanted to keep the South Central Region as a low wage area.[4] But, once again, the tactics of reform were constrained by the impossibility of lowering wages in any sector or among any occupational group. In the final outcome, the South Central reform was accompanied by a 15% rise in the wage bill and a claim that 87.22% of those participating in the reform got a wage increase of some degree. In inter-industry terms, the average wage rise varied from 25.03% in the case of non-ferrous metals to 8.09% for textiles. The reform was *not* therefore successful in reforming the inter-industry wage structure. For even after the reform, cotton remained at the top of the industry wage ranking, although its position was somewhat eroded.[5]

[1] 'Conscientiously elect the Wage Reform Committee', *Ch'ang chiang jih pao*, 26 Aug. 1952; *NFJP*, 8 Aug. 1952.
[2] 'Experience of wage reform in some steel smelting factories in the South Central Region', *Ch'ang chiang jih pao*, 12 Sept. 1952.
[3] 'Firmly implement the eight grade system', *Ch'ang chiang jih pao*, 17 Aug. 1952.
[4] This is discussed in 'What are wage standards?', *Ch'ang chiang jih pao*, 31 Aug. 1952.
[5] *Ch'ang chiang jih pao*, 29 Sept. 1952; *Ch'ang chiang jih pao*, 26 Aug. 1952.

THE WAGE REFORM OF 1956

There were no regional wage reform movements between late 1953 and 1955. The only co-ordinated wage changes in these years took place in the private, construction and handicraft sectors. And in each case, the reforms involved stabilisation or lowering of wages and were undertaken under conditions of strong financial control and the exercise of coercive political and legal power.

By 1955 several factors suggested that the period of regional and sectoral reforms was over and that a national approach to the wage structure was necessary. In the first place, the stabilisation of prices and the development of economic and manpower planning at the national level, made it desirable to abolish non-monetary payment systems and to eliminate inter-regional wage anomalies. The first attempts in this direction took place in the State Organs in 1955, when payment in kind and the complex system of supplements and subsidies were abolished. This reduced wage and salary determination to the use of official occupational wage tables, modified only by special hardship and regional cost of living supplements.[1] This system was not only more satisfactory from the wage point of view, but by its use of formal occupational structures, it lent itself to the control of bureaucratic employment expansion as well. For under the new system, each unit had a formal *piao* (order) which not only specified *the wages* appropriate to each occupation but could also specify *the number of persons* in each occupation.[2]

It was only logical that once the monetisation and unification of wages and salaries had occurred in one sector, it should be extended to other sectors – in particular to industry. The decision to make this extension was the origin of the 1956 wage reform.

In the case of industry, the changes implied by a decision to unify national wage standards were far reaching and it was planned that the reform should also be used to sharpen occupational, regional and industry differentials. In the case of occupational differentials three things were proposed: (*a*) that managerial and technical groups should have greater differentiation vis-a-vis skilled workers; (*b*) that managerial staff should have equal and generally higher wages than technical staff, and (*c*) that differentiation *within* the skilled worker group be increased.[3]

---

[1] *1955 Chin jung fa kuei hui pien* (1956), pp. 549–63; *1956 Chung yang ts'ai cheng fa kuei hui pien* (1957), pp. 472–82.

[2] The relationship between wage reform and bureaucratic employment control is brought out in 'The Tientsin People's Paper factory implements the responsibility wage system', *LT*, 1956, no. 10, pp. 8–9; Wu Tai, 'Talks on enterprise wage work', *CKKY*, 1956, no. 12, pp. 60–3.

[3] Wang Ya-ch'iang (1955), Chap. 15; Sung P'ing, 'Why is it necessary to introduce wage reform', *HHPYK*, 1956, no. 10, p. 75.

These reforms reflected a victory for those who believed that the wage system was potentially an effective instrument for resource allocation and that technical factors should be the sole determinants of wages and salaries. According to Red Guard sources, the reform was inspired by Liu Shao-ch'i, who, impressed by the liberal economic thinking of the post-Stalin thaw, saw wage reform as part of a Chinese programme of economic rationalisation. But contemporary accounts suggest that reform was part and parcel of Chou En-lai's policy of rehabilitating and correctly utilising 'intellectuals', a policy that, in his speech on *The ten great relationships*, Mao supported.[1]

The reforms also reflected the fact that because regular wage evaluation had not taken place after the regional wage reforms, technical and personal development had made earlier reformed occupational wage structures obsolete and counter-productive.[2] At the time of the reform, it was argued that the suspension of evaluation work had been due to managerial error, but the evidence shows that managers had only been acting in accordance with official directives and in response to the strengthening of financial discipline in these years.[3]

These forces for wage reform began operating in 1955, and at that time it was proposed that the reform should be worked out gradually over a two to three-year period and that it should take place without any substantial increase in the average wage. As it turned out, the reform was completed by autumn 1956 and involved a rise in average wages of nearly 20% per annum.[4] The reasons for this reversal are instructive and to understand them fully we shall have to go back to 1953.

The year 1953 was the first of the First Five Year Plan and it was a year

---

[1] The Cultural Revolution materials refer to the 1955 and 1956 reforms as the 'black directives'. For details of this and Liu's 'Libermanism', see 'The counter-revolutionary history of Liu Shao-ch'i', *T'i yü chan pao* (Physical culture struggle paper), 26 April 1967; 'Why were high wages not reduced?', *Shuang ch'en yüeh*, 1958, no. 1 (10 Jan.). For contemporary confirmation of the significance of the reform see Ch'en K'ai, 'Mass wage work is the preparatory stage of the wage reform', *LT*, 1956, no. 3, p. 7; Hsiao Chan, 'Some views on wage reform in industrial enterprises', *CKKY*, 1956, no. 6, pp. 28–31.

[2] A survey in a Chungking factory revealed 19 skilled workers with higher earnings than the factory manager, *Chung ch'ing jih pao*, 4 Aug. 1956; Wang Ya-ch'iang, 'Some views concerning the wage system for skilled and managerial staff', *LT*, 1957, no. 8, p. 14.

[3] Evidence that official control figures made only very small allowance for promotion is contained in an article on the history of wage changes in the banking sector, 'Opinions on wage reform', *1956 Chin jung fa kuei hui pien* (1956 currency laws and regulations) (Peking: Currency Publishing House, 1957), p. 168; see also 'Skill raised; wage grade the same', *KJJP*, 10 June 1956.

[4] The original plan is revealed in 'Serious discussion of labour management problems', *JMJP*, 17 July 1955. The planned rise in average earnings in the reform was to be 14.5%. However, this annual rise was to be achieved by rises starting on 1st April. The full year effect (for 1957) was therefore a rise of 19.3%. *State Council resolution on the wage reform*, *HHPYK*, 1956, no. 15, pp. 175–7.

in which there had been some substantial unplanned wage rises. The government feared that if these continued they would have unacceptable inflationary consequences and lower the high planned rate of domestic savings. In late 1953, therefore, it began a campaign to severely limit further increases in both average wages and the total wage bill.[1]

In this campaign several techniques of wage control were developed. One was a drive to intensify financial discipline in enterprises. This involved a tightening-up of financial control by means of continuous auditing and political pressure on finance cadres; it also involved a specific effort by the Labour Bureaux and others to ensure that unplanned wage expenditure did not take place.[2]

More fundamental than this was the attempt to secure labour force compliance and increased work intensity by the imposition of fierce labour discipline at the enterprise level. The framework for this was provided by the publication of the *Model outline of intra-enterprise disciplinary rules*, and the specific instrument for controlling workers' behaviour (including wage demands) was the newly established Judicial Committee of Comrades (*Ch'i yeh t'ung chih shen p'an hui*).[3] These committees were made up of elected workers and the general responsibility for their organisation rested with the trade unions and the local People's Courts. The committees dealt with a wide variety of infractions against enterprise discipline, although each case had either to be initiated or agreed at the managerial level. The committees had power to organise mass criticism or 'struggle meetings', to lower wages, and to order demotion or dismissal. In some ways, of course, the committees were only taking over responsibility for established practices. However they went further than this, for as one commentator put it, 'the use of trials (*shen p'an*) and punishments in the implementation of disciplinary education give the committees a coercive character, so that those who receive judgement from them have an obligation to submit'. The same commentator added parenthetically that, 'it is not so easy to get results by using [only] the old methods of criticism'.[4]

The effectiveness of these measures to control wage growth in 1954 and

---

[1] A key *People's Daily* editorial reported Mao as taking a keen interest in wage control, *JMJP*, 1 Nov. 1953.

[2] A good example of local control is 'How we implemented wage fund control', *LT*, 1955, no. 5, p. 16.

[3] *Model outline of intra-enterprise disciplinary rules*, KMJP, 14 July 1954; the role of the unions in discipline is detailed in 'The All China Federation of Trade Unions publishes a directive on the consolidation of labour discipline', *CFJP*, 28 Aug. 1953.

[4] 'Some questions on the working of the Judicial Committee of Comrades in production enterprises', *CFJP*, 20 Feb. 1954.

1955 was striking. Even the official data show that average earnings of all workers and staff increased by only 5 % and 3 % respectively in these years, compared with an average increase of 17.4% for the four years 1950–3. Further, it emerged in 1956 that these data concealed real and money wage declines in many areas and sectors of the economy, and the Minister of Labour later admitted that the abolition of lunar bonuses and premium payments had lowered cash earnings in many enterprises by up to 10%.[1]

By 1956, the costs of this policy of strict wage control were becoming apparent. Its success, for example, seems to have been at least partially contingent on levels of activity and employment which could not be tolerated in the longer run. In addition, control was associated with a decline in labour force morale, which at a time when the fulfilment of the First Five Year Plan was in question, could not be regarded with equanimity. Thirdly, the crude techniques employed to slow the growth of average wages precluded the continuous adjustments of the structure of wages which were thought necessary both to secure satisfactory allocation of the labour force and to provide incentives for increased work intensity and skill acquisition. And finally, the disciplinary labour controls developed in 1954 and 1955 gave great discretionary powers to the managers of enterprises. This was at the expense of the Party and Mass Organisations and also of the development of devices to encourage participatory styles of organisation.

There were therefore both political and economic strands in the pressure for a general rise in the wage level in 1956, and the case for reform was strengthened in both respects by the urban socialisation campaigns of January 1956. These campaigns brought the private sector under public control and their success and consolidation were both likely to be enhanced by a popular wage reform.[2]

Thus the gradual, evolutionary, technical reform of the wage and salary system planned in 1955, was overtaken by the struggle for authority within industrial enterprises, by the economic and political storms of the High Tide of Socialism and by the drive to fulfil the First Five Year Plan. As

---

[1] Ma Wen-jui, 'Labour and wages work', a speech at the National People's Congress, *HHPYK*, 1956, no. 15, pp. 115–18.

[2] At the time of the socialisation there were justified fears that the old private sector would have wage reductions. In 1955, socialisation *had* been accompanied by reductions, and in January 1956, a *People's Daily* editorial confirmed that further reductions could be expected. Ch'ien Hua and others, *Ch'i nien lai wo kuo szu ying kung shang yeh ti pien hua 1949–1956* (The transformation of our country's private industry and commerce during the past seven years) (Peking: Finance and Economic Publishing House, 1957), p. 117; 'In the High Tide of Socialism strengthen thought education work among workers and staff', *JMJP*, 17 Jan. 1956.

a result, we find that the wage reform directives proposed that reform be accompanied by a substantial across-the-board wage rise;[1] and as the momentum of the reform grew, raising the average wage became *the primary* object of reform.[2] During the late summer of 1956, this welfare aspect of the wage reform was further emphasised by the emergence of anti-poverty programmes to relieve workers suffering special hardships.[3]

The organisation of the reform followed the patterns developed in the regional reforms. There was the same combination of an activation of work within the normal institutions and departments responsible for wage administration, together with the establishment of *ad hoc* wage reform committees at enterprise, Municipal and Provincial levels.

Political activity was also intense in the 1956 reform, and it took the shape of remarkably open hostilities between the Party, unions and even individuals who were supporting reform on the one hand and managerial staff who wished to retain their discretionary wage powers on the other. Illustrative stories appeared in the press of Party and union members who challenged managers for failing to implement the reform, and the newspapers also reported several prolonged and acrimonious disputes between Unions and managers over the legitimacy of wage deduction as a disciplinary technique.[4]

The results of the 1956 reform were striking. In terms of the average level of wages, the reform fulfilled the rise planned for the whole of the First Five Year Plan. But in terms of the structure of wages, the result was not satisfactory. It is true that new formal rate systems for workers and staff were introduced, but few reports claim that the quality of evaluation work was high. On the contrary, it was widely stated that under intense pressure, cadres had concentrated on raising the average level as expedi-

---

[1] *State Council Resolution on wage reform*, HHPYK, 1956, no. 15, pp. 175–7.

[2] Of the planned rise, 73.27 % was allocated as an across-the-board rise, and the remaining 26.73 % was left for promotion. 'Some opinions and views on wage reform', *LT*, 1957, no. 14, pp. 11–13; Liu Tzu-chiu, 'We must do wage reform work well', *LT*, 1956, no. 7, pp. 31–3.

[3] The key *People's Daily* editorial is 'Pay more and better attention to workers' livelihood', HHPYK, 1956, no. 13, p. 71; The Shanghai programme, aimed at the 5 %–10 % of workers described as living in poverty, was reported in 'Conscientiously help the masses to solve their livelihood problems', *CFJP*, 16 April 1956, and 'Union branches at all levels adopt a variety of approaches to solve the livelihood problems of workers and staff', *HWJP*, 14 July 1956.

[4] The most publicised controversy concerned the implementation of a disciplinary rule system in the Heilungkiang Road Transport System. The following articles describe the long, bitter and at first inconclusive battle over this: 'Should not deduct from workers' wages', *KJJP*, 18 May 1956; 'Fines should not be substituted for correct leadership', *JMJP*, 12 June 1956; 'The Heilungkiang Transport Company and leading staff in the Communications Office refuse to change their mistaken wage fines', *KJJP*, 14 July 1956; 'A double-faced method', *KJJP*, 8 Oct. 1956.

tiously as possible without troubling to make occupational differentiation more rational.[1]

The other unsatisfactory aspect of the reformed occupational wage structure, was that the implementation of the policy of giving above-average increases to cadres went out of control, with cadres reportedly doubling their own salaries.

The macro-economic effects of the reform were also serious. It had been anticipated that real consumption would be able to rise in response to the reform because there was potential output available from excess capacity in the light industry sector and because of the favourable 1955 harvest. It had also been envisaged that a rise of real income in the cities would not on this occasion stimulate rural–urban migration, because rural cooperativisation was expected to increase rural real incomes above even the high levels reached after the bumper harvest of 1955.[2] But by autumn 1956, the stimulation to urban demand given by the reform (which included several months' back pay) was proving unmanageable. Moreover the moderate harvest of 1956 and the loss of peasant income from declining secondary activities, led to a resumption of rural–urban migration.

There can be no doubt, that apart from immediate economic effects, the Party's tactic of seeking support by promoting a wage increase also had an unforeseen ideological and political backwash. In Shanghai, for example, there was a fantastic consumption boom during the summer of 1956. Night clubs were opened, fashionable restaurants were booked for months in advance and a food shortage developed that was so serious that the Municipal Government was reported to have sent vegetable buyers as far afield as Inner Mongolia. This was no environment for the cultivation of economy, self-sacrifice and discipline – values that had been assiduously nurtured in the early Plan years.[3]

At the enterprise level too, the reform had unexpected consequences on discipline, morale and solidarity. The workers, encouraged to state wage grievances in 1956, started in 1957 to demand a variety of concessions, including the right to strike and the revivification of the long defunct

[1] Liu Tzu-chiu, 'Wage reform: the situation and its problems', speech at the Eighth Party Congress, *HHPYK*, no. 21, 1956, p. 208; 'The excessive raising of cadre wages', *KJJP*, 6 Oct. 1956.
[2] This point is made explicitly in a discussion of the appropriate urban wage floor, 'What determines the rate for grade one workers?', *LT*, 1956, no. 5, pp. 13–15.
[3] One factory was reported as employing large numbers of 'underground dance hostesses who, clad in provocative and queer attire, rubbed shoulders with nearly a hundred juvenile delinquents of both sexes, rocking in steps commonly done by American sailors', *HWJP*, 28 Nov. 1956 (*SCMP*, 1956, no. 1441). See also, 'Shanghai's unprecedented boom in the Autumn market', *CFJP*, 22 Oct. 1956; 'Shanghai's livelihood has recently manifested the deviation of extravagant luxury purchases', *CFJP*, 8 Sept. 1956.

Labour Bureau machinery for mediating conflicts with the management. There was also friction at higher levels with bitter complaints among less qualified cadres about the size of the rises given to people with special skills and training.[1]

The upshot was that for 1957 no rise in wage standards was permitted, although the full year effects of the wage reform required an 8.9 % increase in the wage bill.[2] At the enterprise level strict labour discipline was again enforced and the slogans of the 1956 reform re-emerged only to be cynically condemned as rightist deviations.[3]

THE 1963 REFORM

The years 1958–61 were ones in which wage work was at its lowest level. But in the 1960s a revival became necessary. For although dependence on wages was at this time being replaced by an increasing use of direct labour allocation, as long as jobs yielded varying satisfactions and disutilities, direct allocation was bound to stimulate counter-productive dissatisfactions, unless the wage system reflected such variations.[4]

The rule for workers and staff subject to direct transfers after 1957 was, that even if they changed occupations, their new employing unit should maintain their salary at its previous level.[5] As an emergency measure this was defensible, but it rapidly led to a situation in which enterprise wage structures were chaotic, with members of small work groups, engaged in identical occupations, earning quite different wages.[6] This inevitably led to frictions and pressures that limited the efficiency of labour direction. As a result of this problem, in the liberalisation of 1961–3 we find considerable reform activity taking place mainly within individual industries. This activity culminated in the wage reform of 1963. Little is known of this reform except that it was concerned with the sort of irrationality that we

---

[1] 'A discussion of worker and staff "disturbances"', *HWJP*, 14 May 1957; *Shuang ch'en yüeh*, 1968, no. 1 (Jan. 10); 'From the people's letters we see an internal contradiction; we propose the revival of the Ministry of Labour's structure of labour dispute administration', *LT*, 1957, no. 12, p. 4.

[2] *State Council Resolution on the lowering of wage standards of cadres above the tenth grade in State Organs, 1956 Chung yang ts'ai cheng fa kuei hui pien* (1957), pp. 246–7; *State Council notification on not raising wage standards in 1957, 1957 Chin jung fa kuei hui pien* (1958), p. 94.

[3] Two examples of condemned statements that had been basic official policy in 1956 are: 'The enthusiasm of the workers for production depends on cash stimulation' and 'Some people think that engineers should be paid more than workers', *LTJP*, 20 July 1957 and *Chung Kuo ch'ing nien* (China youth) (hereafter *CKCN*), 1 Oct. 1958.

[4] 'A discussion of wage forms', *JMJP*, 28 Oct. 1961.

[5] See Po Yi-po's speech on the 1958 Economic Plan, *HHPYK*, 1958, no. 5, pp. 12–23.

[6] Chou Liang, 'Research into some problems concerning the current implementation of piece-work', *Kung yeh ch'i yeh kuan li wen hsüan*, vol. 4, pp. 132–40.

have been discussing, and that it gave a small overall monetary rise, distri-buted to give above average rises to workers and staff at the lower end of the occupational wage structure.[1]

How far this attempt to compress the wage structure was successful is not altogether clear. Red Guard reports claim that the directive ordering reductions in salaries was not obeyed. This was due to opposition by Liu Shao-ch'i and Po Yi-po. According to these reports, this opposition took the form of a letter, written by Liu, describing his financial difficulties, which was circulated to provincial cadres who then interpreted it to be a covert indication that since Liu, at the peak of the income pyramid, could not manage, there was no need for them to lower their own salaries.[2]

There may have been some truth in this story, but other evidence, including data brought back by Japanese experts, points to the fact that some reduction took place. This would certainly have been justified in economic terms, for by 1963 the educational expansion of the 1950s must have begun to reflect itself in the labour market balance.

THE REFORM OF 1971–2

The latest reform, reported but not publicised in official sources, appears to have taken place in 1971–2. In its first stage, this reform was concerned with lower paid workers who, subject to a length of service criterion, were raised by two grades. This would raise the average wage of all workers in enterprises by approximately 10% – a figure confirmed by visitors to China in the summer of 1972.[3]

If this is correct, the reform must have had the effect of compressing the wage structure. Nonetheless, by spring 1972, reactions to the Cultural Revolution were appearing in many fields and in the case of agriculture, incentive policy underwent a decisive change.[4] A further industrial wage reform that paid serious attention to the wage structure would not therefore be a surprising development.

This concludes our initial review of wage determination. In the next chapter we shall consider the shortcomings of the mechanisms described in this and the previous chapter and the implications of these for the efficiency of wage planning and the development of wage policy.

[1] See *Peking Review*, 6 Dec. 1963 and a refugee account of the reform that confirms the *Peking Review* article, 'The wage reform in Nanchang city', *Union Research Institute*, file no. 3070, 1964–7.
[2] 'Why were high wages not reduced?', *Shuang ch'en yüeh*, 1968, no. 1 (Jan. 10).
[3] 'China a new tranquillity', *Newsweek*, 19 June 1972 and Table 17 above.
[4] *JMJP*, 12 June 1972.

7

The limits of wage control

Chinese wage policy has been conspicuously ambitious and it has also exhibited a capacity to respond to difficulties by making dramatic reversals of direction. It is therefore a fertile field for those interested in observing what wage policy can achieve if vigorously and flexibly pursued, and for those investigating the nature of the constraints faced by wage policy makers – even those placed within the powerful framework of a command economy.

In Chapter 4 we concluded that control of the average level of wages has been fairly successful, but that in the 1950s, although the shapes of the inter-industry and, to a lesser extent, the inter-regional wage structures had developed in the desired direction, control of the inter-sectoral and occupational wage structures had been unsatisfactory. In this chapter we shall attempt to explain these phenomena.

The *successes* of wage policy can be largely explained by reference to the structure and resources of wage administration and to the relationship of particular wage targets to the overall hierarchy of economic policy objectives. The main point about the structure of wage administration is the complexity of the co-ordination involved – even in the annual wage plan. For example, in the case of centrally controlled enterprises, the plan directly involved the enterprise's industrial ministry, its local managing bureau and the organs of local labour administration. Indirectly, wage plans were also the concern of the People's Bank, the finance system, the ministries responsible for the distribution of grain and consumer goods, as well as co-ordinative economic planning agencies at each geographical level of the administrative hierarchy. The combination of this complicated pattern of interdependencies and the paucity of resources allocated to wage work, meant that the planning process could only be effective if it tolerated concentration on a small number of important indicators.[1] The high ranking indicators were the average wage and the total wage bill. These were crucial, because loss of control over them had serious consequences

---

[1] For discussion of the personnel problem see Howe (1971), pp. 77 and 89–91. In Kirin in 1953 it was reported that many companies had only one man working on wages, see 'How to make a realistic wage plan', *LT*, 1953, no. 12, p. 34, while in the post mortem on the 1956 wage reform it emerged that many areas and units still had no specialised offices or staff for wage work at all, see *CHCC*, 1957, no. 8, pp. 9–13.

4 [97] HWP

for inflation and the rate of savings – and their importance was further enhanced by the fact that they could be verified unambiguously.

We suggest, therefore, that control of the average level of wages was relatively successful because average wages ranked high among policy priorities; and because the determination and verification of average wage targets were administratively simple operations. Control of the average level of wages explains control of the inter-industry wage structure. This is because the inter-industry structure was merely a by-product of average wage control in each industry. Finally, control of the inter-industry wage structure can also be used to explain at least partially, why the inter-regional structure appeared to move in the right direction, because the inter-regional wage structure reflects the relative concentration in different areas of industries with differing wage levels. Thus by establishing the heavy industries as the high wage industries, the desired regional wage structure was achieved automatically, because both new and existing investment in this sector were in the areas designated as high wage areas.

Let us turn now to explaining features of the Chinese wage performance that were less satisfactory than control of the average wage level and its dependent wage indicators.

GENERAL CONSTRAINTS ON WAGE POLICY

The problems of the occupational and regional wage structures are mainly quite specific and before analysing them we should like to consider constraints on wage policy of a more general kind. One of the most important groups of these have been political and social objectives that require explicit expression in wage policy. In the 1950s objectives of this kind imparted an upward bias to the average wage. This was notably the case in 1949–50, when wages were used to consolidate political control in the cities, and again in 1956, when wages were an important instrument in the struggle for authority within enterprises. In addition to these specific instances, the general philosophy of this early period favoured the use of wage rises to give industrial workers economic privileges to match the political privileges accorded to them in classical Marxist thinking.[1]

After 1957, the socially divisive implications of rising wages in the urban sector and the consequent increase in the urban–rural differential became recognised, and throughout the 1960s the desire to minimise this differential

---

[1] See, for example, Hsü Ti-hsin, *Chung Kuo kuo tu shih ch'i kuo min ching chi ti fen hsi* (Analysis of the national economy during the transition period in China) (Peking: Scientific Publishing House, 1959).

itself constituted a constraint on wage policy. Similarly, at the time of the Cultural Revolution, the divisiveness of differentials of various kinds *within* cities was also declared politically unacceptable, and this then became an important factor in urban wage policy.

A second basic constraint on wage policy arose from the relationship between the wage structure and the average wage and from the power of the underlying pressures for real wage increases. Experience of wage reform in the 1950s demonstrated that it was extremely difficult to change the wage structure without raising the average wage. This was because price stability meant that a reform in which the average wage was held constant, required that unfavoured workers and staff had their money wages reduced. The evidence discussed in Chapter 6, shows that attempts to implement such reforms led to popular opposition – not only from workers but from managerial staff as well. The only reforms in which the average level of wages was successfully held constant, were those in the basic construction and private sectors in 1954 and 1955; and these reforms were undertaken at a time when the level of activity in these sectors was depressed, and in a coercive atmosphere that lowered work morale.[1] Apart from the evidence of particular reforms, this problem is perhaps most graphically illustrated from the fact that the reforms of the inter-industry and inter-regional wage structures were seen in the early 1950s to require that the average wages in the cotton industry and in the city of Shanghai, respectively, did not rise. Yet in practice, the best that could be achieved was to hold wage increases in this industry and city to levels below those generally achieved.

A third constraint is one whose operations we know little about. This is the influence of the history of pre-1949 wage development. Precisely how powerful this was we cannot know, but it would be contrary to very widespread experience if historic trends in the structure and level of wages had no influence on the ease with which subsequent wage policies were implemented. In the case of the inter-industry structure, the pre-war wage structure was in some respects helpful. This was because, although the wage reformers in some regions were greatly exercised by the fact that the inherited wage structures tended to have textiles and light industry at the top

---

[1] Accounts of the reform in construction in East China and Canton are: 'Education in the general line for advancing socialism gives an impetus to wage reform', *CFJP*, 1 April 1954; 'Labour norms must be introduced into construction enterprises', *NFJP*, 12 Nov. 1954. Wages were held constant and lowered in this sector by setting norms for piecework that workers of average capability could not fulfil. For example in Canton it was reported that in some enterprises 50 % to 60 % of the labour force could not achieve the standard norms, *NFJP*, 13 Nov. 1954.

of the ranking, as we saw in Chapter 2 this was largely a product of wartime conditions, so that the reforms of the 1950s often led to a reversion to the inter-industry structure of the 1930s. The fact that reform did not involve the reversal of long standing inter-industry wage relationships probably made their implementation that much easier.

In other respects, however, the wage structure planned for the 1950s required reversal of historic trends. For example, the general tendency towards compression of differentials had to be changed and in the case of the occupational wage structure, the tendency of heavy industries and industries in which technical progress was fastest to have relatively small differentials between skilled occupations, had to be violently reversed to conform to the plans for the 1950s.

The other relevant aspect of the pre-1949 wage experience is the rise in real wages that took place in some areas during the 1940s. According to Table 15, real wages in Shanghai tripled between 1936 and 1946. Even if the true increase was much lower and related only to a minority of the workforce, rapid increases of any order could not be contemplated during the 1950s; even so, it seems probable that this wartime experience made the imposition of a long term wage freeze in the 1950s impossible. Evidence of the problems created by pre-1949 wage growth is the fact that in articles describing the improved real income of workers and staff, the emphasis is usually on the stability and predictability of income under a regime of relatively stable prices, which is compared with the uncertainties created by hyper-inflation before 1949. The argument that post-1949 wage growth had been faster than pre-1949 growth is rarely found.

Our final constraint is a further result of the imperfections of wage administration referred to earlier. The effect of these imperfections has been the persistence of transactions between enterprises and individuals of the sort found in market economies; and these transactions have been relevant to the control of the average level of wages, the inter-sectoral and occupational wage structures. It should be understood that we are not arguing that the whole urban and wage earning labour force had free occupational choice, or that employing units could hire whom they wanted at any wage. For this would be to claim that the machinery of wage planning and labour allocation built up in the 1950s and 1960s was ineffective, which would be absurd. What is being suggested, however, is that the nature of labour organisation in certain *sectors* and the limited freedom of certain *classes* in the workforce, were such as to enable a small minority of transactions to be of a market nature and that there were mechanisms by which these marginal transactions were able to frustrate wage planning.

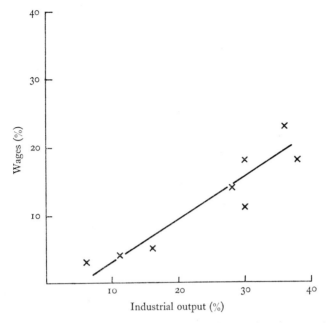

Fig. 4. The relationship between annual changes in industrial output and the wages of all workers and staff, 1950–7.

SOURCES: Wages data as Table 17. Industrial production data are the official figures, from *Ten great years* (1960), p. 87.

NOTES

The relationship between output and wages is clearly significant. The correlation coefficient $r = 0.95$. We have also plotted the regression line on the assumption of a linear relationship. Inspection of the scatter seems to indicate that a gentle exponential curve might give a closer fit. This was tried but did not improve on the linear result.

The most suggestive statistical evidence of the 'market' nature of wage determination in China in the 1950s, is the close relationship between fluctuations in industrial activity and fluctuations in the average level of wages. This is illustrated in Fig. 4. Significant as it is, this diagram is not conclusive. For it could be argued that variations in the rate of increase of wages reflected planners' appreciation of the incentive value of wages, which were therefore regulated according to variations in the planned rate of growth. There is some truth in this. However, it is notable that in years of above average growth wage plans were over-fulfilled and qualitative evidence of labour mobility and wage bargaining is widespread;[1] while in

[1] There were no published wage plans before 1952. In 1953, local plans were certainly over-fulfilled. See for example the experience of Shanghai, 'A significant turn for the

poor years, wage plans tended to be under-fulfilled.[1] The behaviour of wages in the years of high growth is not surprising, since it is the common experience of command economies that in such years emphasis is on physical rather than financial targets; and in the Chinese case, excessive wage expenditure was facilitated by the policy of using enterprise profits rather than turnover taxes to mobilise savings. The liquidity generated by this policy made illicit wage expenditure easy to finance, and as we saw earlier, bank supervision of financial planning was ineffective.

But these factors only partially explain the phenomenon illustrated in the figure. For during the period up to 1958 at least, the behaviour of the private, traditional and construction sectors, and the role of temporary workers in the labour market, were additional factors that increased the sensitivity of wages to fluctuations in activity and aggravated the problems of control.[2] We shall deal with these in turn.

The private and traditional sectors

The private industrial and commercial sector was not finally socialised until January 1956, and even since then there has remained in the cities a certain amount of small scale, unplanned economic activity. The evidence shows that the control of wages in this sector has always been unsatisfactory, although the importance of this may have declined to some extent since 1956.

The only attempt to aggregate the national data available on the behaviour of private sector wages was shown in Table 38 above. The series in this table is short but instructive. It shows that private sector wages were generally higher than those in the public sector and that this remained true

better in plan fulfilment', *CFJP*, 27 Oct. 1953, and 'The development and results of the 1953 National Economic Plan in Shanghai', *WHP*, 30 Sept. 1954. For 1956, see *CHCC*, 1957, no. 8, pp. 9–13. Under-fulfilment in years of low growth (1954–5) is described in: 'Strive to completely fulfil this year's labour plan', *Chung kung yeh t'ung hsün* (Bulletin of heavy industry), 1955, no. 29, pp. 11–14; 'Do wage reforms work well', *JMTY*, 1956, no. 21; 'Improve labour and wage work in mines and factories', *NFJP*, 28 Mar. 1955; 'Wage reform must be given an important place', *LT*, 1956, no. 7, pp. 31–3.

[1] Very revealing accounts of mobility and competitive wage bidding in the early years in Manchuria are in reports in *LT*, 1951, vol. I, no. 7; *LT*, 1951, vol. II, no. 2; see also 'Recruitment of workers and job jumping are serious problems in Shanghai', *CFJP*, 11 Oct. 1951.

[2] Good examples of the sensitivity of private sector wages to accelerations in the rate of growth, and the interaction of public and private wage behaviour in 1951 and 1953 are reported in: 'Communique of the Canton All China Federation of Trade Unions on increasing the wages and salaries of workers throughout the whole Province', *Ch'ing tao jih pao*, 10 Nov. 1951; 'The experience of Chungking city in implementing unified wage co-ordination in the non-ferrous metal industry', *LT*, 1951, vol. II, no. 2, p. 33; 'Enterprises of the First Machinery Ministry wildly grab skilled workers in opposition to the rules of planned assignment', *CFJP*, 14 Jan. 1953.

right up to 1955, by which time the private sector consisted predominantly of supposedly low-wage light industry, and by when its general level of activity was very low. The data in this table for 1953 and 1955 also suggest that the sensitivity of private sector wages to fluctuations in output was greater than that in the public sector. The implications of these data are that the control of wages in the private sector was slight – especially in the years of fast growth – and that the private sector competed for labour with the public sector. These implications are also supported by abundant fragmentary evidence. Many of the wage bargains that made private sector wages responsive to demand were illegal; however it is noticeable that even the terms of official Collective Contracts were responsive to market conditions.[1] This responsiveness and its related problems persisted right up to the end of 1957, when 'capitalist' factories were still reported as recruiting at high wages, and evidence produced during the Cultural Revolution indicates that these phenomena continued at least sporadically in the 1960s.[2]

The problems of private sector wage control were partly a reflection of the fact that most of the resources available for wage administration were directed to the public sector.[3] This was understandable, since the establishment of even rudimentary accounting and planning practices was difficult and it was logical that these should be introduced first into the public sector. Apart from this, there were special characteristics of the organisation of the private sector that compounded the difficulties created by this fundamental bias in the allocation of administrative resources. For example, the rules governing both the distribution of enterprise profits and the determination of business contracts between private and public sector enterprises, encouraged high wage payments. In the case of the former, the policy was to control the personal gains of capitalists by rules governing the allocation of profits between (i) staff bonuses and welfare expenditures, (ii) taxes, (iii) internal accumulation, and (iv) entrepreneurial profits.[4] In practice, the effect of these rules was to increase personal and collective payments to workers and staff and to make it possible for enterprises to

---

[1] 'Opinions on present capitalist wage problems', *LT*, 1954, no. 3, p. 4.

[2] 'Stop the illegal management practices of black firms; appropriate departments should strengthen market management', *Ch'ang sha jih pao* (Changsha daily), 11 Sept. 1957; 'Take action to stop the capitalist drift', *CJJP*, 20 Sept. 1957; 'Stop the capitalist tide in handicraft factories', *Ch'ang chiang jih pao*, 16 Nov. 1957.

[3] This is discussed in Shih Huai-pi, 'Some views on the present wage problems in capitalist enterprises', *Kung shang chieh* (The world of private commerce and industry), 1954, no. 4.

[4] Full accounts of the final laws and their application appear in *Szu ying kung shang yeh ti she hui chu yi kai tsao cheng ts'e fa ling hsüan pien 1953–1957* (Select compendium of policy statements and laws concerning the socialist reform of private industry and commerce 1953–1957) (Peking: Law Publishing House, 1960).

avoid tax payments by distributing their planned profits in the form of wages and salaries or welfare benefits.[1] The effect of this was revealed by a survey of enterprises in Shanghai which found that only 52% of workers' incomes took the form of a basic wage, the rest being made up of bonuses and gifts in kind.[2]

The principle governing public–private contract formation was that prices charged by the private sector should be cost, plus a percentage for profits. The costs here included labour costs and there is no evidence that these were scrutinised in any way. Thus as the percentage of total output governed by contracts of this kind grew, so did private sector indifference to wage costs. By 1955, data for 12 large cities showed that these contracts accounted for 84.5% of private industrial output.[3]

These remarks refer to enterprises in the private sector whose techniques and organisation were comparable to enterprises in the public sector. In addition to the wage problems created by such enterprises, there have also been problems in the less-mechanised, traditional sector. In theory this sector was brought within the ambit of planning by its cooperativisation in 1956, but in practice, illicit, small scale activity has continued.[4] Data on earnings in the traditional sector are rare but an illuminating insight into this sector is provided in Table 40.

This table was the result of a survey of migrant employment and the most revealing aspects of it are the very high earnings at the top of the range and the size of incomes earned in the unorganised sector. Time series data would undoubtedly add another striking dimension to the picture since scattered evidence suggests that earnings – especially in transport – were extremely sensitive to changes in the level of economic activity. Given that entry into this sector was often easy in the 1950s and apparently not impossible in the 1960s, it can be seen that the sector presented a major threat to wage control and constituted an important part of the mechanism by which fluctuations in activity were reflected in general wage levels.

There were periodic drives to control wage levels in the private and traditional sectors. Sometimes these took the form of legal pressure on

---

[1] 'Report on Capital–Labour relations in Shanghai', *CFJP*, 19 Oct. 1950; 'The stable situation of our country', *TKP* (Tientsin), 3 June 1954. A good account of abuses of the premium wage system to avoid taxation is in Liao Li-min, *Pa lao tung ching sai hsiang ch'ien chin yi pu* (Advance labour emulation a step forward) (Canton: South China People's Publishing House, 1954).
[2] Ch'ien Hua and others (1957), p. 148.
[3] Ibid. p. 108.
[4] A revealing account of income determinants in this sector is: 'The wage adjustment in handicraft cooperatives during the past year', *Chung yang ho tso t'ung hsün* (The central cooperative bulletin), 1954, no. 12, pp. 13–14.

TABLE 40. *Earnings of migrants in unskilled and traditional trades in Wuhan* (*yuan per month*)

Occupation	Average monthly earnings	Range of earnings	Type of organisation
Ordinary workers	54.83	47.53–62.53	
Transport auxiliaries	57.58	46.5–64.5	Organised temporaries
Casual transport workers	51.25	40–80	Unorganised temporaries
Cart pullers	88.56	60.84–156.84	Organised
Vegetable traders	47.06	20–79.6	Organised
Casual vegetable traders	50	20–150	Unorganised

SOURCE: 'Adjustment of the wages of ordinary workers: a problem to be given attention', *LT*, 1958, no. 3, p. 30.

capitalists or pressure by political activists within enterprises.[1] On other occasions, individuals who had changed jobs to take high wages in the private sector were subject to intense psychological stress and public humiliation in 'struggle' meetings.[2] In the case of the traditional sector, the only possible action was to control the wage levels in those parts of it that were already cooperativised. This was done in 1954, when cooperative incomes were reportedly lowered by 30% to 40%. Despite these drives for control, nothing very significant seems to have been achieved prior to the complete socialisation of 1956, and even thereafter the problem remained to some extent insoluble.

The construction sector

The other sector where wage flexibility and easy entry created severe problems was construction; and in this case a combination of economic and institutional factors was responsible. In the first place, construction was a sector in which seasonal fluctuations in the work load, superimposed on sharp variations in the level of planned activity, created enormous variations in the demand for labour. This encouraged the employment of persons whose main source of income was agriculture.[3] In the case of unskilled workers, the case for this was so strong that the practice has continued up to the present time; but prior to the collectivisation of agriculture this

[1] 'The Municipality Labour Bureau delivers a severe punishment', *WHP*, 28 June 1954.
[2] The story of a worker who was tempted into the private sector is described in *Shih pao* (The times), Hong Kong, 22 Feb. 1954.
[3] See for example materials in *LT*, 1955, no. 8, p. 45; *LT*, 1955, no. 8, pp. 2–4.

meant that control of entry into the construction work force by any authority external to the employing enterprise was extremely difficult. Thus up to 1956, enterprise wage decisions were bound to reflect variations in demand and supply conditions. And even after 1956, enterprises had to negotiate labour contracts with Collectives (later Communes), which probably meant that the price of labour continued to reflect variations in conditions in the agricultural and construction sectors.

The determination of construction wages was also influenced by certain historic features of work organisation. Before 1949, construction had been dominated by work bosses who constituted an independent, exploitative power in the economy and who were therefore vigorously attacked by the Government and unions. When the old system came under attack, it was at first replaced by a system under which groups (and occasionally individuals) were encouraged to negotiate collectively with employing enterprises to determine a price for each individual job undertaken, the sum total of wages then being distributed within the group as its members pleased.[1] The power and legal status of these groups is indicated by the fact that one of them fought a two-year legal action in the North East Division of the Supreme People's Court for a sum of 30,000,000 yuan.[2]

The result of this system was that construction wages strongly reflected variations in market conditions and that the internal division of income bore little relation to the planned occupational wage structure.[3] This was especially the case in 1953, the first year of the First Five Year Plan. In the Canton area, for example, the effect of wage bargaining in 1953 was to raise the daily rates for construction work by 50 % in six months; and construction managers were reported as remarking that 'the price is indeed high, but if we do not pay, the workers go elsewhere and we are unable to fulfil our tasks'.[4] In 1954, there was a re-organisation of construction labour control in which piece-rates with severe norms were introduced. This had a sharp effect on wages in construction although these were also reflecting the growth of unemployment in this sector following a cutback in construction outlays.[5] But when the system was put to the test in the

---

[1] 'Decision to implement a time wage system', *KCJP*, 22 Feb. 1954; 'The problem of construction workers' time rate wages urgently calls for a solution', *NFJP*, 19 Nov. 1953; 'Enthusiastically support the time rate wages system', *KCJP*, 12 Mar. 1954.

[2] 'Achievements and progress in organising control of temporary workers in Liaoning and the North Western Provinces', *LT*, 1953, no. 11, p. 14.

[3] Some cadres foresaw this problem: see 'Resolutely rely on the worker masses', *JMJP*, 10 July 1951.

[4] *NFJP*, 19 Nov. 1953; *NFJP*, 18 Nov. 1953.

   See numerous articles in *LT*, 1955, no. 1.

upsurge of 1956, there was again substantial over-expenditure of wage bills, in spite of the fact that in some industries at least, the planned rate of increase of construction wages for that year was substantially higher than that for regular production workers.[1]

The role of temporary workers

The proportion of the industrial labour force who worked as temporaries in the 1950s is not known precisely. According to data published in the Cultural Revolution, the total number of temporary workers increased from 2,400,000 in 1957 to 12,000,000 in 1958.[2] The latter figure is equal to 26.5 % of all workers and staff.[3]

The regulation of wages for these workers was very imprecise and appears to have been within the jurisdiction of local rather than central planners. In Kwangtung Province for example, there were Provisional Rules that stated that temporary workers should not be paid less than permanent workers engaged in the same occupations. There is evidence, however, that temporary workers were often paid lower basic wages than permanent staff and did not receive the fringe benefits of enterprise welfare facilities, canteen access etc.[4] In general, we would argue that the evidence on this subject is consistent with the hypothesis that the wages of temporary workers closely reflected local market conditions, and that these terms may well have influenced enterprise attitudes towards employees whose wages and conditions were determined by legal rules and the normal processes of wage determination.[5] The plausibility of this view is greatly enhanced by the fact that the wages of temporary workers were sometimes entered in the accounts under 'miscellaneous expenditures' rather than 'wages'.[6] This practice must have been so persistent and so difficult to rectify, that in the

---

[1] Na Tzu-hung, 'Strengthen labour force assignment work; supply the labour needed for national construction', *LT*, 1956, no. 8, p. 6; *JMTY*, 1956, no. 21; 'Use the wage fund correctly', *HEPJP*, 7 May 1957.

[2] *Black materials on Liu Shao-ch'i and the systems of temporary and contract labour*, 1 Jan. 1967. This was a publication of the Ministry of Labour Red Revolutionary Rebels, republished in Canton in 1968.

[3] Further data on temporaries in Shanghai which confirms the sources quoted in note 1 above are in: *NCNA*, 17 Aug. 1957; *TCKT*, 1957, no. 15, pp. 29–31; *NCNA*, 9 Apr. 1960.

[4] *Notification from the Kwangtung Labour Bureau, NFJP*, 16 Aug. 1952. 'Opinions of a temporary worker', *CHJP*, 15 Aug. 1956; 'Don't discriminate against temporary workers', *CHJP*, 30 Aug. 1956; 'Why lower the wages of temporary workers again?', *KJJP*, 6 Oct. 1956.

[5] In 1956 the market power of temporaries was reflected in the fact that a large number of them were given permanent status. See also an example of temporaries reported as saying, 'If it pays we stay – if not, we go away', *Ho pei jih pao*, 3 Nov. 1954.

[6] 'We investigate the problem of calculating the number of temporary workers in the enterprise labour record', *TCKT*, 1957, no. 4, p. 19.

early 1960s, the State Council published regulations governing the treatment of temporary workers that contained the provision that in 'emergencies', this procedure was permissible.[1]

In concluding this section we must re-emphasise that wage determination was mainly conducted in the manner described in Chapters 5 and 6. However, the evidence does suggest that some sectors and groups fell outside the official procedures, and that in these cases wages were determined by bargaining power. Further, although the extension of the public sector in 1956 eliminated some of the mechanisms by which the demand for labour was reflected in wages, the development of individual and collective contract labour in the 1960s created new ones. In some cases, of course, imperfections of wage control may have resulted in wage bargains that corrected deficiencies in the planned structure – for example illicit payments to Shanghai migrants to Manchuria – but these imperfections undoubtedly also resulted in unwanted pressures on the average wage level, and in distortions in the occupational and inter-sectoral wage structure.

THE SPECIAL PROBLEMS OF THE OCCUPATIONAL WAGE STRUCTURE

The reform of the occupational wage structure involved the imposition in each industry of common occupational structures, and the establishment of common criteria to determine the placing of individuals within the range of income permitted for their occupation. The obstacles to the achievement of these goals fall mainly into two categories: those arising directly from the technological characteristics of Chinese industry, and those arising from the inability of the reformers to control the environment and organisation of wage administration in a way that ensured that the interests of those involved were consistent with, if not actively supportive of, a wage system of this type.

The main technological problem was that inter-enterprise variations in technique were so great that the imposition of a standard occupational structure was sometimes impossible. One indicator of these variations is the size of inter-enterprise variations in costs;[2] and apart from statistical indicators, observers of Chinese industrial enterprises have noted that within industries (for example textiles) the spectrum of technique may pass from processes of an unmechanised, semi-handicraft nature to those using

---

[1] *Chung Hua jen min kung ho kuo fa kuei hui pien 1962–1963* (Compendium of laws and regulations of the People's Republic of China 1962–1963) (Peking: Law Publishing House, 1964), pp. 215–16.   [2] Perkins (1966), p. 112.

highly automated capital equipment. Differences of this sort were bound to make the application of common job structures extremely difficult, and the problem of applying them to small scale enterprises was indeed freely admitted in the early wage reforms in the public sector.

A second technological problem was one that would arise in any economy, irrespective of inter-industry variations in modernity. This is the problem that the whole idea of basing a wage system on the identification of discrete, specialised jobs, can only work in industries where such jobs exist. But as a Chinese critic pointed out, in industries where this is not the case (or in industries where technical progress requires continuous transformation of the occupational structure) the *whole* emphasis in wage evaluation should be concentrated on the personal qualities relevant to work performance.[1]

The adoption of Soviet technology during the First Five Year Plan must have eased the first of these problems; because presumably the classifications used in the Soviet wage manuals adopted by the Chinese were a reflection of the occupational structure of Soviet industrial plants of the kind that were imported into China during the Plan.[2] But towards the end of the 1950s, nationwide standardisation of occupational structures in the public sector received severe setbacks as a result of the socialisation of the private sector in 1956, and later, as a result of the campaigns to develop small scale industrial enterprises that have continued intermittently since 1958. This is because the private sector was characterised by greater variations in technology than the old public sector, and because willingness to use indigenous techniques was an essential part of the small scale industry programme. However, although universal adoption of occupational structures must have ceased to be possible by the late 1950s, the comparatively small sector of industry that remained under control of central ministries after 1957 probably had both the technological homogeneity and the organisational cohesiveness necessary to make substantial standardisation of job structures feasible.

The implication of inter-enterprise variations in technology was that

---

[1] 'An initial summing-up of wage reform in locally managed state enterprises in Canton', *NFJP*, 13 Oct. 1952; 'Opinions and views on wage problems', *LT*, 1957, no. 14, pp. 11–13.

[2] An interesting indication of what was involved in the adoption of Soviet wage practices is obtained by comparing the grades and occupations quoted in the pre-1949 Shanghai wage books with those adopted in the 1950s. In the case of the machinery industry, for example, such a comparison reveals that the 1950s classification involved increasing the number of named occupations from five to forty-five while *decreasing* the grade range for each occupation. In the case of new enterprises the new conventions may have been quite manageable, but for old enterprises there must have been some complicated and confusing changes. See *Shang hai kung ch'ang lao kung t'ung chi* (1947), pp. 86 and 137, and Wang Ya-ch'iang (1955), p. 54.

standardised job structures could not be handed down directly to enterprises and that considerable discretion had therefore to be given to enterprise level authority. Only by doing this could standardised job structures be *re-interpreted* in terms of individual technological situations. When one adds to this the consideration that the other component of wage determination (individual evaluation) was *essentially* an activity that could only be carried out within enterprises, one can see why the powers and attitudes of the groups involved in wage work at the enterprise level were critical determinants of the success of the whole system. We would argue that the three main groups (workers; Party and political activists; and managerial staff) were all either incapable or unwilling to make the system work.

In the case of workers, the origins of hostility varied, but they all reduced to a distrust of the individualism implicit in the system, and a preference for an approach to wage determination that did not undermine the social solidarity of natural work groups. To some extent, this extreme anti-individualism appears to be a particularly Chinese phenomenon, strengthened and nurtured, for example, by Chinese child-rearing practices. The result of these is that while 'the notion of group orientation and group loyalties is not unique to China but is a phenomenon general to human social existence, if indeed it is not the definition of it. What differentiates the Chinese is the singular focus of Chinese group loyalties and the intensity with which ideas of loyal behaviour (such as sacrifice for the collective good) are held.'[1]

The power of natural work groups to attract loyalty and create norms of group behaviour may be due to the fact that such groups provide in China a convenient alternative focus for feelings that can no longer be directed towards their traditional objects such as the family, because these have in some way lost their former prestige and credibility. But whatever its origin, group orientation was certainly a feature of pre-1949 industry and was highly relevant to what was possible, and what was efficient, in work organisation after 1949.[2]

Apart from its general emphasis on individualism, the feature of wage evaluation that was particularly repugnant to Chinese industrial workers was the practice of holding public meetings at which the personal qualities and work performance of individuals were evaluated. For such meetings were bound to lead to some workers undergoing loss of face, fear of which

[1] Richard W. Wilson, *Learning to be Chinese: the political socialization of children in Taiwan* (Cambridge, Mass.: The M.I.T. Press, 1970), p. 20.
[2] The best survey of pre-1949 work organisation is in Jean Chesneaux, *The Chinese labor movement 1919–1927* (Stanford: Stanford University Press, 1968).

may 'come to constitute a real dread affecting the nervous system of ego more strongly than physical fear'.[1]

However plausible this interpretation may seem, it would be a mistake to overemphasise the special Chineseness of these attitudes. Analysts of industrial work organisation in both Western and Asian societies all confirm that the introduction of work methods that abruptly disrupt the informal social organisation of production is usually counter-productive.[2] Only consistency of technical and social organisation will produce a work situation from which participants derive satisfaction and in which satisfactory technical results are achieved; and it is explicit in Chinese sources, that worker opposition to individual evaluation was not based on peculiarly Chinese attitudes alone, but reflected recognition that in many work situations, job similarities and job interdependence created natural social units within which individual wage evaluation was meaningless.[3]

Other sources of pressure for egalitarianism were the rapid influx of new, unskilled workers who stood to lose as a result of any objective appraisal of their merits, and the distrust by skilled workers of wage cadres whose evaluations they believed to be technically incompetent and politically biased. It was as a direct result of these pressures that early attempts at 'democratic evaluation' were replaced by the system of 'guided democratic evaluation'. For, as the cadres complained, with the old system, 'under the guise of democracy, the workers demand a big shareout'.[4]

From these remarks, it can be seen that worker attitudes made establishment of a Soviet style wage system difficult, but the failure of managerial and Party officials to succeed in this reflects their own competence and preferences as much as the intrinsic difficulties of the situation. To begin with, throughout the whole of the period up to the end of the First Five Year Plan, there is evidence that the administrative staff necessary to undertake the sophisticated planning, accounting and evaluation work

[1] Hsien Chin-hu, 'The Chinese concepts of face', *American Anthropologist*, vol. 46, no. 1, p. 45 (quoted in Wilson (1970), p. 24).

[2] A general statement of this and interesting empirical work are in Arnold S. Tannenbaum, *Social psychology of the work organisation* (London: Tavistock, 1966) and Robert L. Opsahl and Marvin D. Dunnette, 'The role of financial compensation in industrial motivation', *Psychological bulletin*, vol. 66, 1966, pp. 94–118. Work on this topic in an Asian context is reported in A. K. Rice, *Productivity and social organization: the Ahmedabad experiment* (London: Tavistock Publications, 1958) and A. K. Rice, *The enterprise and its environment: a system theory of management organization* (London: Tavistock Publications, 1963).

[3] 'How wages were reformed in the Hokang Mining Bureau', *TPKY*, 1950, no. 44, pp. 2–5.

[4] 'The path to a rational wage system', *TPKY*, 1951, no. 47, pp. 25–9; Wu P'in-chia, 'The wage system in the Lushun-Dairen area', *CKKY*, 1950, vol. 2, no. 2, pp. 11–19; *TPKY*, 1950, no. 23, p. 3.

involved in this sort of wage system were never available, and it was not until 1956, that a special school for training labour cadres was established. Moreover, whereas in some types of labour work it was possible to correct administrative weakness by short campaigns in which supplementary staff were mobilised, in the case of wage work, the technical skill requirements were such that supplementary staff could not be expected to achieve high levels of competence. Thus whereas any sort of literate manpower could be mobilised to do a periodic updating of the unemployment registers, only experienced specialists could draw up a draft occupational wage structure. This meant that the only group who had some interest in occupational wage reform – the managers – did not have the administrative manpower to undertake it. Moreover, the period during which their power within enterprises was strongest (1954–5) was a period when stringent external controls of the average wage made occupational wage reform impracticable.

The attitude to the occupational wage structure of Party and political activists was uniformly hostile. These groups were supposed to be particularly active in the wage reform movements, but in fact they were opposed to any wage system in which objective, technical factors were important. In the early years, this hostility was based on the egalitarian ideology of guerilla war and was summed up in the phrase, 'When we have food we all eat; when we have wine we all drink'.[1] This sort of egalitarianism disappeared for a while in the mid-1950s, but re-emerged in 1958 when the ideology of guerilla production work again came to the surface.[2]

The other element in the wage attitudes of Party and political activists was not particularly egalitarian. This was the view that the wage system was an important instrument for securing political compliance and that the use of technical criteria for determining wages was therefore quite wrong. Thus cadres and activists argued that wages should be determined by length of Party membership and performance in current political work and that, 'backward elements who do not speak out at meetings should have their wages lowered'.[3]

Our conclusion therefore is that efficient manipulation of the occupational

---

[1] Egalitarianism was particularly common among cadres with a rural background, see *CKKY*, 1950, vol. 2, no. 2, pp. 11–19.

[2] For example, *CKCN*, Oct. 1958, p. 25.

[3] Cadre opposition to apolitical wage evaluation during the reforms of 1952 and 1956 are vividly described in: 'Firmly implement the eight grade wage system', *Ch'ang chiang jih pao*, 17 Aug. 1952; 'Do well the work of being a member of the wage reform committee', *Ch'ang chiang jih pao*, 27 Aug. 1952; 'Evaluate workers' grades according to technical criteria', *KHJP*, 29 July 1956; *Hsin hu nan pao* (New Hunan daily), 8 Sept. 1956.

wage structure depended critically on the exercise of enterprise level authority and that of the three groups involved, two were hostile to and the third incapable of this kind of work. The only exception to these propositions is that neither the technological factor nor the enterprise power structure precluded the manipulation of the occupational wage structure in the sense of changing the wage relationship between different *groups* (i.e. managers, engineers, cleaners etc.). Thus it would appear that in the early 1950s, reform was successful in improving the relative position of skilled technical staff, and in 1956, managerial cadres and specialists generally achieved exceptional rises.

THE SPECIAL PROBLEMS OF THE REGIONAL WAGE STRUCTURE

The wage system was expected to perform an important role in facilitating a shift in the geographical distribution of the labour force, but the evidence suggests that in this respect it was not very effective.

One reason for this was that the nature of the inherited wage structure and the inability of planners to reduce wages, meant that a major re-ordering of the regional wage structure would have required increases in the average wage and the wage bill that would have been incompatible with a high rate of savings and the maintenance of a reasonable rural–urban differential. It is true that Manchuria, an important employment growth point, was already a high wage area; but this was largely the result of the concentration of heavy industry there and unfortunately, the main source of unemployed persons and underutilised skilled labour was Shanghai which had initially and kept, a 'pure' wage differential. This meant that even if it had been possible to hold average wages in Shanghai *constant*, very large increases in key point areas would have been necessary to establish even a small monetary differential. Added to this, was the fact that the real income differentials created by disutilities of movement to areas with foreign climatic characteristics, different dietary patterns and unfamiliar social environments, probably meant that *no* restructuring of money wages would have been wholly satisfactory.

The other problem connected to the issue of regional wage variations, related these to the overall non-agricultural income structure, and to the question of the rural–urban differential. This was the problem that the erection of common wage structures throughout China implied that in real terms, the *entry point* into these structures was to be the same throughout the economy. For although there were a few genuine regional supplements applicable to specific sectors and areas, the normal 'regional wage coefficient' was strictly a correction for inter-regional price variations. The effect of this system therefore was to fix (in real terms), *one side* of the inter-sectoral wage differential. This was of course highly irrational, since it ignored the fundamental point that if the differential was to fulfil any allocative function, local entry points would have to be related both to variations in local agricultural incomes, and to variations in the transfer costs of urban immigrants.[1]

Variations in agricultural income were important not only between broadly defined regions, but even between neighbouring localities. In the case of Provincial variations, the survey cited in Chapter 3 showed per capita peasant incomes in Kiangsu Province to be 74% higher than a comparable figure for Szechuan.[2] The size of intra-Provincial variations is shown in the case of Kiangsu, by a survey that reported that the highest locality surveyed had an average income 83% higher than the lowest.[3] Whatever the data problems in these surveys, it is obvious that a common real wage entry point into the industrial and non-agricultural wage structures must have involved substantial variations in the inter-sectoral differential, and that a differential adequate to areas where agricultural incomes were above average would be too high for other areas.

The question of transfer costs was raised in Chapter 2, where we pointed out that these tend to be lower for migrants moving to small towns. We suggested that this factor could partially explain why unskilled wages appeared to be lower in Kunming than in Shanghai, and why therefore, the skilled–unskilled wage differential was much smaller in the larger city. As operated during the First Five Year Plan, there was no allowance for this factor in the wage system. This meant that if the differential was appropriate to large cities, it must have been far too high for smaller ones.

Thus, to sum up, we would argue that although the planners were moving the broad aggregates of the inter-regional wage structure in the right direction, the adoption of a wage system that eliminated regional and local variations in the point of entry suggests that, prior to 1957, the planners had not related their thinking on the regional wage structure to the realities of variations in agricultural income or to the effect of city size on migration costs. None of this is an argument against gradually reducing dysfunctional

---

[1] The theory of the inter-regional structure of income is hard to find. By far the most important contributions to this subject are in: August Lösch, *The economics of location*, 2nd edn (New Haven and London: Yale University Press, 1954), esp. pp. 75 and 240–4.

[2] *TCKT*, 1957, no. 13, pp. 4–5.

[3] 'A preliminary research survey into the agricultural:industrial income differential in Kiangsu Province', *LT*, 1957, no. 21, pp. 18–21.

regional variations in the *average* wage; on the contrary, this is desirable, but the path to income equalisation must allow for rational solutions to the problems analysed above.

CONCLUSION

We have been concerned in this chapter to explain the degree of success achieved by the Chinese in their efforts to use the structure of wages as an instrument of labour control. We have found, that although policies towards the average wage and the inter-industry wage structures were implemented moderately successfully, the occupational, inter-sectoral and inter-area wage structures proved difficult to manipulate. We explained this mainly by reference to the behaviour of special sectors and groups of workers, and to the fundamental relationship between wage bill and wage structure that makes reform without rises very difficult. Later, we examined technological, administrative and political factors that made centralisation of wage decisions difficult and inefficient.

The socialisation of urban commerce and industry and the collectivisation of agriculture in 1956 removed some of the problems relating to the private sector and the control of temporary workers; but by 1957, it had finally become apparent that the rise in the average wage of workers and staff that had taken place was creating an intolerable strain on the demand for wage goods, especially food, and was widening the inter-sectoral differential to the point where control of rural–urban migration was impossible. Thereafter the overriding priority in wage policy was given to the control of the average wage and the wage bill. Given the experience of wage administration in the 1950s, this implied that the use of wage structures would have to be abandoned, since apart from all the other problems, even limited reform required a rising wage level.

The implications of this change in policy were far reaching. For the abandonment of wage structures did not imply that skill acquisition and labour allocation were less important, but it did imply that new means would have to be found to reach these established objectives. In the case of skill acquisition, emphasis was shifted to direct training programmes and campaigns of persuasion that attempted to establish skill acquisition as an indicator of political excellence. While to secure desired transfers of labour between enterprises, industries and sectors, we find that direct controls were developed and made more comprehensive than they had been in the mid-1950s.

Perhaps the most interesting changes of all were those that followed from recognition of the difficulties of using the wage structure to secure inter-area movements and of the implications of regional equality of the transfer wage into the non-agricultural work force.

One response to the first problem was the policy of reviving the economic importance of the seaboard cities. This policy was initiated in 1956, and in the case of Shanghai was accelerated markedly after 1958 with the development of heavy industries in the city. This development was totally contrary to the thinking of the First Five Year Plan and must reflect recognition of the costs and problems involved in transferring existing and newly trained skilled labour from Shanghai to inland cities. The other policies towards the location of industry during the 1960s that reflect the wage experience of the 1950s, are those of insisting that key point areas of priority growth, limit their material demands on the rest of the economy, and do this in part by the use of persuasive techniques to motivate migration to and work performance in them. In the 1950s the priority of key point areas had been absolute and their wage increases, although probably inadequate, were exceptionally large. In the 1960s numerous articles appeared on the importance of key point areas developing without special economic support, and it was no accident that the oilfield of Taching – the most publicised key point of the 1960s – was the origin of labour heroes and work techniques of legendary selflessness and efficiency, which became models for emulation throughout China.

The response to the problems created by the common entry wage into the non-agricultural workforce was also very significant. In an important directive in December 1957, the State Council decreed that unskilled workers entering the non-agricultural workforce *after* the date of the directive, should have their wages related to local agricultural incomes.[1] The declared aim of this measure was to lessen the importance of inter-sectoral income differentials as incentives for migration. This presumably meant that after 1957, it ceased to be possible to publish national wage and salary structures extending over the whole range of occupations as had been done in 1955 and 1956. Certainly none has been published – although common national scales were probably in use for senior personnel up to 1966 and have been revived in 1972. This practice would not however create any problem, since for senior personnel the inter-sectoral differential is not very relevant. The revival of bureaucratic salary scales will however create problems if it is extended to lower level personnel – unless the new scales allow very much greater flexibility than the old ones.

---

[1] *State Council draft temporary directive concerning the wage treatment of ordinary and miscellaneous workers hired by enterprises, units and State Organisations, HHPYK,* 1957, no. 24, p. 92.

The other development not explicitly related to the inter-sectoral wage problem, but none the less highly pertinent to it, was the expansion of urban municipality jurisdiction over substantial areas of adjacent country-side. The significance of this was that it enabled the urban authorities to think and plan in terms of bands and gradations of income, rather than having to handle a sharp urban–rural dichotomy. By taking over areas which were the main source of temporary and migrant labour, the urban authorities could begin to control the intra-regional allocation of income in a way that avoided the creation of sharp income discontinuities between those working in the built-up areas and those who are following agricultural pursuits close to the cities. For however tight direct controls over migration may be, it is inconceivable that they can be effective if income differentials between immediately adjacent areas are very large.

Most of the arguments for limiting the role of the wage system based on the experience of the 1950s still hold true. But in one aspect the situation has changed significantly. We argued above that manipulation of the wage structure involved a continuous rise in the average wage, which given the slower growth of agricultural incomes, led to an increasing urban–rural income differential. The validity of this point rests of course on the assumption that price levels of all kinds are taken as fixed. But if the planners are willing to manipulate these, they will be able to bring about changes in the level and distribution of income that offset unintended by-products of wage structure reform. In the 1950s, price policy was constrained by the overriding necessity of eliminating the spectre of hyper-inflation and by the need to finance the First Five Year Plan. Since 1958, however, there have been reports of a new flexibility in this area, and if the possibilities inherent in this were fully utilised, it would become possible to make considerable use of the wage structure without having to worry about the effect of this on the real urban wage or the rural–urban income differential.

8

The overall incentive structure:
wage forms, job tenure and emulation

Up to this point, our discussion of the Chinese wage structure has focused on the broad aggregates of basic rates and average earnings. We have not enquired into variations in types of wage payment or the allocation of other material benefits to the employed population; and although we have referred in passing to the role of punitive sanctions in industrial enterprises, we have yet to analyse the functions of that peculiarly socialist device – the emulation campaign.

These omissions must now be rectified, since the efficiency of the wage system cannot be analysed without distinguishing its components and relating it to other elements in the structure of rewards and sanctions operating at the enterprise level. In this chapter therefore, we shall consider four topics: piece-work wage systems; premium and welfare payments; variations in job security; and the functions of the emulation campaign. With these subjects behind us, we shall be able to proceed to some conclusions about Chinese wage experience, and relate these to the problem of formulating an optimal Chinese incentive policy.

PIECE-WORK SYSTEMS

Piece-work systems were adopted in the 1950s as a part of the development of a Soviet wage system. The principle of directly relating income to work performance was a thoroughly Stalinist one, and was accepted in China as a legitimate device at a stage of development during which lack of socialist consciousness made it economically expedient.

The forms of piece-work were very variable and will not be explored in detail here. But the basic principle of the system was the payment of a monetary bonus or the imposition of a penalty, whenever a worker's performance, measured by objective criteria, exceeded or fell short of a norm. Variations in the system arose from the use of group rather than individual performance, and from variations in the relationship between performance and reward. In general, although progressive systems were advocated by Mao in the Yenan period, the Chinese appear to have preferred systems in which gearing is low – i.e. systems in which above norm performance results in less than proportionate changes in income. This is in contrast to Soviet practice, where before the 1962 wage reform, progressive systems were fairly important.[1]

The implementation of piece-rate systems lasted from 1949 to 1956, tending to accelerate during the wage reforms. In 1957, this trend was reversed, and in 1958 widespread abolition of the system was reported.[2] According to Cultural Revolution materials the abolition in 1958 was less drastic than contemporary reports suggest; but it is interesting to note that these materials do not claim that the revival of wage work in the 1960s included the systematic restoration of piece-work. Thus these materials, taken together with the fact that the penetration of piece-rates was never high by Soviet standards (42% coverage of the industrial workforce which may be compared to a peak of 72% in Russia), suggest that the difficulties of implementing the system in China were considerable, and were recognised throughout the spectrum of political and economic opinion.[3] What were these difficulties?

One group of problems arose from the familiar constellation of technical and administrative factors. To be efficient, piece-rate systems must be *equitable* and this is only possible in an environment that is predictable and technologically uniform, and where the administrative skills necessary to design and administer the system are available. None of these conditions has held in China. Predictability has never been achieved because the level of activity in enterprises has been strongly influenced by cyclical factors and by failures of planning co-ordination – particularly with regard to raw materials supply. This has meant that where piece-rates operate, fluctuations in workers' incomes reflect factors outside of workers' control. Under these conditions, piece-rates rapidly become unpopular and counterproductive.[4]

A second difficulty has been that inter-enterprise variations in technical conditions have precluded the application of industry-wide piece-rate norms.

---

[1] Chapman (1970), p. 34.

[2] 'The labour and wages situation in 1956', *HHPYK*, 1957, no. 10, p. 115; 'We propose the abolition of piece-work', *Chung Kuo ch'ing nien pao* (China youth daily) (hereafter *CKCNP*), 6 Oct. 1958; 'We abolish piece-work', *WHP*, 29 Oct. 1958.

[3] Chapman (1970), p. 34; Sun Shang-ch'ing, 'Current questions on the nature and future of our country's piece-work wage system', *Ching chi yen chiu* (Economic research) (hereafter *CCYC*), 1959, no. 4, p. 19.

[4] 'A summary of the results of an investigation into piece-work wage systems undertaken by the Ministry of Industry of the North East People's Government', *TPKY*, 1951, no. 50, pp. 11–15. The examples in this discussion are taken from early experience, but the same problems were reported right up to 1957.

This meant that implementation was difficult, and that because workers could not make meaningful inter-personal and inter-factory comparisons, piece-rates produced open disputes and hidden dissatisfactions that 'disturbed the workers' internal solidarity'.[1]

Thirdly, the administration of piece-rate systems, in particular norm setting work, requires skills and time which wage cadres, struggling even to introduce wage planning of the most rudimentary kind, could not handle. This too led to counter-productive inequities which were a constant source of friction.[2]

The net effect of these planning, technological and administrative factors have been uncertainties and inequities that undermined worker support for piece-rate systems. These feelings have been reinforced both by a general preference for egalitarianism and, in the early 1950s, by the hostility of the large numbers of new, unskilled workers, who as we saw earlier, were particularly distrustful of wage differentiation of any kind.[3]

Another aspect of piece-work revealed by reports from Manchuria is that managers found that the positive effects of these systems were offset by the negative results of anxiety to avoid the *penalties* that accompany below norm performance. Many workers were reported as taking the view that in the implementation of piece-work, penalty avoidance was *more important* than attempting to win the rewards of above norm performance. This meant, that rather than responding positively to piece-work, workers put a premium on conservative work performance and the avoidance of any local-ised technical innovation or outstanding work effort that might eventually lead to norm revision or the hostility of other members of their work group.[4]

Although the problems analysed above all emerged in the early 1950s, they were not sufficient to halt the progress of piece-rate implementation, and in 1956, as a result of the wage reform, piece-rate penetration reached a peak coverage of 42%. In 1957 however, the changing climate of opinion in wage matters led logically to the curtailment of piece-work, and in 1958 the issue became acute, because the application of 1956/7 norms to the levels of output reportedly reached in that year began to produce a rapid upsurge in wage bills. The result was a bout of norm revision and piece-work abolition. In 1959 however, there was probably some restoration of

---

[1] 'To correctly grasp wage policy is the prerequisite of adjusting time work', *TPKY*, 1952, no. 87, pp. 21–4.
[2] *TPKY*, 1951, no. 50, pp. 11–15.
[3] Ch'eng Chi-chung, 'The combination of time and piece-work wages', *LT*, 1959, no. 16, p. 20.
[4] 'Standards too high – punishments unpredictable', *TPKY*, 1950, no. 36, pp. 20–2; *TPKY*, 1951, no. 50, pp. 11–15.

abolished systems, because it was reported that such systems still covered 35 % of the workforce.[1] There are no statistical materials on the subject for the 1960s, but as we pointed out earlier, the revival of interest in the wage instrument in the 1960s did not apparently extend to piece-rate systems. Instead, effort was concentrated on the resumption of premium wage systems, to which we now turn.

PREMIUM AND WELFARE PAYMENTS

Premium payment systems have varied substantially in both their importance and terms, owing to shifts in official policy towards them and lack of control over individual enterprise schemes. In this section we shall consider the extensiveness of their application; the criteria used for making awards; and the problems raised by their operation.

For most of the 1950s, premium schemes were available for all industrial workers and staff in the State sector. It has been suggested by some scholars that leadership personnel were excluded from the premium schemes and that in this respect, Chinese incentive practices have departed significantly from the Soviet model. In fact, several sets of regulations published in the 1950s explicitly include staff, and there is evidence that these regulations were operative.[2] In their early form, managerial incentives were progressive in the sense that premium payments for over-fulfilment were greater for senior staff, and in the case of managers, payments up to 90% of basic salaries were allowed.[3] It is true however that in 1957 staff premiums came under attack, and in the 1958 regulations, the factory leadership were excluded from obtaining premiums.[4]

During the First Five Year Plan, the most important regulations, those of 1952/3, related the payment of premiums to the fulfilment of the enterprise plan for gross value of output, profits and profit remittance.[5] In addi-

---

[1] *CCYC*, 1959, no. 4, p. 19.

[2] *Temporary regulations of the North East People's Government Ministry of Industry on piece-work, TPKY*, 1951, no. 76, pp. 47–9 and no. 77, pp. 42–3; 'Staff premium evaluation work', *TPKY*, 1950, no. 30, pp. 25–6; *Communication of the Ministry of Industry of the North East People's Government concerning rewards for administrative and leadership personnel in factories, TPKY*, 1952, no. 101, p. 19; 'Workers and staff premium methods ought to be changed', *Chi hsieh kung yeh* (Machinery industry) (hereafter *CHKY*), 1957, no. 6.

[3] *TPKY*, 1951, nos. 76 and 77, as note 2, above.

[4] See a series of articles in *CKKY*, 1957. The 1958 rules are discussed in an account of the National Labour and Wages Conference, *LT*, 1959, no. 15, pp. 18–23.

[5] *Chung yang jen min cheng fu fa ling hui pien 1952* (Central People's Government compendium of laws 1952) (Peking: People's Publishing House, 1954), pp. 169–71. A good discussion of these rules is Ch'en Kuan-hua, 'Research into the conditions for premium awards in State enterprises', *CKKY*, 1957, no. 11, pp. 50–2.

tion, enterprises were sometimes required to demonstrate a good record of adopting Soviet techniques before the premium fund could be distributed. According to these regulations, the sources of premium payments were to be both planned and unplanned profits. In the 1952 rules, enterprises were divided into three groups and the highest rates of premium payments were to be made in heavy industry. In this sector premium funds could be taken from profits at the top rates of 5% from planned and 20% from unplanned. Total annual payments were restricted to 15% of the annual basic wage bill. In the case of light industries, the rates were 2.5% from planned and 12% from unplanned profits – again to a maximum of 15% of the wage bill. In the revised version of 1953, maximum premium payments were to be between 6% and 12% of the wage bill according to the category of industry. Apart from monetary payments, premium work in the 1950s also frequently involved the provision of feasts and small awards in goods, especially where individuals were involved.

Despite much talk about premium system revision in 1956, the 1952/3 regulations seem to have remained the basis of premium work until the publication of new regulations in 1958. In these, the source of payments was to be profits retained by the enterprise in accordance with the 1957 rules for decentralisation, and the maximum level of payments was to be reduced to the equivalent of 5% of the monthly wage bill. These regulations there-fore continued the downward trend in the level of permitted payments manifested in the earlier rules.

In 1961 and 1962, although we know of no further official regulations, it is clear that there was a substantial revival of premium systems and it was emphasised that one of the main reasons for increasing enterprise profits was, 'to ensure that the need to set up an enterprise bonus fund will be met'.[1] It is clear that the system got out of hand and it was reported that rates of payment in the 1960s rose to around 20% to 50% of the wage bill[2]. These figures may include welfare payments which under the old system

---

[1] Hsiao Min, 'A preliminary study of the problem of profit in socialist enterprises', *KMJP*, 11 Dec. 1961 (*SCMP*, 1961, no. 2661); Sung Hsin-chung, 'The system of retaining a percentage of profits by our enterprises', *TKP* (Peking), 12 May 1961 (*SCMP*, 1961, no. 2543).

[2] One important turning point in premium work was a meeting of leadership personnel from the mining industry. It is reported that at this meeting, the restoration of premium systems was advocated by Po Yi-po, Ch'en Yün and Chang Lin-chih, *Tung fang hung pao* (The east is red daily) (Peking), 4 July 1970; 'Is he a leader of the working class or a traitor?', *Hsi ts'ang jih pao* (Tibet daily), (hereafter *HTJP*) 7 Oct. 1967. For data on the level of payments see: 'Some problems concerning bonus work in commerce enterprises', *TKP* (Peking), 1 Jan. 1962. Materials published in the early 1960s largely confirm Red Guard accounts of the development of premium work at this time; in particular it is clear that the revival of industry after 1962 generated substantial profits which were the source of premium funds.

were calculated separately, but even so, they indicate levels of payment far in excess of those permitted under the 1958 rules.

In 1966 it was reported that premium systems had been abolished, and although there are some reports that suggest that 'open violation' of this directive continued, visitors to China in 1971 reported that there were no individual premium schemes in enterprises visited by them.[1] However, there have also been reports that in place of performance-related group and individual bonuses, there is now a monthly bonus which keeps the total enterprise wage bill at the pre-abolition level. Without this, bonus abolition would have caused an unacceptable drop in money wages.

The above developments relate only to premium regulations in which the criteria for awards were plan fulfilment. Apart from these, there have also been systems based on other criteria. For example, regulations were published in 1949, 1950, 1954, 1957 and 1963 that gave awards to the originators of technical innovations at various levels of the industrial and research systems.[2] There have also been various supplementary payment schemes. For example, payments have been reported for special working conditions; to encourage geographical mobility; and supplements of up to 50% have been available for workers with particularly rare skills.[3] Lastly, workers whose performance won them the title of *Advanced Production Worker* or *Model Worker* have also been given premiums in accordance with special regulations drafted on an industry basis. We shall return to the implications of this in the last part of this chapter.

The extent to which premium awards have actually been made is not easy to establish. Certainly the existence of regulations alone is no guarantee that they were ever implemented. We would argue for example that the draft regulations for staff premiums published towards the end of the First Five Year Plan were almost certainly a dead letter. They could not have been implemented in the atmosphere of 1957, and by 1958 new rules had made the drafts obsolete.

[1] 'Letters from revolutionary masses', (*SCMP*, 1968, no. 4122); 'China's affluent austerity', *The Financial Times*, 29 April 1971.

[2] *A communication concerning premium awards*, TPKY, 1949, no. 10, p. 7; *Central Government directive concerning awards for inventions relevant to production, technical improvements and rationalisation proposals*, CFJP, 17 Aug. 1950; 'An explanation of some problems in the implementation of temporary regulations for rewarding production inventions, technical improvements and rationalisation proposals', *Chung Hua jen min kung ho kuo fa kuei hui pien 1954–1955* (Compendium of laws and regulations of the People's Republic of China 1954–1955) (Peking: Law Publishing House, 1956), pp. 430–4; 'Our country's first evaluation for scientific prizes', *WHP*, 26 Jan. 1957; the 1963 rules are in *JMJP*, 2 Dec. 1963.

[3] The best general introduction to premiums is *Sheng ch'an chiang li pan fa chieh shao* (An introduction to production premium methods) (Shanghai: Labour Publishing House, 1951).

Despite this qualification, there is evidence, on both a regional and industry basis, that premium systems were widely implemented. For example, we have an article on premium payments in the Manchurian chemical industry that shows that the early premium rules were in use in this sector, and an article on the machinery industry published in 1954, stated that by the end of 1953 *most* machinery enterprises in Manchuria were operating premium systems.[1] Other regional data are supplied in an article on heavy industry in Taiyuan city in 1957;[2] and even more interesting, is a survey of premium payments in the first quarter of 1957 in the city of Shenyang. This reported that over 26 % of the industrial workforce received premiums amounting to 5 % to 7 % of their incomes and also that some 6,000 managerial and technical staff had received payments of a similar order.[3]

The conclusions to be drawn from this sort of information are (a) that in the 1950s premium schemes were quite widespread; (b) that the official levels of payment as a proportion of total income were low by Soviet standards, but (c) that large profits and bad accounting in Chinese enterprises made substantial illicit premium payments quite common. There are no industry or regional data for the 1960s, but it seems likely that premium systems remained widespread up to 1966.

The main function of premiums was to improve workers' performance in the framework of a wage system in which income was determined by job and qualification, rather than by current work performance. Premiums were thus to some extent a substitute for piece-work. Premiums also had the function of providing incentives to enterprises to fulfil their tasks in a more balanced way than they would otherwise have done, and to pay attention to tasks that lay outside the enterprise plan altogether – for example, safety work.[4] The difficulties and costs of achieving these ends seem to have been considerable.

One problem was that premium criteria did not usually relate directly to cost targets and financial performance; and since enterprise profits were so large that they did not usually limit premium payments below the levels permitted by the wage bill percentage limit, the pursuit of premiums en-

[1] 'The path to a rational wage system', *TPKY*, 1951, no. 47, pp. 25–9; Wu Tai, 'Wage problems in our country's machine building industry', *CKKY*, 1954, no. 3, pp. 1–4.
[2] *CHKY*, 1957, no. 6.
[3] 'The wage income of our city's workers and staff is strikingly increased', *Shen yang jih pao* (Shenyang daily), 5 Oct. 1957.
[4] The early rationale for premiums is given in *Sheng ch'an chiang li pan fa chieh shao* (1951). For the 1960s see Shih Hsin-lin, 'A tentative discussion on the incentive system in industrial enterprises', *JMJP*, 6 March 1962 reprinted in *Communist China Yearbook 1962* (Hong Kong: Union Research Institute, 1963), and Fu Te-huang, 'The use and application of premiums', *LT*, 1962, no. 7, pp. 154–8.

couraged profligate use of inputs. Even more serious was the effect of premium systems on the control of aggregate wage bills and wage structures. In the case of wage bills, some payments (for example innovation payments) fell outside the definition of the wage bill used for planning, and they therefore constituted a loophole for enterprises wishing to violate the wage bill target. Further, since profits rarely constituted a constraint on premium fund size, the principle of relating payments to a percentage of the wage bill meant that maximisation of premiums made it in the interests of enterprises to maximise the planned wage bill! The 1953 regulations were particularly bad in this respect, since, in these, premiums were related to the wage bill for *all* workers and staff, irrespective of their function. The premium rules thus became a major cause of the expansion of the numbers of 'unproductive' employees. In 1955 the rules were amended to exclude (for premium fund calculation) that part of the wage bill belonging to non-productive workers and staff.[1]

These undesirable results of the premium system all arose as a result of enterprises following the rules. There is plenty of evidence however (not all of it from suspect Red Guard sources) that the rules were often not adhered to, and that enterprises converted profits to premiums in total disregard of them. Thus especially in the 1960s, when the authorities were trying to hold down the average wage, it is possible that premium payments from illicit sources tended to frustrate this aim.[2]

The problem of controlling enterprise premium systems would have been less serious if managers had used these funds in accordance with the principles of the overall wage system (i.e. if they had related payments to objective skill and scarcity factors). But the evidence suggests that the value of premium funds to enterprise managers was precisely that they enabled them to satisfy egalitarian pressures from below, and thereby to undermine the incentives to skill acquisition and mobility provided by the basic wage system. In the 1950s this tendency was condemned.[3] But in the 1960s, the use of premium funds to make across-the-board increases was encouraged; and whether or not the role of individuals in this was exactly as described, one can readily believe that the pressures for an increase and the means of satisfying it were both present.[4]

[1] 'Reform the methods for applying premiums in enterprises', *CHKY*, 1957, no. 2; *State Council directive concerning the definition of the wage bill for determining enterprise premium funds, Chung hua jen min kung ho kuo fa kuei hui pien 1954–1955* (1956), p. 427.
[2] Fu Te-huang, *LT*, 1962, no. 7, pp. 154–8.
[3] Wang Ju-shan, 'A discussion of premium wage system problems in industrial enterprises', *CKKY*, 1953, no. 6, p. 18.
[4] Ma Wen-kuei, 'On the character and tasks of our State industrial enterprises', *JMJP* 3 March 1964 (*SCMP*, 1964, no. 3191).

The egalitarian consequences of premium systems were greatly reinforced by practices in the field of welfare and supplementary wage payments. These payments were partially the responsibility of Trade Unions, and partially under management control. The range of expenditures varied from massive collective welfare items such as canteens, clubs, housing, medical facilities etc., to small items for individuals such as soap, towels, theatre tickets and small cash benefits for those with special needs. According to the regulations, up to 1958, total welfare expenditures were limited to 10.5% of the wage bill. But, in practice, in the early 1950s between 40% and 50% of Manchurian wages were made up of welfare payments, and in the late 1950s expenditures of up to 20% were reported as common. These payments were sometimes related to need and sometimes corruptly appropriated by cadres. Typically, however, they were distributed equally, as for example in the Loyang factory, where the welfare fund was distributed equally and was known as 'the 9 yuan system'.[1] With factors such as these determining payouts, the welfare system must have undermined and distorted enterprise wage structures.

The costs of these payments and their effect on the urban–rural differential began to be appreciated by the end of the First Five Year Plan period; and in accordance with the spirit of the 'rational low wage policy' they were abolished. In some cases, however, it was reported that when enterprises had abolished welfare payments, they merely transferred the burden of them to the premium account – thus illustrating the interchangeability of the two systems in the eyes of enterprise leadership.[2]

In 1962 there was a revival of welfare work under trade union leadership, together with some relaxation in the rules governing welfare funds that enabled welfare administrators to increase the proportion of funds going to expenditure on individuals rather than collective items.[3] According to Red Guard materials, this expansion of welfare work was closely related to the revival of premium systems under the leadership of trade union and anti-Party leaders. It is not possible to quantify the levels of expenditure that

[1] For the early 1950s see: 'Research in wage work problems', *TPKY*, 1951, no. 55, pp. 14–15. For the late 1950s see: Wei Li, 'The supplementary wage system needs to be greatly changed', *CHCC*, 1958, no. 5, p. 12. The system as operated in the 1960s can be seen from *Kung yeh k'uai chi ho suan* (1965), p. 146 and articles in *Kung hui ts'ai wu kung tso shou ts'e* (A handbook of union finance work) (Peking: Workers' Publishing House, 1963). The 9 yuan system and corruption are described in: 'The hardship fund cannot be distributed equally', *KJJP*, 1 Nov. 1956; 'Irrational supplementary payment work in a non-ferrous machinery factory', *CCJP*, 18 Nov. 1956.

[2] *LT*, 1959, no. 15, pp. 18–23.

[3] *State Council regulations concerning the methods for enterprise workers and staff supplementary payments, Chung hua jen min kung ho kuo fa kuei hui pien 1962–1963* (1964), pp. 215–16.

took place, but it seems probable that it was sufficient to make some impact on differentials within enterprises and between the rural and urban areas.

THE QUESTION OF JOB TENURE

The distribution of job tenure throughout the labour force is an important part of the total pattern of incentives, because the predictability of income, and variations in working conditions and fringe benefits associated with tenure, must be relevant to workers' valuation of the net benefits of work. Up until the mid-1960s, workers with tenure had their wages determined in accordance with comparatively centralised criteria and enjoyed a comprehensive range of individual and collective welfare benefits; they thus enjoyed the satisfaction that their work rewards were predictable, secure and by comparison with the population at large, generous. In contrast to this, wages of temporary workers were less predictable, more vulnerable to downward pressures when the level of activity was low and not supplemented by welfare benefits.[1] These differences have undoubtedly been relevant in a number of ways to the morale of the workforce and one of the few striking attempts to change economic organisation that took place during the Cultural Revolution was the attempted abolition of temporary worker status.

The emergence of the temporary worker problem in the 1960s had been anticipated by rumblings from temporary workers in the 1950s. Up to the end of the First Five Year Plan, however, the ability of the economy to absorb temporary workers and the rising average wage, kept the number of temporaries low and their dissatisfactions below boiling point. But although the temporary workers were not at that time a serious social problem, they were a problem for the Ministry of Labour. This was partly because their hiring was typically casual and undocumented and therefore made hiring control difficult, and partly because the irreversible absorption of temporaries into the permanent workforce in the upswings of activity had become a major cause of overmanning, and therefore a real source of economic inefficiency.

This problem of securing efficient labour utilisation in an economy prone to fluctuations and in which occupational flexibility is common, is not of course peculiar to China. In Japan, for example, the economic system has

---

[1] 'Temporary and contract workers! rise up and rebel!' *Shou tu hung wei bin* (Capital city Red Guards), 13 Sept. 1966. It is claimed by Red Guard sources that the crucial decision to exclude temporary workers from labour insurance was taken by the Minister of Labour in 1958. In fact this was current practice before that date. See *Black materials on Liu Shao-ch'i and the system of temporary and contract labour*, 1 Jan. 1967.

responded to a similar situation by the creation of a core of skilled, committed workers, backed by temporary workers who move in and out of industry from the agricultural or urban household economy in response to industrial cycles. Even with the high degree of industrialisation now reached in Japan, this system is still important in some prefectures and cities.[1] By the late 1950s, writers in China were arguing for a system with a similar sort of flexibility.[2] As a result we find the development of three new devices: (*a*) Collective Contracts for the supply of groups of workers from the rural sector; (*b*) contracts stipulating terms and duration of work for individuals, and (*c*) the creation of special arrangements for workers to be employed in both agriculture and industry. Work systems of the latter type, involving the rotation of employees between agricultural and non-agricultural occupations, started in 1958 and continued vigorously in the 1960s. The precise character of the rotation varied according to the requirements of particular areas and industries. Most of these schemes were located in the urban periphery and were reported to be particularly important in the mining, logging, construction, water conservancy, sugar refining and light industry sectors.[3]

During the 1960s, the preference of labour administrators for labour working on these terms appears to have increased. So much so, that according to Red Guard material, there was widespread resistance to a ruling that all pre-1960 entrants to the labour force who were included in the 1963 labour plan be made permanent; and in his confession of errors, the former chief of planning in the Ministry of Labour, Wang Chieh, reported that secret drafts of the Third Five Year Plan circulating in the Ministry proposed that the share of permanent workers in the workforce be lowered by a third.[4]

Quite why this preference for temporaries occurred and at precisely what levels of labour administration it was manifested, is not convincingly explained in the Red Guard materials. But when one considers the inter-

[1] See for example a discussion of the implications for agricultural labour supply of changes in the Japanese industrial growth rate, in *The Japan economic review*, vol. III, no. 11, 1971, p. 8.
[2] Cheng K'ang-ning, 'Summarise the experience of 1956; reform labour and wage work', *CHCC*, 1957, no. 8, pp. 9–13.
[3] See 'The Head of the planning bureau of the Ministry of Labour, Wang Chieh confeses his views on the conversion of apprentices to temporary workers during the Third Five Year Plan', *Lao tung chan pao* (Labour battle weekly), 3 Feb. 1968. This confession, together with the *Black materials* cited above (p. 127, n.1), are the two documents produced during the Cultural Revolution that reveal most convincingly the nature of employment planning in the 1960s. For multiple sector employment see: 'The labour system of industrial and farming work in rotation is actively tried out all over China', *NCNA* (Peking), 27 Dec. 1965.
[4] See note 3 above.

dependence of the rural and urban sector and the historical experience of Japan, it seems improbable that the share of temporaries in the labour force actually reached, or was planned to reach, an economically irrational level.

Why then did the matter become so important? Basically because the real income differentials between permanent and temporary workers became so great, that they became ideal material for exploitation in a political conflict. Indeed, the explosiveness of the issue was such that it ultimately led, in the early evening of 26 December 1966, to the summary dismissal of the Minister of Labour and the dissolution of the All China Federation of Trade Unions.[1]

Looking at the matter in retrospect, it appears that the Cultural Revolution was an instrument for the release of tensions created by an inequality that had become unsustainable. None the less, if the above discussion is related to our earlier account of the welfare and premium systems, the fundamental ambiguity and weakness of the Cultural Revolution 'policies' towards labour organisation and incentives becomes apparent. The *ambiguity* was that while on the one hand welfare and bonus privileges in their old form were abolished, on the other the attack on the contract system capitalised not only on aspirations for job security, but precisely on demands for the privileges that were being abolished. The *weakness* was that, while the attack on welfare and premiums had a valid economic rationale (they were creating excessive inter-sectoral differentials and undermined enterprise wage structures), the attack on the contract/temporary system did not. High levels of workforce permanency had proved inefficient in the 1950s and 1960s and the logic of a system that combines a core of permanent skilled workers with a flexible periphery of the less skilled, seems inescapable at least for the present.

At the present time it does indeed appear that although there have been modifications – particularly in regard to payment practices – the temporary system has been retained. The positive value of the Cultural Revolution will, therefore, probably prove to be that it provided the planners with a warning of the destabilisation that can follow from permitting real income differentials within enterprises and cities to become too great.

[1] *A record of the conversation between comrades of the Central Cultural Revolutionary Small Group and representatives of the National Red Revolutionary Rebels*, a pamphlet published originally in Peking by Red Revolutionary Rebels of the Ministry of Labour; it was subsequently reprinted in Canton on 4 Jan. 1967.

EMULATION AND MODEL WORKERS

The emulation campaigns of the 1950s had the function of providing incentives to supplement and reinforce the wage and premium systems. The view that we should distinguish sharply between emulation campaigns as a 'non-material incentive' and wage systems as 'material incentives', and that incentive policy simply involves switching from one to the other has no great foundation in fact. In the Soviet Union, Stakhanovite workers were paid fantastic wages, and even in Yenan the early development of emulation was not apparently inconsistent with Mao's advocacy of cumulative piecework and the payment of large differentials to cadres for meritorious performance.[1]

In China in the 1950s, the links between material rewards and emulation were made explicitly in special regulations that governed the distribution of awards to Advanced Production Workers and Labour Models.[2] The important sense in which emulation and wage work were alternatives, was that shortage of personnel made their simultaneous development very difficult. In spite of this, it is a remarkable fact that 1956, the year of the most extensive wage reform, was also a record year for numbers of emulation heroes.

Emulation campaigns were also used as incentives for manual and clerical workers and their organisation was shared by union, managerial and to some extent Party authorities.[3] Campaign objectives in the 1950s were both to increase work intensity, and also (as with premiums) to influence aspects of work behaviour that the wage system either left uncontrolled, or in some cases, distorted. For example, emulation was used to encourage accuracy in accounting, speed in statistical work, ideological remoulding among capitalists, improvements in safety and quality control and all forms of technical innovation.[4] In the case of office staff, the formu-

---

[1] A useful account of the origins of Yenan emulation work is in Mark Selden, 'Yenan legacy: the mass line', in A. Doak Barnett (ed.), *Chinese Communist politics in action* (Seattle and London: University of Washington Press, 1969).

[2] See the premium regulations cited earlier and *Temporary regulations concerning the question of premiums for socialist emulation, 1956 Chung yang ts'ai cheng fa kuei hui pien* (1957), p. 179; 'Answers to questions concerning the temporary regulations on socialist emulation premiums', ibid. pp. 52–3. A revealing article in the 1960s reported that after a worker had been selected as a model, 'the masses unanimously agreed to reward him', see 'Bring to enterprises the PLA's excellent style of work', *NFJP*, 21 July 1964 (*SCMP*, 1964, no. 3291).

[3] 'A discussion of problems in the organisation of socialist emulation', *Chung Kuo fang chih kung jen* (Chinese textile worker), 28 July 1956, pp. 1–4.

[4] The best chronological list of emulation campaigns is in *Shin Chūgoku nenkan 1970*. More detailed accounts of objectives in the 1950s are: 'The foreman of an advanced shop', *NFJP*, 5 July 1954; Chao Hung-wan, 'How a union in a private factory im-

lation of success criteria was very difficult. Quantitative criteria stimulated unnecessary bureaucratism and qualitative criteria were hard to define. Thus in the end, the usual solution was to relate office premiums to the most relevant indicator in the enterprise plan (i.e. the Finance Department would be judged by financial indicators, the Labour Department by labour indicators etc.). This did not of course solve the problem of competition *within* the office.[1]

There can be no doubt that although there were many experiments in emulation during the 1950s, the dominant type of emulation work was the search for individual heroes and the organisation of campaigns to copy them. The typical product of the time was Wang Jung-lun, a legendary steel worker from the Anshan Iron and Steel complex. The prodigious progress of Wang and others in fulfilling their tasks for the First Five Year Plan were reported throughout China and campaigns of emulation were organised on the basis of the standards and work styles adopted by them.

Although these campaigns were very extensive, they seem to have been unpopular and to have had only limited success. One factor in their unpopularity was that the glorification of individuals (on the Soviet pattern), was disliked by the workers who feared that model performance had too much influence on standard work norms.[2] With time moreover, the emulation of living heroes, whose plan fulfilment was always ahead of everybody else's, became somewhat unrealistic. For example, at the rate of progress achieved by Wang Jung-lun in 1953, Wang could be expected to be half-way through the Fourth Five Year Plan when the rest of the labour force was completing the First.[3]

The opposition of cadres and managers to emulation campaigns was partly due to their sensitivity to shop floor feeling on the matter. But there were more substantial issues involved as well. For example, 'storming' in emulation competitions led directly to increases in the incidence of sickness among the labour force and to 'endlessly soaring accident rates'.[4] Another problem associated with emulation was that campaigns tended to erode managerial authority; for as one cadre put it: 'if we develop emulation, we

plemented the policy of "use, restrict, reform" in labour emulation', *LT*, 1954, no. 11; 'Some experience of statistical emulation in State Textile Factory No. 4', *Ch'ing tao jih pao*, 8 May 1956.

[1] 'Some views on office emulation', *KJJP*, 20 Dec. 1956.

[2] 'The experience of the Hua Hsiang Mining Bureau in implementing individual piece-work', *Ch'ang chiang jih pao*, 12 Oct. 1952.

[3] 'Is Wang Jung-lun's task of completing the first year of the First Five Year Plan a blind, rash advance that destroys balanced production within the enterprise?', *CKCNP*, 25 Dec. 1953. See also Wang Jung-lun, 'My resolve', *JMJP*, 1 Jan. 1954.

[4] 'The speech of representative Wei Hung', *Ch'ing tao jih pao*, 4 June 1956; *HHPYK*, 1951, no. 7, p. 38.

get a flood of proposals that create leadership passivity'.[1] Related to this, and perhaps most important of all, managers complained that the *individual* competitiveness of campaigns undermined internal work co-ordination, and that violent outbursts of increased work intensity and innovation frustrated their efforts to make the internal planning system work. Hostility based on these factors should not be confused with the self-interested inertia reported in Soviet management. The context of the latter has been a planning system functioning, within tolerable limits, in the manner it was supposed to. In China in the 1950s, however, the creation of a measured, predictable environment within which plan fulfilment was possible was still a thing of the future. The obstacles to the establishment of such a system – inexperience, communication costs, fluctuations etc. – became insuperable, when on top of them were placed the dislocations associated with 'storming' and emulation.

Because of these factors the response of industrial systems to emulation campaigns were attempts to reduce the 'shock' elements to a minimum, thereby making emulation campaigns detailed, technical exercises backed by material incentives. After the violence of the Korean War campaigns, there was also an attempt to switch the emphasis of campaigns away from fulfilment of targets by increases in intensity and hours worked, and towards the development of technical innovations that increased productivity.[2]

The character of emulation changed significantly in the 1960s. The emphasis in award work for example, switched from the individual to the collective; for although individual awards continued, the small group, the shift and the factory became much more important.[3]

There was also an important shift in emulation criteria. This shift involved moving away from exclusive concentration on the narrow, technical criteria of plan fulfilment, towards more general criteria, some of which were related to work and organisational styles, and some of which were purely political. Thus whereas the model worker of the 1950s was the man who prefulfilled his tasks in the National Economic Plan, in the 1960s he was the man who developed indigenous techniques, who co-operated in the

[1] 'Struggle to fulfil the National Plan by fully developing labour emulation', *Ch'ang chiang jih pao*, 1 May 1955; see also a very revealing account of opposition to emulation work at the enterprise level and above: 'Stir up a production high tide', *NFJP*, 28 Feb. 1956.

[2] Lai Jo-yü, 'Improve emulation work', *LT*, 1953, no. 11, p. 1; 'Some problems of enterprise administration in the organisation of socialist emulation to promote a high tide of production', *Ch'ang chiang jih pao*, 28 Mar. 1956.

[3] 'The All China Federation of Trade Unions calls a forum of Trade Unions to exchange experiences on the production work of the masses', *KJJP*, 7 May 1965 (*SCMP*, 1965, no. 3464).

development of democratised factory management under Party leadership, and above all, who 'worshipped Chairman Mao immensely and with boundless love and who studied hard, fruitfully implemented, enthusiastically propagated and courageously defended the thought of Mao Tse-tung'.[1]

The years in which this change of emphasis took place were 1958 to 1960, and an interesting indication of the struggle involved in the suppression of old style emulation, is the Red Guard exposure of Tu Chen-hsiang, an official of the Canton Finance and Trade Department. Tu's crime was that he had persisted in the use of plan fulfilment criteria in emulation work, and that he had given premiums to emulation heroes, both of which had been common practice in the 1950s.[2]

The changing criteria for emulation success were reflected in the choice of heroes. (Individual models could of course be emulated by collective units.) Some of the heroes of the 1960s were drawn from the ranks of workers who had made significant contributions to technical progress. But, towering above these were men such as Wang Chieh and Lei Feng, both members of the People's Liberation Army, and Li Feng-chou, a political instructor in a branch of the People's Bank.[3] Apart from the fact that none of these men was actively engaged in industrial work, the significant point common to all three is that by the time they became heroes they were dead. The use of dead heroes is arguably the most ingenious and useful advance in emulation work that took place in the 1960s. For dead heroes have the great advantages that they cannot embarrass the living with prodigious performances, nor can they be corrupted, trivialised or bureaucratised, nor can they collapse with exhaustion from overwork – fates that overtook some of the most famous labour heroes of the 1950s.[4] The dead heroes simply stand as embodiments of certain values relevant to the economic and political roles of industrial workers.

In the 1970s, there has been a revival of living models, but dead ones have remained important; and an interesting and perhaps unique example

---

[1] 'The political department for Finance and Trade of the Central Committee of the Chinese Communist Party calls on Finance and Trade workers to emulate Li Feng-chou', *NCNA* (Peking), 8 Sept. 1966.

[2] *Down with Tu Chen-hsiang the chief follower of the capitalist road within the Party in the Canton Finance and Trade system*, pamphlet dated 15 May 1967.

[3] Lei Feng and Wang Chieh left diaries which served as materials for emulation study: *Lao tung jen min ti hao erh tzu Lei Feng* (Lei Feng: a good son of the labouring people) (Peking: The China Youth Publishing House, 1963); *Yi hsin wei ko ming* (All the heart for revolution) (Peking: The China Youth Publishing House, 1965).

[4] Li Li-san, 'Summary report of the all China conference of representatives of industrial, agricultural and military model workers', *HHYP*, 1951, no. 1. According to one report, of an early group of 192 model workers, 76 subsequently collapsed from overwork and 90 others got into some kind of trouble, 'Basic summary of patriotic labour competition', *KJJP*, 19 April 1951.

of a man who was a great model when alive and who has remained an important figure for emulation since he died, is Wang Chin-hsi of Taching. Wang also achieved the unique distinction of membership of the Party Central Committee.

The effectiveness of emulation campaigns would be difficult to evaluate under any conditions; at a distance all we can do is to make some tentative suggestions. First, in the 1950s, the number of workers who received awards was considerable. In 1954, for example, there were 153,900 Model Workers and 220,450 Advanced Production Workers; and Shanghai data for 1955 and 1956 suggest that about 3% of those engaged in emulation competitions got awards.[1] In this period, it seems probable that the campaigns did have some success in increasing work intensity, especially when they were combined with patriotic movements at the time of the Korean War. Against this, the reports cited earlier confirm that increased work intensity had its counter-productive aspects, that it lowered the quality of work and that it made the establishment of industrial planning systems very difficult. Efforts to switch the emphasis from plan fulfilment achieved by increased intensity and long hours towards technical creativity, qualitative indicators and balanced plan fulfilment do not seem to have made headway.

In the 1960s, the politicisation of emulation must have lessened its impact on purely economic objectives. On the other hand, the switch towards technical innovation may well have been more successful than in the 1950s, and the shedding of some of the Soviet features of emulation probably made it more acceptable than it had been. On balance, therefore, we think that the net benefits of emulation may have been greater in the 1960s than in the 1950s. This belief is based not only on the factors mentioned above, but follows from the basic point that in a period when average wages were either constant or at best growing very slowly, the links between emulation and material rewards were more vital than ever before. These links remained important in the 1960s even if the old premium rules lapsed. Thus at the level of factory awards, 'management of the workers' welfare' was one of the five criteria used to select 'Five Good' factories,[2] and winners of emulation competitions of all kinds were certainly eligible for gifts in kind, holidays in Trade Union rest homes, and perhaps most important of

---

[1] *Chinese workers march towards socialism* (Peking: Foreign Languages Press, 1956), p. 22; 'The city's conference for representatives of the 1955 Labour Models and Advanced Production Workers opened yesterday', *CFJP*, 6 Apr. 1956; the same title, *HWJP*, 19 May 1956; 'Production jumps ahead in the new joint-managed enterprises', *CFJP*, 3 Feb. 1957.

[2] The five were: (1) political work, (2) plan fulfilment, (3) use of military work styles, (4) administrative efficiency, (5) management of livelihood.

all, privileged access to the scarce stock of residential housing.[1] It is also probable that emulation success was a key to promotion, which in the period of wage standstill was the only legitimate way up the income scale.

[1] This is based on conversations and observations made by the author in 1965 and 1966. In many cities only a minority of the population live in post-1949 housing, and several persons connected with the allocation of new housing stock emphasised to me that the criteria in allocating this are: (*a*) need, and (*b*) production performance. In fact, with one exception, every apartment visited by me had certificates on the wall that indicated that at least one of the occupants, and sometimes more than one, were winners of emulation or innovation awards.

9

Optimal incentive policy and the future of the Chinese economy

We have now completed our analysis of the functioning of the Chinese wage system and related this to some of the most important non-wage incentives. In this chapter we shall put our material into perspective both by looking at the Chinese system of incentives in the light of basic theoretical thinking and by drawing out from our account of the past some propositions about the future.

THE FUNCTIONS AND EVOLUTION OF INCENTIVE SYSTEMS

The functions of the incentive system in an economy undergoing industrialisation may be summarised as follows: (*a*) to secure the entry and commitment of workers into the industrial and modern non-agricultural sectors, (*b*) to motivate workers to acquire skills, (*c*) to motivate workers to achieve high standards of work performance, and (*d*) to ensure that the labour force is used in an optimal manner. In the case of (*c*), we would distinguish two types of work performance. These are: (*i*) performance that follows predetermined patterns of work activity, in which therefore, a good performance is typically measured by indicators that reflect careful adherence to standard work practice and intensive effort, and (ii) performance evaluated in wider terms, in which a good performance reflects workers' ability to perceive and co-operate in the implementation of technical and organisational improvements. For convenience we shall call these intensity and creativity performance respectively.

The instruments in the incentive armoury include the whole range of rewards and sanctions that exist in a society and can be manipulated to achieve any of our four basic purposes. The most useful classification of these is that which makes the distinction between *external* and *internal* incentives.[1] External incentives are rewards allocated by persons external

---

[1] This section is based mainly on papers by Katz, Maslow and Leavitt in Victor H. Vroom and Edward L. Deci, *Management and motivation* (London: Penguin Books, 1970); Rensis Likert, *New patterns of management* (New York: McGraw Hill, 1961); Reinhard

to the recipient, usually on the basis of objective criteria of performance; internal incentives are rewards and penalties that arise within a person as a result of his work experience. These basic types of incentives can be further subdivided as follows:

external incentives (1) system (or collective) material rewards, e.g. welfare privileges, job security, etc.;

(2) individual material rewards, e.g. wage systems based on qualification and performance;

(3) coercive pressures and sanctions.

internal incentives (1) satisfaction from work as physical, technical or social activity;

(2) satisfaction from the achievement of collective goals with which an individual has identified himself.

It will be seen that under this classification, external incentives include both material and non-material elements. Within this group we have *system rewards*, which we define as material advantages of any kind accruing to a person purely by virtue of membership of a factory, industry, sector or other collective entity. These may include special welfare benefits, job security or high average wages unrelated to individual performance. We also have *individual material rewards* which are material benefits allocated according to individual qualities and performance, primarily through the wage system; and coercive sanctions, which are defined as sanctions ultimately involving the use of some kind of physical or psychological violence as a penalty for unsatisfactory work performance.

The most important distinction within the internal incentive group is that between (1) satisfactions that workers derive from the physical, technical or social characteristics of the job itself, and (2) the satisfaction that an individual gets as a result of identifying personally with the goals of his shop, factory, industry and ultimately, society, and seeing these achieved as an end product, however remote, of his work. The development of internal incentives is usually thought to require an increased degree of worker participation in making decisions relevant to his own activities, since this will make identification with the wider enterprise goals easier.

One unsolved problem concerning both external and internal incentives

Bendix, *Embattled reason: essays in social knowledge* (New York: Oxford University Press, 1970), Chaps. 8–9; Chris Argyris, *Integrating the individual and the organization* (New York: John Wiley, 1964).

is the relationship between 'satisfaction' or 'morale' (however induced), and work performance. Empirical enquiry has identified cases where the two are positively related and others where productivity appears to be a function of low pay, insecurity and dissatisfaction. It is clear, however, that even if in some circumstances dissatisfaction is related to high performance – there is a limit beyond which this becomes intolerable and a violent breakdown of the system is possible.[1] Further, it seems to be the case that the technical conditions under which low morale and good performance are linked are fairly limited.[2]

Categorisation of this sort prompts two questions. First, what policy principles will enable us to combine different types of incentive into an optimal incentive bundle? And second, how will the composition of the bundle and the character of its components change through time?

One approach to the first question is to make deductions from empirical research on the relationship of specific incentive instruments to particular goals of policy. This has shown that different goals are most easily achieved if a particular type of incentive is used. Material system rewards, for example, are effective for recruitment and for building up labour force commitment; while individual material rewards have been found to be powerful motivators of intensive work performance, and less conclusively, of skill acquisition. Individual material rewards in the form of the wage system also have the function of providing indicators that facilitate rational labour allocation.

Internal incentives may also be used to motivate work intensity and skill acquisition, but are particularly appropriate in situations where imaginative and flexible work performance is vital – situations that is, where the importance and possibility of shop floor innovation, or the general unpredictability of the environment, preclude the standardisation of work procedures. One point on which most authorities agree, is that in the long run, coercive controls alone are not viable for any purpose, except perhaps to recruit and retain labour in labour camps. The reason for this is that however efficient coercive controls are, the nature of modern industrial activity is such that it cannot function without the assent of its participants. Coercion does not create such assent and is more likely to lead to such practices as work to

---

[1] Abraham K. Korman, *Industrial and organizational psychology* (New Jersey: Prentice-Hall, 1971), Chap. 7.
[2] This is discussed in Reinhard Bendix, 'Human relations and technological and institutional imperatives', and William J. Goode and Irving Fisher, 'Technology, collaboration and morale', in R. Dubin (ed.), *Human relations in administration* (New Jersey: Prentice-Hall, 1954); see also J. P. Davison and others, *Productivity and economic incentives* (London: George Allen and Unwin, 1958).

rule, concealed sabotage, a mechanical performance of duty and other manifestations of alienation likely to lower efficiency below tolerable standards.[1]

Given these relationships, the resources allocated to different components of the incentive bundle should be related first to the relative importance of the various objectives of the whole system, and then to the feasibility and relative costs of the incentive alternatives. The feasibility factor has several dimensions. For example, the operation of wage systems that reward individual performance, require that such performance can be measured and that logical and obviously equitable rewards can be related to it. This will depend on the degree of worker interdependence, which will in turn be determined by technological factors that will vary by industry and sector. It will also depend on the availability of the administrative capacity necessary to devise and maintain such systems. The feasibility of some forms of internal incentives will also hang on technological factors. This is because such incentives often involve toleration of a degree of worker discretion over the choice of methods of production, or even over the nature of the final product. In some cases this will be technically impossible, and again, there will be inter-industry and possibly inter-enterprise variations in this.

With regard to costs, there is a presumption that the costs of internal incentives will be less than the costs of erecting the wage structures and welfare systems associated with external rewards. Thus, where the budget constraint is vital, this will create a bias towards internal rewards.

Variations in objectives, feasibility and cost considerations, give rise to numerous possible permutations of policy. For example, if the dominant problem is inadequate labour supply and lack of commitment, and if the budget constraint is not vital, then the use of wage and welfare systems would seem most appropriate. If, on the other hand, creative work performance is at a premium and wage goods are scarce, then reliance on internal non-material incentives is called for. In many cases, of course, the choices will not be so simple, because of conflicts between policy objectives, cost and feasibility determinants. In these cases, policy objective considerations must be primary, or at least given relatively heavy weighting.

The evolution of incentive systems has been the object of enquiry by economists, psychologists and sociologists and each group has contributed important insights into the problem. The main point emphasised by economists is that the specialisation and interdependence that accompany economic development require that incentive systems increase in com-

---

[1] See Argyle, in Vroom and Deci (1970), p. 174 and Bendix (1970).

plexity, in rationality and in predictability.[1] In advanced economic systems, it is argued, human resources cannot be increased, allocated and motivated efficiently, if rewards do not reflect objective factors which are perpetually differentiating themselves. In terms of wages the hypothesis is that payment in kind will be replaced by cash wage systems within which the level and type of rewards will be determined by objective factors. In the early stages of development, the dominant objective factor is the need to recruit labour and to retain it while it acquires skills. For this purpose collective benefits are appropriate. Later, when allocation considerations become dominant, individual rewards will be more efficient.

The most influential hypothesis produced by psychologists is based on the theory that human needs fall into a natural hierarchy in which physical and security needs are primary, and aspirations for esteem and self-actualisation are secondary.[2] Given this hierarchy, the relative efficiency of any incentive is determined by its relationship to the human needs or aspirations dominant at each stage of economic development. Thus at low levels of per capita income, individual and collective material rewards are appropriate, since these satisfy dominant physiological and survival requirements. At higher levels of income, these incentives lose their force because satisfaction of primary needs is taken for granted; it therefore becomes necessary to develop internal incentives that utilise energy being channelled to the newly dominant social and psychological needs.

The main line of sociological argument is that, at low levels, work is predominantly a question of the application of physical effort, for which individual material rewards (especially piece-work) are appropriate; but as society reaches higher levels of per capita income (with industry declining as a proportion of the National Product) work increasingly becomes a question of the production and dissemination of knowledge. The appropriate incentives for this it is argued, are the security of collective rewards and the prospects of long term material benefits.[3]

It can be seen from this brief survey that there do exist currents of thought that can be used to interpret incentive experience. Since these currents have different disciplinary inspirations it is not surprising that they are not yet unified, and in addition to disciplinary considerations, differences arise from the fact that these theories are the result of reflection on situations with distinct historical and cultural boundaries. The views of the economists and psychologists, for example, differ more in emphasis

[1] John T. Dunlop, *Industrial relations systems* (New York: Henry Holt, 1958).
[2] A. H. Maslow, 'A theory of human motivation', in Vroom and Deci (1970), pp. 27–41.
[3] A. L. Stinchcombe, 'Social structure and organization', in J. G. March (ed.), *Handbook of organizations* (New York: Rand McNally, 1965).

than crucial substance. Thus in the economists' view, the changing requirements of the *economy* are the main dynamic factor in the incentive system, whereas the psychologists emphasise the changing needs of the *individual* – although these needs are none the less themselves determined by the economic phenomenon of rising incomes. The one important difference between the three lines of thought is that neither the economists nor sociologists have much to say about internal incentives. In the case of economists, this can be explained by their basic methodological bias towards the quantifiable. In the case of the sociologists, however, there seems to be no reason why the framework of security and long term material prospects that they see to be necessary in post-industrial society should not be combined with some development of internal incentives.

Let us now see how these ideas can be related to the Chinese scene.

THE EVOLUTION OF THE CHINESE SYSTEM OF INCENTIVES

The Chinese experience of incentives has now been very wide. Of the three types of external incentive discussed, *system rewards* in the industrial and State bureaucracy have taken the forms of high average wages, job security and welfare benefits; *individual rewards* have taken the form of a wage system based on qualification, occupation and performance; and *coercive controls* were certainly experimented with in 1954–5 and possibly at other times.[1]

The development of internal incentives has taken a variety of forms. There has, for example, been the use of the educational and propaganda systems in conjunction with emulation work, to encourage individuals to internalise values relevant to their economic performance ('quicker, faster, better, more economically' etc.). There have also been efforts to encourage workers to identify with collective goals and relate fulfilment of these to fulfilment of their own work tasks. In the 1950s, making the connection was not too difficult, since the emphasis was on enterprise and national economic plans. In the 1960s, however, the collective goals took the form of national and international political goals whose relationship to basic level economic work must at times have appeared tenuous.[2]

The efficiency of these incentive instruments has been variable. In the

[1] Red Guard materials tend to equate coercion with bureaucratic administration of any kind. On this basis, they incorrectly see a long struggle between democratic and coercive styles of management. See: 'The struggle between the two roads in factory management', *Kung jen tsao fan pao* (Workers' rebellion paper), 1968, no. 7 (28 Nov.).
[2] Victory in Vietnam was one international objective used in the 1960s. I recall being told by one worker that, 'to work here on the shop floor and fulfil my tasks, is as good as to fight in Vietnam'.

case of external controls, it is indisputable that the collective benefits offered by the industrial and bureaucratic sectors were powerful enough to ensure adequate entry and commitment to these sectors. The problem with this class of incentive, however, has been that it created forms of dualism that appeared so inequitable that they led ultimately to the destabilisation of the whole system. In the 1950s, dualism took the form of an urban–rural differential that caused uncontrollable migration. In the 1960s, this remained a problem,[1] but on top of it was placed the explosive dualism within urban areas – remembering that these areas had been expanded to include the rural hinterland. As a result of this expansion, urban dualism came to include both agricultural/non-agricultural differentials, as well as those between established workers in the modern sector and those who worked in the traditional sector, or as temporary workers in the modern sector.

The unresolved issue here is the extent to which these differentials (especially the intra-urban one) were necessary. We would argue that the evidence of over-supply in industrial and bureaucratic organisations in the 1950s and early 1960s shows that system benefits were excessive. However, in the long run we think that the skills necessary to the efficient operation of these organisations will never be acquired without substantial labour commitment, and that this requires that a premium be paid to ensure that a solid core of workers remains attached to these organisations, whatever the temporary attractions of small-scale enterprises or self employment outside may be. In other words, we agree with Liu Shao-ch'i's defence of the industrial wage differential and think that attempts to eliminate all forms of income dualism cannot be effective in the long run. This view is supported by evidence that in the post-Cultural Revolution period systems benefits, in the form of welfare payments, have been restored to levels even higher than those reported in the mid-1960s.[2]

The development of the wage system (individual material rewards) has

---

[1] It is interesting that Red Guard sources quote Liu as saying that, 'Unions are the main organisational form of the *urban* people' (our italics). This suggests that the destruction of the Trade Unions in 1966 was a part of the attack on rural–urban differentials, *as well as* an attack on intra-urban differentials; Unions were supposed to have contributed to the latter by their support of the development of contract and temporary labour. See *HTJP*, 7 Oct. 1967.

[2] 'The true face of Liu Shao-ch'i in the 1957 anti-rightist struggle', *Tung fang hung* (East is red), 4 Jan. 1967. Liu is reported here as saying that the differential was justified because, 'the workers' life is hard; they work an eight hour day; the air is bad; the work is intensive and life expectancy is shorter than that of peasants'. A report from Shanghai quoted a case of welfare expenditures running at a level equal to 36 % of the wage bill. See 'The essential distinction between two systems of distribution', *Hung ch'i* (Red flag) (hereafter *HC*), 1972, no. 7 (translated in *Selections from China mainland magazines* (hereafter *SCMM*), 1972, no. 72–7).

been the main focus of this book. The adoption of a Soviet system has undoubtedly been an irreversible watershed on the road to the establishment of a modern wage system. Payment in kind has largely disappeared, and the adoption of Soviet wage criteria, however briefly, has at least introduced the concept of using systematic, technical criteria for purposes of wage determination. Also, as argued earlier, wage systems have performed some allocative functions – particularly in regard to labour movements between industries and occupations and, in varying degrees, between sectors and regions. The extent to which the system stimulated skill acquisition is not clear, but even in this respect we think that it was of some importance.

One problem posed by the Soviet wage system was that its essentially individualistic basis was somewhat alien to the Chinese scene; but much more important than this, the system was premature in terms of the economic, technological and administrative capacity of the Chinese economy. These factors were relevant both to the decision in the 1950s to place heavy emphasis on wages as against other incentive forms, and also to the adoption of a Soviet rather than any other type of wage system.

The main economic factors of importance were as follows:

(*a*) The very low levels of initial per capita income in the economy, and the reliance on largely internal sources of savings, meant that the use of wage structures whose establishment and evolution involved a continuously rising wage level was bound to cause excessive demand for wage goods, income dualism and insuperable difficulties in the area of population and employment control.

(*b*) The supply of skilled labour was so small in relation to the demands of the First Five Year Plan, that what was needed was a wage system that would enable enterprises to offer a career prospect to encourage workers to remain in specific occupations and acquire skills and experience. A system in which the fastest way up was to switch jobs was quite wrong; and the Soviet system, in which income is determined primarily by occupation or job, is bound to stimulate just this sort of unwanted mobility. By the end of the 1950s this was recognised, and we find Chinese writers arguing the case for a Japanese type of system, in which pay increases are related to seniority of service.[1]

(*c*) A third economic factor that differentiates the Chinese situation from others in which Soviet type wage systems have been used, is that in China it has been impossible to dispense with the small scale, urban production sector. Nor has it been possible to leave this sector outside the domain of

---

[1] Chang Ming-fang, 'Some views on the reform of the wage grade system for workers in the machinery sector', *LT*, 1958, no. 3, pp. 22–3.

public control – whether centralised or not. This means that the wage system has to apply to enterprises which differ widely in technique and in organisational and financial characteristics, and whose sources of labour supply go to the roots of the household and agricultural economy. The effect of this is to make centralised standardisation and control of the type required by a Soviet wage system inefficient, if not unworkable.

The problems raised by this last factor have been compounded by the lack of administrative resources available to the wage system. For as we showed earlier, this lack hindered the establishment of the system in the first place, and made the problems created by inter- and intra-industry variations in technology and economic circumstances insoluble.

This mutually reinforcing constellation of economic, technological and administrative factors goes a long way towards explaining why the Chinese developed a propensity to experiment with coercion and with internal forms of incentive – although, whatever the propaganda, these systems were *never* mutually exclusive. The only prolonged experiment with coercion was in 1954–5, when wages and system benefits were widely reduced in real terms, and coercive, quasi-judicial discipline was developed at the enterprise level. In 1955, the effectiveness of enterprise level controls was reinforced by the Hu Feng counter-revolutionary movement, which was the last upheaval prior to the Cultural Revolution in which a substantial number of people suffered severe penalties for 'counter-revolutionary' activities.[1]

This early experiment in coercion was of a formal, bureaucratic kind in which use was made of quasi-legal rules. In 1957 and possibly at other times, there were experiments with other forms of coercion in which the Party used mass meetings and other *ad hoc* coercive devices. These experiments were not a success in industry, and the 1954–5 exercise led to a decline of morale that was only revived by the massive and unrepeatable increase in average incomes permitted during the 1956 wage reform.

The costs and implementation problems associated with external incentives – whether material or coercive – made a compelling case for the use of internal incentives; and this case has been reinforced by other factors. One of these is that the Chinese have had long experience of value internalisation as a means of social control and the use of emulation models as a means of accomplishing this.[2] This long experience probably reflects

---

[1] Hu Feng was a rightist author whose exposure triggered a widespread purge, notably in Shanghai.

[2] This phenomenon and its political implications are discussed in Lucian W. Pye, *The spirit of Chinese politics* (Cambridge, Mass.: The M.I.T. Press, 1968), pp. 29–31. See also for an illuminating discussion of the role of models in traditional Chinese society

the fact that external controls have always been difficult to operate in a society where communication costs are high.

Another factor in favour of internal controls has been that the objectives of the incentive system are such as to make them particularly appropriate. We saw earlier that according to sociological argument, economies in which important objectives of the incentive system are encouragement of creativity and workers' willingness to cooperate with others, should not rely heavily on individual wage incentives. In its original setting, this argument was used to explain the diminishing role of individual wage incentives in post-industrial societies. But, if these objectives are also important in economies in the early stages of industrialisation, the argument against individual wage incentives remains valid. The difference is that whereas wealthy societies can afford to replace them with lavish, collective material rewards and long term earnings prospects, in the pre-industrial, or transitional society, the constraint of poverty excludes this alternative. This is very much the case in China. For in the Chinese case there are many parts of the economy where capital shortage, inter-enterprise variations of technique, the secrecy traditions of craft workmanship and the impediments to the creation of an efficient bureaucracy all make the growth of output sensitive to the discovery and dissemination of inexpensive technical improvisations, and to the willingness of the workforce to respond to the demands of the economy in an imaginative and flexible way.[1] Thus in these parts of the economy at least, it is not appropriate to rely on wage systems that involve rigid work procedures and quantifiable performance criteria; for high quality work performance here involves precisely the qualities that individual wage incentives seem unable to stimulate. In place of such incentives, the cost factor points to the desirability of internal motivation.

The third condition that has made China conducive to internal incentives is that the sort of enterprise and planning reorganisation necessary for the expansion of individual or small group discretion over techniques and other decisions has been more feasible in China than it would have been in an economy where a high degree of co-ordination was necessary because capital intensity was uniformly high, and mass or flow production techniques the only ones used.

Arthur F. Wright, 'Values, roles, and personalities', in Arthur F. Wright and Denis Twitchett, *Confucian personalities* (Stanford: Stanford University Press, 1962), pp. 3–23.
[1] These problems and their relation to emulation and propaganda work are discussed in: 'Everything for the great fatherland', *JMJP*, 1 Jan. 1952; 'Views on, experience in, and improvements from emulation linking three bicycle factories', *KJJP*, 12 Jan. 1956; '6,000 workers sign mutual technical assistance pacts', *Kung jen sheng huo* (Workers' livelihood), 30 July 1956.

Although the conditions for a flexible approach to organisation were present, the actual discovery of the relationship between work performance and enterprise organisation has been gradual and related to growing recognition of the value of creative work performance and the role that internal incentives can play in stimulating this.

The earliest forms of worker participation were Joint Production Committees and Worker and Staff Representative Committees in the public sector, and Labour–Capital Consultative Committees in the private sector.[1] In theory, these all provided opportunities for worker participation in enterprise decisions, and it was claimed that these types of democratisation liberated both intensive and creative work performances. However, the establishment of Soviet planning techniques in the early 1950s was inevitably accompanied by the growth of a hierarchical, specialised type of management that severely limited the meaningfulness of these sorts of organisation. Soviet management, based first on Lenin's Taylorism and his ideal of the 'iron discipline', and later on Stalin's system of one-man management, had no genuine place for decision making below the managerial level.[2] It was not until the decentralisation of power to enterprises and local planning bodies in 1957 that the relationship between work performance and participative styles of organisation were talked about again with any seriousness.

By the 1960s, however, it was argued explicitly that poor work performance was a result of 'bureaucracy, restriction and compulsion' and that increases in productivity would follow from the development of informal, unstructured industrial organisation. 'Practice shows', stated one article, 'that every enterprise which practices democracy in production can turn to better account the zeal and creative character of its workers, improve the relations between cadres and the masses, advance technical innovation and

---

[1] A crucial distinction between the organisation of worker-management bodies in the public and private sectors, was that in the public sector, wage and welfare issues were strictly excluded from the field of discussion, but in the private sector, these issues were of dominating importance; see: 'Strictly implement Joint Production Committees', *Ch'ang chiang jih pao*, 29 May 1951; Shih Fu-liang, 'The tasks and status of the Labour Bureau in the rationalisation and regularisation of Labour–Capital relations', *CCCP*, 1950, Ser. 10, no. 16, p. 7.

[2] Critics of Stalin (especially Trotsky) have often compared Stalinist styles of government and control with genuine Leninism, which is taken to be more liberal and democratic in nature. However, the authoritarian flavour of Lenin's approach to economic organisation is revealed in the following: 'We must learn to combine the "public meeting" democracy of the working people – turbulent, surging, overflowing its banks like a spring flood – with *iron* discipline while at work, with *unquestioning obedience* to the will of a single person, the Soviet leader, while at work' (original italics). V. I. Lenin, *The immediate tasks of the Soviet Government, Collected works*, 4th edn, vol. 27 (Moscow: Foreign Languages Publishing House).

revolution of management, and make its production plans advanced yet reliable.'[1]

The Cultural Revolution accelerated the implementation of these principles by abandoning completely the old managerial distinctions, rules and nomenclatures and by creating new Revolutionary Committees to run enterprises. These committees were reported to be abolishing the last vestiges of bureaucratic management and to be reverting to extreme forms of democratisation.[2]

This situation did not, however, persist for long. The first signs of the turn of the tide against democracy, creativity and unstructured organisation were demands for a return to minimal standards of discipline. 'In the name of "rebellion" and opposing slavishness, they [the undisciplined] in reality stir up anarchy', wrote the *People's Daily* in 1969.[3] These attacks on lack of discipline were directed particularly at Shanghai and at the railway system, where the collapse of order had been most serious.[4] Beyond the issue of discipline, the effect of the attacks on foreign techniques and oppressive organisational systems was also to discourage interest in formal training and technical procedures of any kind. In the case of training, it was reported that young workers feared that any interest in technical expertise would leave them open to charges of political deviance for 'putting techniques first';[5] and the *People's Daily* summed up the general problem of order and its reimposition by the Party as follows: 'Under the influence of the evil tide of anarchism some of the factory's rational rules and systems had at some point been eliminated. After the formation [reformation?] of the Party Committee it was proposed that they be promptly restored. However, some people under the influence of the theory that "systems are useless", said that since the Cultural Revolution had raised the consciousness of the masses, production could be stimulated without systems and rules so that the question of their revival was irrelevant.'[6]

---

[1] 'The All China Federation of Trade Unions calls a forum of Trade Unions for exchanging experiences on masses productive work', *KJJP*, 7 May 1965 (*SCMP*, 1965, no. 3464). In the early 1960s there was a revival of democratic bodies within enterprises in the form of Workers Congresses. These, however, were welfare rather than production oriented, and their establishment was seen as entirely compatible with hierarchical and disciplined organisation. See Li Jun-chih, 'Concerning the system of Workers and Staff Congresses in state enterprises', *HC*, 1962, no. 2, pp. 33–7.
[2] 'Tientsin industrial workers win new victories in revolution and production', *NCNA*, 7 Sept. 1968 (*SCMP*, 1968, no. 4256); *Kung jen tsao fan pao*, 1968, no. 7 (28 Nov.).
[3] 'Strictly preserve revolutionary discipline', *JMJP*, 15 July 1969.
[4] 'Strengthen discipline, seize even greater victories', *JMJP*, 21 July 1969; 'Go in for Mao Tse-tung thought study groups in a big way and resolutely overcome anarchism', *JMJP*, 15 Feb. 1968.
[5] 'Strengthen Party leadership, grasp production management', *JMJP*, 13 Dec. 1971.
[6] 'Grasp ideology, systems and techniques', *JMJP*, 8 Oct. 1971.

By 1972, the pendulum had certainly swung back towards normalisation. But it would be a mistake to think that nothing had been gained by the Cultural Revolution. There is no doubt that the sort of changes in attitude and organisation that were encouraged during 1966–8 did partially reflect real economic imperatives – however much non-economic issues became entangled with them – and the post Cultural Revolution situation may well have been healthier as a result of the shake-up in rules and organisation that had taken place.

The problem posed for the present incentive system by the theoretical considerations and the history of policy changes discussed above is this: how flexible can one be in combining different types of incentives in a unified incentive policy? For not only may different objectives of the same enterprise call for use of different types of incentive, but more important, the incentive requirements in different sectors will also vary. Thus incentives appropriate to modern, bureaucratic organisations and capital intensive industry will not suit handicraft cooperatives and petty commerce. In the former, wage and external systems of different kinds combined with hierarchical forms of organisation are probably more appropriate, while in the latter, the development of internal incentives within a framework of less structured organisation is more likely to be efficient. In the case of Chinese industry, the fact that many modern enterprises are centrally controlled and therefore organisationally separate from the small scale, unconventional technology sector, must be a help in maintaining different types of incentive practice within that sector as a whole. But given that use of internal incentives involves influencing people's basic attitudes to work and organisation, and that this must be partly done through the educational system and media common to *the whole* workforce, it must in general be very difficult to implement an incentive mix which satisfies simultaneously the efficiency requirements of the whole economy. Even allowing for these difficulties, however, it should be possible to achieve combinations of some sort.

Such combinations will call for a mixture of rule adherence and flexibility, control and creativity, even though it would be unrealistic to expect that these can be held in permanent equilibrium. The trick must be to avoid extremes.

THE FUTURE OF THE SYSTEM

Unless the Chinese economic system is overtaken by a demographic catastrophe, the process of industrialisation that has been under way since the 1930s may be expected to continue. This process should result in the incorporation of a growing proportion of the workforce in the modern sector, and the application there of incentive systems appropriate to large scale, specialised organisations. The route to this maturity however is likely to be difficult. The Chinese leaders themselves have often emphasised the length of the journey; but the narrowness of the path and the depth of the crevasses on either side need emphasis too. The wage and incentive system will undoubtedly have an important role to play in this future, and from the analysis contained in this book, it is possible to suggest some of the dangers that will arise in this sphere.

In the case of the wage system, there are three problems that will need careful control. The first is that the modern sector will be bound to offer system rewards of some kind; for however thorough are attacks on dualism, the technical factors governing work conditions and the necessity of stabilising skilled and apprentice labour are bound to win out. This means that there will always be a fringe of unsatisfied potential entrants to the permanent workforce. Provided growth in the modern sector is rapid and even, and provided the system of labour organisation and population control can handle the problem of migration, this will not present serious problems. This is because there will be a continuous process of absorption from the ranks of the dissatisfied. If, however, the economy develops a growth pattern which includes long swings, then the possibility of serious social strife in the periods of relatively slow growth (or even of decline) will be real. This is what happened in the 1960s when the rate of growth dropped to about half that achieved in the 1950s. The reasons for this particular deceleration are not wholly clear to us yet, but whatever they were, swings of this kind could create a threat to the whole system.

The second problem arises from the reforms of 1957 which, it will be recalled, allowed the bottom of the wage structure to be placed firmly on the ground of local income situations, and gave appropriate powers of wage co-ordination to local planning authorities. This was a rational development. But as long as restrictions on labour mobility remain, there is always the possibility that regional income inequalities could become progressively larger. Precisely how the regional wage structure develops will depend not only on labour policy, but also on policy towards the inter-regional distribution of agricultural income, and towards the nature of financial controls over industrial enterprises. If all these factors were working in the same direction, the dangers would be substantial.

The third problem in this group is a consequence of the demotion of wage structures as an allocative mechanism in favour of the development of direct controls over inter-enterprise labour transfers. The issue raised by this is not simply whether other incentives can be found to encourage skill acquisition, but whether, in the absence of wage variations indicating the relative skills of workers, the utilisation of skilled labour can be made tolerably efficient. For if relative skills are not reflected in wages, then even effective financial pressures to minimise labour costs will not encourage enterprises to economise in the use of skilled labour. And further, to the extent that labour planners above the level of the enterprise are imperfectly informed of the skill characteristics of the labour force, they will have no rational criteria on which to base labour transfers. At present, the costs of direct allocation are probably more than compensated for – if indeed there is even a choice. But in the longer run, this problem will have to be looked at again.

Turning now to the future of the incentive system as a whole, we would argue that the ability of the system to function efficiently will depend critically on the quality of the Chinese political process. The importance of this is illustrated by two developments in the 1960s that show how the political system can pose a threat to rational incentive policy. At the crudest level, the ruthless exploitation of dissatisfactions created by income differentials during the Cultural Revolution is an example of how political conflict can use tensions that are bound to be present in any incentive system without sufficient concern for the long run consequences of this. Activity of this kind is particularly dangerous in a society where lack of legitimate outlets for tensions such as these (e.g. formal bargaining procedures and interest group organisations) makes the precise character of tensions unknown and their intensity relatively much greater. This episode, however, is only part of the larger problem, which is that political conflict in the 1960s has led to an extreme polarisation of thinking in the field of incentive policy. At the polemical level at least, the alternatives are presented as completely antithetical.[1] But as we have seen, all the evidence we have discussed underlines the truth, that to be effective, the incentive system must accommodate itself to the technical, spatial and administrative dimensions of the Chinese economy; and in the future must be flexible enough to adapt to the requirements of an economy that will be characterised by increasing capital intensity, specialisation and interdependence. In such an economy, flexible and creative work performance will be less important than discipline and predictability. The sort of conflicts likely to be associated with this transition have already become apparent in the 1960s, not only in conflicts

[1] In the literature, the Maoists favour internal incentives and enterprise organisation on the lines of the Anshan Constitution; and opponents favour material rewards and Soviet style management practices summarised in the Seventy Theses.

between 'creativity' and the maintenance of minimal standards of discipline and organisation, but also in the discovery that popular interpretation of the value of 'self reliance' was taking the form of industrial conglomerates, whose administration was inefficient, and which rejected commercial and technical co-operation with rival enterprises.[1] The correction of this latter deviation was not too difficult, but the problems of shifting the whole emphasis of the incentive system on to new lines will be.

We cannot of course expect that the fine tuning of an optimal incentive mix will ever be achieved and maintained anywhere, but if an oversimplified system is applied too rigidly for too long, or if policy alternates erratically from one extreme to another, the Chinese economy may never reach the point of maturity where its objective characteristics justify a homogenous and stable system, let alone the utopian state, where the nature of human norms makes a governmental incentive policy unnecessary.

[1] 'Specialisation and co-operation are important means of achieving greater, faster, better and more economical results', *JMJP*, 20 Feb. 1965 (*SCMP*, 1965, no. 3416).

10

Analytical summary

1. Before 1949, the industrial workforce was relatively small and concentrated in Manchuria and Shanghai. Data on wage patterns in those areas suggest that the long term trend (1919–49) of all wage differentials was downward. When this period is broken up, however, it becomes clear that the narrowing of differentials, both between industries and between persons of different occupations and skill levels, was strongly influenced by wartime (post-1937) conditions. Of particular importance in this narrowing process were the incidence of governmental wage controls, inflation and the pattern of inter-industry output growth.

2. Data on real wage changes in this period are slight, but the pattern appears to have been that in the 1930s real industrial wages declined somewhat, whereas during the war they rose quite sharply.

3. Since 1949, inter-industry differentials have continued to decline, while the skill and occupational differentials of manual workers increased in the 1950s, declined in the 1960s but are now back to their 1949 level. Most of our data on wages are for workers and staff but we do also have information that indicates that substantial differentials between sectors and different workforce categories developed at various times (i.e. between urban and rural workers, between temporary workers and permanent workers and staff and between workers in the modern and traditional sectors). In the case of the urban–rural differential, this grew in the 1950s, but was stabilised and by some criteria perhaps diminished in the 1960s. In the case of the temporary–permanent differential, this probably increased after 1957/8 as a result of tighter controls on labour mobility, and a decline in the rate of growth of the non-agricultural economy. The main cause of attention to this differential in recent years has been its role in political and social conflict.

4. The long term trend of real wages of industrial and other non-agricultural workers and staff since 1949, has been upward. The growth rate of real wages for this group between 1952 and 1972 has been about 1.9% per annum. Most of this increase, however, took place before and during the First Five Year Plan that finished in 1957. By 1957, wages of workers and staff were fairly high relative to the past and very high relative

to the rest (i.e. the other 80% to 90%) of the working population. The years 1959 to 1962 probably saw declining real wages with some recovery in 1963. Between that year and the wage reforms of 1971/2 the data suggest that the policy of wage stabilisation was successful, since even on the most favourable assumptions, no increase in real wages seems to have taken place.

WAGE POLICY

5. There is not much that could be described as *wage* policy in China before the development of wartime controls; although it would be true to say that the Kuomintang's *labour* policies (as expressed for example in their labour legislation) initiated the process by which that part of the workforce employed in relatively large, modern factories in the cities became a privileged group in the labour force as a whole.

6. In the period between 1949 and 1957, there was an active wage policy in the sense of there being a willingness to use both the level and structure of wages as instruments to stimulate work effort and allocate labour resources. This active policy was accompanied by persistent efforts to construct a system of wage planning based on the Soviet example.

7. The years 1957/8 marked a watershed in wage policy. After this point there was a marked diminution of interest in the wage instrument and this was accompanied by a rise in the comprehensiveness and efficiency of direct controls over labour allocation. The main reason for this switch of policy was that experience showed that continuous adaptation of the wage structure involved a continuous and unacceptable rise in the real average wage. This was partly due to the constraint of the policy of stable prices and partly to the nature of the wage determination mechanism. A second problem with the wage system of the 1950s was that a detailed copy of the Soviet system was inappropriate in the relatively primitive economic, technical and administrative environment of China at that time. Finally, a third problem was that the highly differentiated Soviet system could not handle contemporary Chinese pressures for egalitarian and group-oriented payments systems.

8. Although there was a real policy turning point in 1957/8, it would be wrong to suppose that the whole administrative apparatus relevant to wage determination was abandoned. It is true that there was some decentralisation and that the emphasis between different wage criteria shifted somewhat, but up to 1966 there is evidence that both a spirit of rationality and the use of bureaucratic procedures continued in wage administration. The disappearance of the old Ministry of Labour must have been something of

a setback, but the fact that most wage work had been transferred to the industrial ministries during the 1960s and the determination of the Government, even at the height of the Cultural Revolution, to stop a drastic dismantling of wage administration, suggest that the revival of wage work in the 1970s has been based on meaningful foundations.

THE INCENTIVE SYSTEM

9. The control and significance of changes in the pattern of basic wages cannot be understood without reference to other incentive devices. These other devices include premium and bonus systems, fringe benefits, variations in job security and emulation campaigns. In the 1950s, these developed on Soviet lines. Thus premium schemes were based on plan fulfilment criteria, and emulation campaigns that started as 'shock' movements based on Korean War fervour were regularised to become detailed technical exercises backed by material incentives. By the late 1950s it was recognised that premiums, fringe benefits, and the maintenance of a high proportion of the labour force in permanent tenure was economically expensive and the privileges were curtailed.

10. In the 1960s, the links between premiums and plans were weakened. At the same time emulation campaigns became more politicised in their objectives and their value for stimulating localised technical creativity emphasised. It is thought that since 1967/8, premiums have been consolidated into an automatic monthly bonus, but with the revival of planning, this step may be reversed.

11. Future incentive policy will remain bound by the necessity for controlling the growth of real consumption and preventing the emergence of economically inefficient and socially divisive income differentials. Within these limits, what is called for is a flexible policy that recognises the existence of variations in the efficiency of different incentive instruments in different situations. In some ways this will be extraordinarily difficult, because use of internal incentives involves controlling both the character of work organisation and prevalent social values; and while it is possible to envisage mixes of different types of external incentives, it is less easy to envisage mixed systems of work organisation or the possibility of varying the formation of people's values according to their work situations. In any event, what cannot be expected of the present or future is any rigid form of stability, for apart from changes brought about by economic growth, the incentive system will have to respond to the shifting demands of the wider social system of which it is a component.

Bibliography

MATERIALS IN ENGLISH

Argyris, Chris, *Integrating the individual and the organization*, New York: John Wiley, 1964.

Aspects of labor economics, National Bureau of Economic Research, Princeton: Princeton University Press, 1962.

Average annual money earnings of workers and staff in Communist China, Washington: Central Intelligence Agency, 1960.

Barnett, A. Doak (ed.), *Chinese Communist politics in action*, Seattle and London: University of Washington Press, 1969.

Bendix, Reinhard, *Embattled reason: essays in social knowledge*, New York: Oxford University Press, 1970.

Bergson, Abram, *The economics of Soviet planning*, New Haven and London: Yale University Press, 1964.

The structure of Soviet wages, Cambridge, Mass.: Harvard University Press, 1954.

Brown, Emily Clark, *Soviet trade unions and labor relations*, Cambridge, Mass.: Harvard University Press, 1966.

Capital formation and economic growth, Princeton: Princeton University Press, 1955.

Chang, John K., *Industrial development in pre-Communist China*, Chicago: Aldine Publishing Co., 1969.

Chapman, Janet, *Wage variation in Soviet industry: the impact of the 1956–1960 wage reform*, Memorandum RM-6076-PR, Santa Monica: The Rand Corporation, 1970.

Chen, Nai Ruenn, *Chinese economic statistics*, Edinburgh: Edinburgh University Press, 1966.

Chesneaux, Jean, *The Chinese labor movement 1919–1927*, Stanford: Stanford University Press, 1968.

China News Analysis, Hong Kong.

Chinese workers march towards socialism, Peking: Foreign Languages Press, 1956.

Communist China yearbook 1962, Hong Kong: Union Research Institute, 1963.

Davison, J. P. and others, *Productivity and economic incentives*, London: Allen and Unwin, 1958.

Deutscher, Isaac, *The Soviet trade unions*, London: Royal Institute of International Affairs, 1965.

Dewar, Margaret, *Labour policy in the USSR 1917–1928*, London: Royal Institute of International Affairs, 1956.

Donnithorne, Audrey, *China's economic system*, London: Allen and Unwin, 1967.

Dubin, R. (ed.), *Human relations in administration*, New Jersey: Prentice-Hall, 1954.

Dunlop, John T., *Industrial relations systems*, New York: Henry Holt, 1958.

(ed.) *The theory of wage determination*, London: Macmillan, 1957.

Emerson, John Philip, *Nonagricultural employment in mainland China 1949–1957*, Washington: U.S. Department of Commerce, 1965.

Etzioni, Amitai, *The active society*, New York: The Free Press, 1968.

Howe, Christopher, *Employment and economic growth in urban China 1949–1957*, Cambridge: Cambridge University Press, 1971.

INTERNATIONAL LABOUR OFFICE, *Review* and *Towards full employment*, Geneva, 1970.

Korman, Abraham K., *Industrial and organizational psychology*, New Jersey: Prentice-Hall, 1971.

Kuznets, Simon, *Modern economic growth*, New Haven: Yale University Press, 1966.

Lenin, V. I., *Collected works*, Moscow: Foreign Languages Publishing House, various dates.

Li, Choh-ming, *Economic development of Communist China*, Berkeley and Los Angeles: University of California Press, 1959.

Likert, Rensis, *New patterns of management*, New York: McGraw Hill, 1961.

Lösch, August, *The economics of location*, 2nd edn., New Haven and London: Yale University Press, 1954.

Mainichi Daily News, Tokyo.

March, J. G. (ed.), *Handbook of organizations*, New York: Rand McNally, 1965.

Meij, J. L. (ed.), *Internal wage structure*, Amsterdam: North Holland Publishing House, 1963.

Morris, Morris D., *The emergence of an industrial labor force in India: a study of the Bombay cotton mills, 1854–1947*, Berkeley: University of California Press, 1965.

New China News Agency, Peking, Shanghai, Canton.

New Society, London.

Newsweek, New York.

Palekar, S. A., *Problems of wage policy for economic development, with special reference to India*, London: Asia Publishing House, 1962.

Peking Review, Peking.

Perkins, Dwight H., *Market control and planning in Communist China*, Cambridge, Mass.: Harvard University Press, 1966.

Psychological Bulletin.

Pye, Lucian W., *The spirit of Chinese politics*, Cambridge, Mass.: The M.I.T. Press, 1968.

Reynolds, Lloyd G., and Cynthia H. Taft, *The evolution of wage structure*, New Haven: Yale University Press, 1956.

Rice, A. K., *Productivity and social organization: the Ahmedabad experiment*, London: Tavistock Publications, 1958.
   The enterprise and its environment: a system theory of management organization, London: Tavistock Publications, 1963.

Schwarz, Solomon M., *Labour in the Soviet Union*, London: Praeger, 1953.

Selections from China mainland magazines, Hong Kong.

Shih, Kuo-heng, *China enters the machine age*, Cambridge, Mass.: Harvard University Press, 1944.

Shinohara, Miyohei, *Structural changes in Japan's economic development*, Economic Research Series, No. 11, The Institute of Economic Research, Hitotsubashi University, Tokyo: Kinokuniya Bookstore, 1970.

Smith, Anthony D. (ed.), *The labour market and inflation*, London: Macmillan, 1968.
   Wage policy issues in economic development, London: Macmillan, 1969.

Survey of the China Mainland Press.

Swaniewicz, S., *Forced labour and economic development*, London: Royal Institute of International Affairs, 1965.

Taira, Koji, *Economic development and the labor market in Japan*, New York and London: Columbia University Press, 1970.

Tannenbaum, Arnold S., *Social psychology of the work organisation*, London: Tavistock Publications, 1966.

Ten great years, Peking: Foreign Languages Press, 1960.

The China Quarterly, London.

The Financial Times, London.
The Japan Economic Review, Tokyo.
The Manchoukuo yearbook 1934, Tokyo: East Asian Economic Research Bureau, 1934.
The Manchoukuo yearbook 1942, Hsinking: The Manchoukuo Yearbook Company, 1942.
The Sunday Times, London.
The Times, London.
Turner, H. A., *Wage trends, wage policies, and collective bargaining. The problems for underdeveloped countries*, Cambridge: Cambridge University Press, 1965.
Vroom, Victor H., and Edward C. Deci, *Management and motivation*, London: Penguin Books, 1970.
Wiles, P. J. D. (ed.), *The prediction of Communist economic performance*, Cambridge: Cambridge University Press, 1971.
Wilson, Richard W., *Learning to be Chinese: the political socialization of children in Taiwan*, Cambridge, Mass.: The M.I.T. Press, 1970.
Wright, Arthur F. and Denis Twitchett, *Confucian personalities*, Stanford: Stanford University Press, 1962.
Wu, Yuan-li, *An economic survey of Communist China*, New York: Bookman Associates, 1956.
Young, John, *The research activities of the South Manchurian Railway Company 1907–1945 – a history and bibliography*, New York: The East Asian Institute, Columbia University, 1966.

MATERIALS IN CHINESE

Books

Chao Yi-wen, *Hsin Chung Kuo ti kung yeh* (New China's industry), Peking: Statistical Publishing House, 1957.
Chiang Hsüeh-mo, *She hui chu yi ti fen p'ei* (Socialist distribution), Shanghai: Shanghai People's Publishing House, 1962.
Ch'ien Hua and others, *Ch'i nien lai wo kuo szu ying kung shang yeh ti pien hua 1949–1956* (The transformation of our country's private industry and commerce during the past seven years), Peking: Finance and Economic Publishing House, 1957.
Ch'üan kuo ke chung yao shih hsien kung chih shu (Index numbers of wages in important cities), Chungking: Statistical Office of the Ministry of Social Affairs of the National Government, 1945–6.
Chung Hua jen min kung ho kuo fa chan kuo min ching chi ti yi ke wu nien chi hua (The First Five Year Plan for the development of the economy of the Chinese People's Republic), Peking: People's Publishing House, 1955.
Chung Kuo chih kung yün tung ti tang ch'ien jen wu (Present tasks of the Chinese workers and staff movement), vol. 4, Peking: Workers' Publishing House, 1951.
Hsü Ti-hsin, *Chung Kuo kuo tu shih ch'i kuo min ching chi ti fen hsi* (Analysis of the national economy during the transition period in China), Peking: Scientific Publishing House, 1959.
Kung hui ts'ai wu kung tso shou ts'e (A handbook of union finance work), Peking: Workers' Publishing House, 1963.
Kung jen yün tung wen t'i (Problems in the workers' movement), vol. 4, Peking: Workers' Publishing House, 1951.
Kung yeh ch'i yeh kuan li wen hsüan (Select documents on management in industrial enterprises), vol. 4, Peking: Chinese Industry Publishing House, 1964.

Kung yeh k'uai chi ho suan (Industrial accountancy calculation), Peking: Chinese People's University Publishing House, 1965.
Lao tung jen min ti hao erh tzu Lei Feng (Lei Feng: a good son of the labouring people), Peking: The China Youth Publishing House, 1965.
Lao tung t'ung chi kung tso shou ts'e (Handbook of labour statistics), Peking: Statistical Publishing House, 1958.
Lao tzu kuan hsi yü chi t'i ho t'ung (Labour–Capital relations and collective contracts), Shanghai: New China Bookshop, 1950.
Liao Li-min, *Pa lao tung ching sai hsiang ch'ien chin yi pu* (Advance labour emulation a step forward), Canton: South China People's Publishing House, 1954.
Mao Tse-tung, *Ching chi wen t'i yü ts'ai cheng wen t'i* (Economic and financial problems), Hong Kong: New Democracy Publishing House, 1949.
Shang hai chieh fang ch'ien hou wu chia tzu liao hui pien (A compendium of Shanghai commodity prices before and after liberation), Shanghai: Shanghai People's Publishing House, 1958.
Shang hai kung ch'ang lao kung t'ung chi (Statistics of Shanghai's factory labour), Shanghai: Shanghai Bureau of Social Affairs, 1947.
Sheng ch'an chiang li pan pa chieh shao (An introduction to production premium methods), Shanghai: Labour Publishing House, 1951.
Su Ch'ün, *Kuo chia ch'i yeh kung tzu chih tu ti chi ke wen t'i* (Some problems in the wage system in state enterprises), origin unknown, 1952.
Szu ying ch'i yeh k'uai chi chih tu (The accounting system in private enterprises), Peking: The China Book Bureau, 1954.
Szu ying shang yeh ti she hui chu yi kai tsao (tzu liao) (The socialist reform of private commerce: materials), Peking: San Lien Bookstore, 1963.
Wage rates in Shanghai, Shanghai: Shanghai Bureau of Social Affairs, 1935. (In English and Chinese.)
Wang Ya-ch'iang, *Kung yeh ch'i yeh kung tzu ti li lun yü shih chien* (The theory and practice of wages in industrial enterprises), Peking: Machinery Industry Publishing House, 1955.
Wo kuo kang t'ieh, tien li, mei t'an, chi hsieh, fang chih, tsao chih kung yeh ti chin hsi (Our country's iron and steel, electricity, coal, machinery, textiles and paper industries – past and present), Peking: Statistical Publishing House, 1958.
Yi hsin wei ko ming (All the heart for revolution), Peking: The China Youth Publishing House, 1965.

Journals

Chi hsieh kung yeh (Machinery industry).
Chi hua ching chi (Planned economy).
Ching chi chou pao (The economics weekly).
Ching chi yen chiu (Economic research).
Chung kung yeh t'ung hsün (Bulletin of heavy industry).
Chung Kuo ch'ing nien (China youth).
Chung Kuo fang chih kung jen (The Chinese textile worker).
Chung Kuo hai yuan (Chinese sailors).
Chung Kuo kung yeh (Chinese industry).
Chung yang ho tso t'ung hsün (The central cooperative bulletin).
Hsin Hua pan yüeh k'an (The new China semi-monthly).
Hsin Hua yüeh pao (New China monthly).
Hsüeh hsi (Study).
Hung ch'i (Red flag).
Jen min tien yeh (People's Electricity).

Kung jen sheng huo (Workers' livelihood).
Kung shang chieh (The world of private commerce and industry).
Lao tung (Labour).
T'ung chi kung tso (Statistical research).
Tung pei kung yeh (North Eastern industry).
Yüan tung kuan ch'a (Far east perspective) (Hong Kong).

Newspapers

An hui jih pao (Anhwei daily), Hofei, Anhwei province.
Ch'ang chiang jih pao (The Yangtze river daily), Wuhan, Hupei province.
Ch'ang ch'un jih pao (Changchun daily), Changchun, Kirin province.
Ch'ang sha jih pao (Changsha daily), Changsha, Hunan province.
Ch'eng tu jih pao (Chengtu daily), Chengtu, Szechuan province.
Chi lin jih pao (Kirin daily), Kirin, Kirin province.
Chiang hsi jih pao (Kiangsi daily), Nanchang, Kiangsi province.
Chieh fang jih pao (Liberation daily), Shanghai, Kiangsu province.
Ch'ing tao jih pao (Tsingtao daily), Tsingtao, Shantung province.
Chung ch'ing jih pao (Chungking daily), Chungking, Szechuan province.
Chung Kuo ch'ing nien pao (China youth daily), Peking, Hopei province.
Fu chien jih pao (Fukien daily), Foochow, Fukien province.
Ha erh pin jih pao (Harbin daily), Harbin, Heilungkiang province.
Hang chou jih pao (Hangchow daily), Hangchow, Chekiang province.
Hei lung chiang jih pao (Heilungkiang daily), Harbin, Heilungkiang province.
Ho nan jih pao (Honan daily), Kaifeng, Honan province.
Ho pei jih pao (Hopei daily), Peking, Hopei province.
Hsi ts'ang jih pao (Tibet daily), Lhasa, Autonomous Region of Tibet.
Hsin hu nan pao (New Hunan daily), Changsha, Hunan province.
Hsin wen jih pao (Daily news), Shanghai, Kiangsu province.
Hsing tao jih pao (Star island daily), Hong Kong.
Hsing tao wan pao (The star island evening news), Hong Kong.
Hu pei jih pao (Hupei daily), Wuhan, Hupei province.
Jen min jih pao (The people's daily), Peking, Hopei province.
Kan su jih pao (Kansu daily), Lanchow, Kansu province.
Kuang chou jih pao (Canton daily), Canton, Kwangtung province.
Kuang hsi jih pao (Kwangsi daily), Nanning, Kwangsi province.
Kuang ming jih pao (The enlightenment daily), Peking, Hopei province.
Kung jen jih pao (Workers' daily), Peking, Hopei province.
Liao ning jih pao (Liaoning daily), Shenyang (Mukden), Liaoning province.
Lü-Ta jih pao (Lushun–Dairen daily), Dairen, Liaoning province.
Nan ching jih pao (Nanking daily), Nanking, Kiangsu province.
Nan fang jih pao (Southern daily), Canton, Kwangtung province.
Nei meng ku jih pao (Inner Mongolia daily) Huhetot; Hai-la-erh; Wu-lan-hao-te,
    Autonomous region of Inner Mongolia.
Shan hsi jih pao (Shansi daily), Taiyuan, Shansi province.
Shen yang jih pao (Shenyang daily), Shenyang (Mukden), Liaoning province.
Shih pao (The times), Hong Kong.
Szu ch'uan jih pao (Szechuan daily), Chengtu, Szechuan province.
Ta chung pao (Masses daily), Tsinan, Shantung province.
Ta kung pao (Impartial daily), Tientsin and Peking, Hopei province; Hong Kong.
T'ien chin jih pao (Tientsin daily), Tientsin, Hopei province.
Wen hui pao (The cultural contact daily), Hong Kong; Shanghai, Kiangsu province.

Red Guard materials

These materials are from the *Survey of the China mainland press*; the files of the Union Research Institute (Hong Kong); and the *RG* series of microfilms issued by the Center for Chinese Research Materials, Washington.

A record of the conversation between comrades of the Central Cultural Revolutionary Small Group and representatives of the National Red Revolutionary Rebels, Peking and Canton, 1967 (Union Research Institute file series 307).

Black materials on Liu Shao-ch'i and the system of temporary and contract labour, 1 Jan. 1967, republished Canton, 1968 (*RG* ser. x).

Down with Tu Chen-hsiang the chief follower of the capitalist road within the Party in the Canton Finance and Trade system, 15 May 1967 (*RG* ser. xii).

Kuang t'ieh tsung szu (Canton railways General Headquarters).

Kung jen tsao fan pao (Workers' rebellion paper).

Lao tung chan pao (Labour battle weekly).

Shou tu hung wei bin (Capital City Red Guards).

Shuang ch'en yüeh (Frosty morning moon).

T'i yü chan pao (Physical culture struggle paper).

Tung fang hung (East is red).

Tung fang hung pao (The east is red daily).

Legal compilations

Chin jung fa kuei hui pien 1949–1952 (Compendium of currency laws and regulations 1949–1952), Peking: Finance and Economic Publishing House, 1956.

1955 Chin jung fa kuei hui pien (The 1955 compendium of currency laws and regulations), Peking: Currency Publishing House, 1956.

1956 Chin jung fa kuei hui pien (1956 currency laws and regulations), Peking: Currency Publishing House, 1957.

1957 Chin jung fa kuei hui pien (1957 compendium of currency regulations), Peking: Currency Publishing House, 1958.

Chung Hua jen min kung ho kuo fa kuei hui pien 1954–1955, 1962–1963 (Compendium of laws and regulations of the People's Republic of China 1954–1955, 1962–1963), Peking: Law Publishing House, 1956, 1964.

Chung yang jen min cheng fu fa ling hui pien 1949–1952 (Central People's Government compendium of laws and regulations, 1949–1952), vol. 2, Peking: People's Publishing House, 1952.

Chung yang jen min cheng fu fa ling hui pien 1952 (Central People's Government compendium of laws 1952), Peking: People's Publishing House, 1954.

1956 Chung yang ts'ai cheng fa kuei hui pien (The 1956 compendium of Central Government financial laws and regulations), Peking: Financial Publishing House, 1957.

Chung yang ts'ai ching cheng ts'e fa ling hui pien (Central Government compendium of financial and economic regulations and policy statements), Series 1–3 (9 vols), Peking: New China Bookstore, 1950–2.

Hua Tung ch'ü ts'ai cheng ching chi fa ling hui pien (Compendium of finance and economic regulations for the East China Region), Shanghai: East China People's Publishing House, 1951.

Szu ying kung shang yeh ti she hui chu yi kai tsao cheng ts'e fa ling hsüan pien 1953–1957 (Select compendium of policy statements and laws concerning the socialist reform of private industry and commerce, 1953–1957), Peking: Law Publishing House, 1960.

MATERIALS IN JAPANESE

Tsuji Hideo, *Chinkin kōzō* (The structure of wages), Tokyo: Rōmu Gyōsei Kenkyū Shō, 1955.

Chūgoku keizai hatten no tōkei kenkyū II (Studies in the statistics of China's economic development), Tokyo: Ajia Keizai Kenkyū Shō, 1962.

Chūgoku sōkan 1971 (The 1971 China compendium), Tokyo: Ajia Chōsa Kai, 1971.

Hokushi rōdōryoku no tai-Man shūryū ni tomonau shomondai ni tsuite (Hisoka) (Concerning problems related to the mobility of North Chinese labourers in Manchuria) (Secret), Peking: *MMT*, Hokushi Keizai Chōsajo, 1940.

Jihen to nyū-Man rōdōsha mondai (Problems relating to workers entering Manchuria after the 'China Incident'), Harbin: *MMT*, Hokkei Keizai Shīryō, 1938.

Jinmin Chūgoku (People's China), Peking.

Kako jūgonenkan no Manshū ni okeru Nihonjin oyobi Chūgokujin shukōgyō rōdōsha chingin no sūsei (Wage trends of Chinese and Japanese manual workers in Manchuria during the past fifteen years), Dairen: *MMT*, Shachōshitsu Jinjika, 1927.

Kita Shina rōdō jijō gaikan (A survey of labour conditions in North China), No place: Kita Shina Kaihatsu Kabushiki Kaisha, 1941.

Man-shi ni okeru rōdōryoku jijō ni kansuru chōsa (Gokuhi) (A survey of the labour situation in Manchuria and China) (Top Secret), Tokyo: *MMT*, Tōa Keizai Chōsakyoku, 1944.

Manshū keizai tōkei nempō 1936 (The Manchurian yearbook of economic statistics for 1936), Dairen: Dairen Chamber of Commerce and Industry, 1937.

Manshū kōgyō rōdō gaikyō hōkoku (Report of a survey of industrial labour conditions in Manchuria), Hsinking: *MMT*, Shinkyō Shisha Chōsashitsu, 1944.

Manshū kōgyō rōdō jijō (Labour conditions in Manchurian industry), Dairen: *MMT*, Shomubu Chōsaka, 1925.

Manshū rōdō mondai no sūteki ikkōsatsu (A statistical investigation of Manchurian labour problems), Tokyo: *MMT*, Tōa Keizai Chōsakyoku, 1927.

Nichi-Man rōdō mondai zadankai yōroku (A summary record of a conference on Japanese–Manchurian labour problems held at the Yamato Hotel, Hsinking), Hsinking: Keichō Dai Ichibu, 1934.

Nihon keizai shinbum (The Japan economic daily), Tokyo.

Nihon teikoku shūgi ka no Manshū (Manchuria under Japanese imperialism), Tokyo: Manshū Shi Kenkyū Kai, 1972.

Shin Chūgoku nenkan, 1966–1970 (The new China yearbook), Tokyo: Chūgoku Kenkyū Shō, 1966–70.

Shinohara Miyohei and Funahashi Naomichi (eds.), *Nihongata Chingin kōzō no kenkyū* (Studies in Japanese wage structure), Tokyo: Rōdō Hōgakai Shuppan, 1963.

Shōwa jūgonendo nyū-Man kuryokusho tōkei (Statistics on labourers entering Manchuria in 1940), No place: Tōya Haigan Kabushiki Kaisha, 1941.

Takei, Gōichi, *Manshū no rōdō to rōdō seisaku* (Manchurian labour and labour policy), Tokyo: Canshō Shōten, 1941.

Ueda, Teijirō, *Nihon jinkō seisaku* (Japan's population policy), Tokyo: Chikura Shobō, 1937.

Index of subjects

accidents, caused by emulation campaigns, 131
administration, *see* State Administration, wage administration
Advanced Production Workers, 123, 130; number of (1954), 134
agriculture: collectivisation of (1956), 115; incentive policy in, 96; wage entry point into other employment from, 113–14, 116; workers alternate between other employment and, 105, 128
All China Federation of Trade Unions, dissolved (1966), 78, 129
Anshan Constitution, 150n
area differentials, *see* regional differentials
auditing, tightening of financial control by continuous, 91

bonus payments: abolished, 92; not included in official wage records, 35; resumed, to keep wage bill at pre-abolition level, 154; *see also* premium payments
bureaucracy, *see* State Administration

cadres: in finance, 91; oppose emulation campaigns, 131; in wage administration, 111, 112, 120; in wage reform, 88, 93–4
'character', as criterion for determining wage, 81
cities: extension of jurisdiction of, over adjacent countryside, 117; policy of reviving economic importance of those on seaboard (from 1956), 116; size of, and skill differential, 114
civil aviation, wage span in, 83n
clothing industry, wages in, 6, 12
coal mining: skill differential in, U.S.S.R., 11, 12, 13; wage ranking of, 44, 45, 46, 47
Collective Contracts, 72–3, 79–80, 103, 106; for supply of groups of workers from rural sector, 128
command economies: wage policy in, 9–13, wage problems in, 13–15
Communist Party: Central Committee of, and wage system, 73–4; length of membership of, as criterion for determining wage, 80, 81; salary position of secretary of, in factory, 39, 40; in wage determination, 80, 110, 112; in wage reform, 78–9, 84, 87, 88, 92; work hero on Central Committee of, 134

Communist Party Labour and Wage Committees, at enterprise level, 79
construction industries: growth of wages in (Inner Mongolia), 48; skill differential in (Manchuria), 20–1; wage changes in, involving stabilisation or lowering, 89; wage control in, 99, 105–7
contracts: between private and public sectors, 103, 104, 106, 108; *see also* Collective Contracts
cooperative sector: average income in, 51, 105; conversion of traditional sector to, 94, 104
cost of living: index for, Shanghai and Nanking, 33; regional wage adjustments for, 71–2, 89
cotton industry: wage control in, 99; wage ranking of (South Central Region), 88
Cultural Revolution: attempted abolition of temporary worker status in, 127; effects of, 41, 129, 147, 148; opposing views on wage policy developed during, 58; possible break in accounting continuities during, 28; reactions to, 96; wages during, 61, 73

decentralisation in economic administration: in 1956 wage reform, 57, 90; after 1957, 69, 76, 79, 146, 153
dependency denominators, in calculating urban–rural differentials, 50

earnings, average money: growth of, in seven industries, 44, 45; in public and private sectors, 62; in U.S.S.R., 13; by years, 31, 32; *see also* wages, average
earnings, real: by industries, in Shanghai, 25; *see also* wages, real
economies, different types of, *see* command, industrialised, low-income, *and* market economies
education: expansion of, in 1950s, 96; wage differentials and demand for, 67
egalitarianism: general preference for, 120, 153; Mao on (1942), 59; in 'Maoist' wage policy, 59, 60; premium systems and, 126; pressures for, 38, 111, 112; of Russian trade unions, 10; in South Central Region, 88
electricity industry, wage ranking of, 43, 44, 45
emulation campaigns, 118, 130–5, 154

Index of persons and place names

Africa, skill differentials in, 4–5
Algeria, 5
Anhwei, 54
Antung, 18–20
Argentina, 5, 6
Argyle, Michael, 139n
Argyris, Chris, 137n
Asia, skill differentials in, 4–5

Barnett, A. Doak, 130n
Bendix, Reinhard, 137n, 138n, 139n
Berg, Elliot, 5n, 8n
Bergson, Abram, 9n, 10
Brazil, 5
Brown, Emily Clark, 14

Canton: inter-industry differentials in, 23–4, 46–7; skill differentials in, 42; place in inter-regional ranking, 52–3; construction wage bargaining in, 106; wage reform in, 99n; 16, 48
Chang Chih-ang, 73n
Chang, John K , 17n
Chang Lin-chih, 122n
Chang Ming-fang, 143n
Chang Yen-hsing, 52
Changchun, 18–20, 33, 54
Chao Hung-wan, 130n
Chao Yi-wen, 32
Chapman, Janet, 9n, 11–13, 119n
Ch'en K'ai, 90n
Chen, Nai Ruenn, 48
Ch'en Yün, 122n
Ch'eng Chi-chung, 120n
Cheng K'ang-t'ing, 77n
Chengtu, 52, 54, 64
Chesneaux, Jean, 110n
Chiang Chen-wu, 34n
Chiang Hsüeh-mo, 73n
Ch'ien Hua, 92n, 104n
Chile, 5
Chou En-lai, 57, 90
Chou Fei-kuang, 39
Chou Feng-ching, 30n
Chou Liang, 95
Chungking, 47
Columbia, 5
Congo (Brazzaville), 5
Congo (Kinshasa), 5
Czechoslovakia, 14

Dairen, 18–20

Davison, J. P., 138n
Deci, Edward L., 136n, 139n
Deutscher, Isaac, 9n
Dewar, Margaret, 9n
Donnithorne, Audrey, 75n
Dubin, R., 138n
Dunlop, John T., 140n
Dunnette, Marvin D., 111n

East China Military Region, wage reform in, 99n
Eastern Europe, economic reforms in, 14, 15
Emerson, John Philip, 29n, 30

Fe Te-huang, 77n, 124n, 125n
Fisher, Irving, 138n
Fukien, 52, 54
Funahashi, Naomichi, 8n

Galenson, W., 9n
Gellner, Ernest, 14n
Ghana, 5
Goode, William J., 138n

Hangchow, 52, 54
Harbin, 52–4
Heilungkiang, 52–4, 93n
Hong Kong, 5
Hopei, 50
Howe, Christopher, 31n, 35n, 76n, 97n
Hsiao Chan, 90n
Hsiao Min, 122n
Hsieh Chien-yün, 34n
Hsieh Chi-ch'un, 77n
Hsieh Chin-hu, 111n
Hsü Ti-hsin, 98
Hu Fan-hsüeh, 57n
Hu Feng, 144
Hupei, 33, 50, 52, 54

India, 5–7
Inner Mongolia, 48, 54, 64, 94
Ishikawa, Shigeru, 36, 63n
Ivory Coast, 5

Japan: occupational differentials in, 3n; sectoral differentials in, 7; and Manchuria, 16, 18–21, 23–6; seniority payments (*nenkō jōritsu*) in, 6, 8, 143; temporary workers in, 8, 128